Dangerous Liaisons

The publication of this book, and the SAR seminars from which it resulted, were inspired and generously supported by Eric and Barbara Dobkin through their commitment to scholarly enterprises that foster positive social change in our world.

The School for Advanced Research gratefully acknowledges the co-sponsorship of the Society for Applied Anthropology in developing this volume.

**School for Advanced Research
Advanced Seminar Series**

James F. Brooks
General Editor

Dangerous Liaisons

Contributors

Eyal Ben-Ari
Department of Sociology and Anthropology, Hebrew University of Jerusalem, Israel

R. Brian Ferguson
Department of Sociology and Anthropology, Rutgers University, Newark, New Jersey

Douglas P. Fry
*Conflict Resolution and Peacemaking, Åbo Akademi University, Vasa, Finland;
Bureau of Applied Research in Anthropology, University of Arizona*

Danny Hoffman
Department of Anthropology, University of Washington, Seattle

Anne Irwin
Department of Anthropology, University of Calgary, Canada

Laura A. McNamara
*Computation, Computers, Information and Mathematics, Sandia National
Laboratories, Albuquerque, New Mexico*

David Price
Department of Anthropology, St. Martin's University, Lacey, Washington

Robert A. Rubinstein
Maxwell School of Syracuse University, New York

Maren Tomforde
Staff and Command College of the German Armed Forces, Hamburg, Germany

Dangerous Liaisons

Anthropologists and the National Security State

Edited by Laura A. McNamara and Robert A. Rubinstein

SAR
PRESS

School for Advanced Research Press

Santa Fe

School for Advanced Research Press
Post Office Box 2188
Santa Fe, New Mexico 87504-2188
www.sarpress.sarweb.org

Managing Editor: Lisa Pacheco
Editorial Assistant: Ellen Goldberg
Designer and Production Manager: Cynthia Dyer
Manuscript Editor: Maya Allen-Gallegos
Proofreader: Catherine Cocks
Indexer: Margaret Moore Booker
Printer: Cushing Malloy, Inc.

Library of Congress Cataloging-in-Publication Data

Dangerous liaisons : anthropologists and the national security state / edited by
Laura A. McNamara and Robert A. Rubinstein.
    p. cm. — (Advanced seminar series)
  Includes bibliographical references and index.
  ISBN 978-1-934691-49-6 (alk. paper)
  1. Political anthropology. 2. National security. 3. Terrorism. 4. World politics.
I. McNamara, Laura A. II. Rubinstein, Robert A., 1951-
  GN492.D36 2011
  306.2—dc22
                            2011002801

Cover illustrations: *top left*, IT Systems Administrator phone support, © ryasick, iStockphoto.com;
top right, Afghan young man posing with woman wearing burka in the background, © Juanmonino,
iStockphoto.com; *bottom left*, U.S. Army soldiers with the 214th Military Police Company provide
medical supplies to the Tal Kayf clinic in Tal Kayf district, Mosul, Iraq, in support of Operation New
Dawn on May 3, 2011. Department of Defense photo by Spc. Aaron J. Herrera, U.S. Army. Use of
DoD photo does not constitute or imply endorsement of this book or the opinions stated within.;
bottom right, Brigade General Qazi Abidus Samad (Bangladesh) at the African Union-United Nations
Hybrid Operation in Darfur (UNAMID) commemoration of the International Day of United
Nations Peacekeepers at the Arc Compound. UN Photo/Albert Gonzalez Farran.

Contents

Figures

Tables

Abbreviations and Acronyms

AAA	American Anthropological Association
AAS	Association for Asian Studies
ACLU	American Civil Liberties Union
AFRICOM	United States Africa Command
ARPA	Advanced Research Projects Agency
BAU	Behavioral Analysis Unit (FBI)
CDF	Civil Defense Forces
CF	Canadian Forces
CIA	Central Intelligence Agency
CITF	Criminal Investigation Task Force
CO	Commanding officer
COIN	Counterinsurgency
CORDS	Civil Operations and Revolutionary Development Support
DDR	Disarmament, Demobilization, and Reintegration
DHS	Department of Homeland Security
DoD	Department of Defense
ECOMOG	Economic Community of West African States Cease-fire Monitoring Group
EO	Executive Outcomes
EUFOR	European Force (NATO)
FBI	Federal Bureau of Investigation
FOB	Forward operating base
FOIA	Freedom of Information Act
FULRO	Front Unifié de Lutte des Races Opprimées
GAA	German Association of Anthropology
GVN	Government of South Vietnam
GWOT	Global War on Terror
HTS	Human Terrain System
HTT	Human Terrain Team
HUMINT	Human Intelligence
IDF	Israel Defense Forces
IPA	International Peace Academy (now International Peace Institute)
ISAF	International Security Assistance Force
KAF	Kandahar Airfield
KFOR	Kosovo Force (NATO)
KUBARK	Code name for CIA cold war interrogation manual
JPRA	Joint Personnel Recovery Agency

JTFG	Joint Task Force Guantánamo
LAV	Light Armored Vehicle
MKULTRA	Code name for CIA cold war mind-control research program
NATO	North Atlantic Treaty Organization
NCA	Network of Concerned Anthropologists
NCTC	National Counterterrorism Center
NGO	nongovernmental organization
NPFL	National Patriotic Front of Liberia
OC	Officer commanding a company (company commander)
OGA	Other government agency
OLC	Office of Legal Counsel
PAE	Pacific Architects and Engineers
PAFFO	Public affairs officer
PPCLI	Princess Patricia's Canadian Light Infantry
PRISP	Pat Roberts Intelligence Scholars Program
PRT	Provincial Reconstruction Team
PSYOP	Psychological Operations (Center)
RMA	Revolution in Military Affairs
RUF	Revolutionary United Front
SA	Special agent
SEDAG	Southeast Asian Development Advisory Group
SERE	Survival, Evasion, Resistance, and Escape
SfAA	Society for Applied Anthropology
SFOR	Stabilization Force (NATO)
SMC	Student Mobilization Committee
SOWI	Bundeswehr Institute of Social Sciences
UNDPKO	United Nations Department of Peacekeeping Operations
UNEF	United Nations Emergency Force
UNTSO	United Nations Truce Supervision Organization
USAID	United States Agency for International Development
USIA	United States Information Service
VSA	vital signs absent

Introduction

Scholars, Security, Citizenship: Anthropology and the State at War

Laura A. McNamara and Robert A. Rubinstein

This is a book about intersections. It is a product of two years' worth of discussions among a small group of ethnographers from four different countries, each with a variety of experiences studying war, violence, the military, and the state. In some ways this book is distinctly a product of our times due to the terrorist attacks on American embassies in Tanzania and Kenya and the later attack on the United States on September 11, 2001, the United States' declaration of a Global War on Terror (GWOT), and the subsequent invasions of Afghanistan and Iraq. Throughout the first decade of the new century anthropologists have watched with both interest and concern as government agencies—particularly those with military and intelligence functions—have sought their professional assistance in understanding terrorists' motivations, stabilizing nascent wartime governments, and countering insurgencies. Large and very powerful government agencies such as the US Department of Defense (DoD) are investing substantial sums of money in social science research and calling for the involvement of social scientists in mapping "the contours of [an] international arena... much more complex than at any time during the Cold War" (Gates 2008). Such trends have raised fears that anthropology is under threat of colonization, that anthropologists' moral and epistemological commitments will be inevitably subverted as they align their research priorities to meet the demands of the state.

This book also explores long-standing tensions in anthropology having to do with the discipline's relationship to the state. This challenge is hardly unique to anthropology: knowledge underwrites power, which is why governments invest in research, seek the consultation of scientists, and create bureaus and functions to house and deploy expert resources. Decision makers (particularly in the military) have long looked to scientists (particularly in the physical and mathematical sciences) as sources of reliable knowledge about the physical world. For example, modern weather forecasting in the United States has roots in military-funded math and physics research dating to the late nineteenth century. In return, scientists have come to rely heavily on government support for research and development activities. As Sheila Jasanoff describes it, the post–World War II social contract between science and government set expectations on both sides: given adequate fiscal support for free and unfettered inquiry, scientists would generate foundational knowledge that would provide practical benefits to government and industry alike. Yet the contract has always been somewhat fraught, not least because the direct affiliation with policy threatens the normative neutrality of science, but also because the contentious nature of decision making—which often takes place at the ragged edge of scientific research where uncertainties abound and knowledge is not fixed—may undermine the epistemological authority of science as a special form of knowledge (Jasanoff 1987).

Although Jasanoff's work focuses on the dynamics of regulatory science in American policymaking, the tensions that she identifies are as prevalent in the social sciences as they are in the physical, biological, and mathematical sciences. In the first half of the twentieth century applied anthropology was considered problematic because its proponents were pursuing technocratic aims rather than legitimate scientific knowledge. Consider, for example, John Embree's 1945 essay, "Applied Anthropology and Its Relationship to Anthropology," published in *American Anthropologist*. For Embree (1945:635), a technocratic anthropology was less of an ethical problem than a threat to the epistemological legitimacy of anthropology qua proper science: "the application of techniques to carry out specific policies…cannot be called true science," he wrote. In fact, "it would save anthropology some future embarrassment if its representatives in government would not insist on calling all of their present activities true anthropology (e.g., work in military intelligence, psychological warfare, administration)" (Embree 1945:635).

ANTHROPOLOGY AND THE STATE AT WAR

Not coincidentally, Embree's examples of technocratic anthropology revolve around functions of war: intelligence, information operations, governance. Like many sciences, anthropology attracts the attention of war makers. From the perspective of governments, it makes sense to involve social scientists in developing and implementing foreign policy during times of conflict. In this regard, anthropology is perhaps particularly relevant: it is the discipline most visibly associated with the close and continued study of other places, populations, and cultures and is perceived as holding valuable knowledge about the social and political dynamics of other peoples and countries. Moreover, anthropologists have a long history of studying violence and warfare, either as integral aspects of larger fieldwork experiences with particular social groups, or as part of a broader effort of cross-cultural comparison aimed at understanding what it means to be human. During times of conflict it is little wonder that the state sees anthropological knowledge as beneficial to its goals.

Yet for anthropologists, the benefits are not so clear. The fraught relationship between science and policy described by Jasanoff is particularly complicated in anthropology because it has such an unwieldy history in relation to government institutions. Peter Pels (1997:165) describes anthropology as "an academic offshoot of a set of universalist technologies of domination" that took shape with the modern imperial state. As a result, the practical deployment of anthropology as an applied endeavor in service of the state has long been a topic of debate among anthropologists.

This has been particularly true since the 1950s with the emergence of educated indigenous elites in Asia, Africa, and Latin America. These new intellectuals articulated sophisticated critiques of the political, economic, and epistemic structures that Western colonialism had imposed on much of the world, including the role of anthropology in realizing the imperial project by providing knowledge that could be used to control local communities. For anthropologists, this critique cut deeply because indigenous leaders pointed out the many ways in which anthropological scholarship had benefited the governing strategies of colonial governments. As Murray Wax (1987:5) points out, indigenous political movements and decolonization shaped the worldview of an entire generation of post–World War II anthropologists who perceived complicated intersections among research, ethics, and politics, and for whom employment with military and intelligence entities represented "a prostitution of valuable professional talents for monies and prestige…[and] a betrayal of the peoples whose welfare anthropology had claimed to cherish."

With this disciplinary narrative in mind anthropologists have argued passionately about the implications of conducting research on behalf of government bureaucracies. This is arguably the most divisive and painful topic in many disciplinary debates about what anthropology is and what anthropologists do, and it extends deeply into their disciplinary history, at least in the United States. It assumes a charged significance during times of war, when questions about the ethics of putting one's knowledge into the service of the state are most pointed. Moreover, it is during wartime that anthropologists have most publicly embraced roles as citizen-experts with a clear stake in affairs of the state: critiquing blind patriotism in the United States during World War I, offering expert opinions in support of guiding racial ideologies in the Third Reich, assisting with psychological operations in the Pacific during World War II, conducting research on tribal cultures in southeast Asia, or holding sit-ins and teach-ins to protest the war in Vietnam, to name a few examples.

This brings us to the 1960s, an especially tumultuous time for anthropology during which grand debates about the nature of anthropology and the role of anthropologists were triggered and contextualized by US counterinsurgency efforts in Latin America, Southeast Asia, and elsewhere. This time is a touchstone for much of today's debate about whether and how anthropologists should (not) engage with military and intelligence institutions in the post–cold war era. The Vietnam War generated particularly sharp debates about anthropologists' engagement with the state-at-war and saw members of the American Anthropological Association (AAA) passing multiple resolutions stating the ethical, scientific, and political concerns of their association. In 1966 the AAA was still reacting to the controversy that engulfed the discipline with the revelation that the government was seeking anthropological participation in Project Camelot, a US counterinsurgency project in Latin America (Horowitz 1967), and there was growing opposition to the war in Vietnam. In this context a group of members, frustrated with the paucity of topics dealing with the "confrontation between the discipline of anthropology and the political and moral dilemmas of the modern world," circulated a petition at the 1966 AAA meetings demanding that the AAA organize symposia on the "effects of war on the human species" (Fried, Harris, and Murphy 1968:x). In response, Morton Fried, Marvin Harris, and Robert Murphy organized a panel that included fifteen of their colleagues presenting and discussing papers on a range of topics related to war: the biological effects of war, human aggression, war and disease, primitive and modern warfare, war and society, the psychology of war, the recruitment and deployment of soldiers, and alternatives to war. The presenters' papers, their discussants' comments, and the remarks of symposia attendees and participants were documented in the 1968 volume *War: The Anthropology of Armed Conflict and Aggression.*

The two years following the publication of the Fried, Harris, and Murphy book moved the intellectual and political confrontations within the AAA to more immediate and public forums. The events of those years, 1969–1971, hold lessons and resonances for current conversations.

In 1968 the executive board of the AAA formed an ad hoc ethics committee that received a one-year charge to develop recommendations about the role, scope, and structure of the activities of a standing ethics committee should have within the association. Joseph Jorgenson and Eric Wolf served on this committee, which "proposed the creation of detailed ethical standards as part of its function, but this along with other suggestions, was rejected by the Executive Board" (Wakin 1992:155). The following year a standing ethics committee was formed to continue this work, and both Wolf and Jorgensen also served on this committee, with Wolf as chair.

There soon followed an episode in the history of anthropology that is now both revered and contested in the retelling (consult Wakin 1992 for the most thorough treatment of the relevant events and background):

A graduate student at UCLA representing the Student Mobilization Committee (SMC), a group opposed to the war in Vietnam, sent Wolf and Jorgensen covertly copied papers from the files of the professor for whom she was working, Michael Moerman. Jorgensen and Wolf quickly determined that Moerman was working on behalf of the US government's counterinsurgency strategy in Southeast Asia. Lauriston Sharp from Cornell University and Herbert Phillips from the University of California were also implicated. In response, Wolf and Jorgensen issued a statement condemning that work as violating anthropological ethics but maintained the confidentiality of the anthropologists involved. At around the same time, the SMC published an issue of its newsmagazine, the *Mobilizer*, that was dedicated to exposing US counterinsurgency activities in Southeast Asia and that named the anthropologists involved in the work condemned by Wolf and Jorgensen. The SMC distributed this issue of the *Mobilizer* along with the statement by Wolf and Jorgensen at the annual meeting of the Association for Asian Studies (AAS).

Together, the Wolf and Jorgensen statement and the revelations in the *Mobilizer* hit like a bombshell. The atmosphere within American anthropology was already quite charged, and the nature of the revelations, the way they came into Wolf and Jorgensen's possession, how they became public, and the devastating professional and personal consequences of the revelations combined to throw the discipline and the AAA into intense turmoil (Jorgensen and Wolf 1970; Foster 2000; Wakin 1992).

Eventually, the AAA executive board admonished Wolf and Jorgensen for their actions, asserting that Wolf and Jorgenson had plainly exceeded the charge given the ad hoc committee and that they had misrepresented themselves as speaking for the association (Foster, Hinton, and Köbben 1971; Foster 2000:210). Others saw the admonishment as an overly bureaucratic act (Jorgensen and Wolf 1970), which some recall as their being reprimanded for "blowing the whistle" (Johnson 2007). At the 1970 AAA annual meeting, Margaret Mead, who had chaired a committee appointed by the board to look into the controversy, announced the board's findings at the business meeting of the association, and she was loudly and widely booed (Foster 2000:211). Wolf and Jorgensen resigned from the ethics committee and published their now-classic paper, "Anthropology on the Warpath in Thailand," in the *New York Review of Books*. Professional relationships and personal friendships were destroyed, some not to be repaired for decades, if ever.

Further details regarding these events can be reviewed elsewhere, as noted. Here we want to point out a few resonances with discussions taking place today by calling attention to several themes that characterized the debates of the 1960s and that run through many of the chapters of this book.

Firstly, one of the most difficult issues that anthropologists faced in the 1960s was the intersection of ethics, politics, and science in anthropology. Normatively, science is independent of politics: professionals have science, citizens have politics, and merging the domains is potentially damaging to the epistemological independence and vitality of science. However, the war in Vietnam sparked debates about whether or not anthropologists should give up the pretense of science as a shield against politics, acknowledge the discipline's embeddedness in the turmoil of the day, and assess the political and ethical implications of anthropology's epistemological commitments to respecting the cultural, political, and social autonomy of other peoples. As this volume illustrates, similar discussions are occurring today in the context of conflicts in Afghanistan and Iraq.

Secondly, closely tied to the intersection of science, ethics, and politics is the question of how anthropologists ought to engage with the US government. During the Vietnam era American anthropologists by and large recognized that one's identity as a citizen necessarily implied responsibility for and engagement with the war. How to put that responsibility into practice was the difficult question: while some anthropologists believed that employing their skills in service of the government might minimize the damage of conflict, others believed that engaging the government with antiwar activism was the most ethically and politically appropriate stance for anthropologists.

In practical terms this raised questions about whether anthropologists should try to keep their knowledge production activities independent from the political turmoil of the Vietnam era; whether anthropology as a science could or should be leveraged in Vietnam to minimize conflict and harm; and whether anthropologists had a moral commitment to stand outside the structures of the state and work as citizen-activists against the war. Even those passionately opposed to anthropological involvement in counterinsurgency work recognized that the question for anthropology was not whether to participate, but how. As Berreman (1968:395) put it in arguing against those he saw as urging that anthropology be separate from current affairs, "They are involved whether they wish it or not. The question is not 'Shall I get involved?' but 'How can I be involved responsibly—in a way consistent with humanity as I understand it?'"

Thirdly, the 1960s brought revelations that anthropologists were involved in counterinsurgency work, which other anthropologists met with rapid, vociferous, and widespread condemnation. Roughly forty years later, whether or not these accusations were indeed founded in reality is questionable. As Keith Brown (2009) points out, anthropologists investigating allegations of disciplinary malpractice have in the past failed to apply to themselves the careful empirical and reflexive practices they champion for studying others. For example, early in the 1960s reports about the existence of Project Camelot led to accusations of widespread unethical behavior on the part of participating anthropologists, including deceptive research tactics. Subsequent documentary research would show that anthropological involvement was actually rather minimal and incidental (Horowitz 1967). Similarly, the incriminating materials Wolf and Jorgensen received were poor-quality photocopies "so voluminous that they fill a file cabinet drawer" (Foster 2000:210). Wolf and Jorgensen apparently reported their findings before they had carefully examined the entire corpus of the material, and when Wolf later spoke forcefully about the direct contribution of anthropology to military efforts in Thailand, he quoted a report written by a D. J. Blakeslee. Yet the Blakeslee who authored the report in question was not an anthropologist holding membership in the AAA, despite Wolf's assumption and assertions to the contrary (Wakin 1992:210, 226).

Similar dynamics continue to permeate the discipline today, with anthropologists in an uproar over a range of issues from the use of anthropological knowledge in torture to the employment of anthropologists in US Army Human Terrain Teams (HTTs). Some of these concerns are less well founded (for example, anthropologically informed torture; see McNamara this volume) than others (the potential for misuse of information collected by the army's HTTs). Recently, both Keith Brown (2009) and Robert Rubinstein (2009) have suggested that Mary Douglas's analysis of the dynamics of ritual pollution might profitably be used to understand anthropologists' visceral reactions to allegations of improper behavior on the part of their colleagues who are seen as morally defiled by their contact with the national security state.[1] Often this is coupled with a further suggestion that such association by some anthropologists raises concerns of fieldwork accessibility and safety for all anthropologists. It is worth noting that this is not a trivial concern given the dispersion of anthropological research sites throughout the world.

Once again, such concerns are contiguous with the past. For example, one of the reasons that anthropologists in the 1960s responded so quickly to allegations that their colleagues were participating in counterinsurgency (or working on behalf of the army, the intelligence community, or in some other function supporting the government at war) was a fear that such activities might tarnish anthropology's reputation for openness and honesty, creating dangerous conditions for anthropologists in the field and perhaps limiting access to field sites. These are not new concerns and indeed have a long history, reaching back to Franz Boas's (1919) revelation that some anthropologists had been working as spies for the US government. Today, many of us worry that individual anthropologists will be unable to pursue fieldwork safely, while others believe that being professionally associated with anthropologists who are pursuing work in, for, or on behalf of the national security state will affect their own careers negatively. These issues are discussed in several of the chapters in this volume (especially Ben-Ari, Ferguson, and Rubinstein).

The debates triggered by anthropological encounters with the national security state raise questions about whether anthropology is properly conceived of as a science—and if so, whether this status excludes a politically committed form of anthropology—and they also raise questions about the proper political role of the AAA in anthropology more generally. The fact that the AAA has a code of ethics is a direct outcome of the ferment of the Vietnam era. Back then many anthropologists believed that the AAA should consider changing its role to that of a professional organization with the standing to license, sanction, investigate, and assume political positions. During the Vietnam era many AAA members believed that the organization was ineffectual, slow, and overly bureaucratic—as, for example, did Jorgensen and Wolf (1971), who wrote that the "emphasis on procedures rather than on issues...caused us to reject what seemed to us 'a bureaucratic interpretation of the role of the committee.'" Others argued that the AAA was more properly an organization for disciplinary advancement, having neither sanctioning nor coercive authorities, nor explicit political alignments. These issues are arising once again: since 2006 the AAA has impaneled two committees to address issues of ethics and practice at the intersection of anthropology and national security, including the Commission on the Engagement of Anthropology with the US Security and Intelligence Communities and the Task Force for Comprehensive Ethics Review. Debates have also occurred regarding changes to the AAA's code of ethics as proposed by Terence Turner at the 2007 AAA meetings.

Lastly, it is worth emphasizing what several of our non-American seminarians pointed out to us: the debates of both the 1960s and today have been dominated by American concerns. In the wake of the war in Vietnam A. J. F. Köbben, citing comments made by New Zealand-Canadian anthropologist Cyril Belshaw, argued that the questions being asked in the debate were out of touch with their non-American perspectives (Foster, Hinton, and Köbben 1971). Similarly, three of our contributors come from outside the United States (Irwin, Tomforde, and Ben-Ari), and their chapters speak to the issue of how American historical and political framings dominate American perspectives about the international challenges of anthropology.

SEMINARS, DISCUSSIONS, AND A BOOK (OR TWO)

Our Seminars

The School for Advanced Research (SAR) in Santa Fe, New Mexico, sponsored two seminars upon which this volume is based. SAR has a long history of providing scholars with a quiet setting in which to consider momentous and contentious topics for anthropology. The precipitating events for our seminars were both international and disciplinary in scope. The encroachment of state objectives on disciplinary trajectories is a trend that many anthropologists—glancing back to Project Camelot, Vietnam, and Project Phoenix—find deeply worrisome. Given this history, many anthropologists were concerned that declarations of war in Afghanistan and later Iraq would eventually bring military attention to anthropological research in particular, as this is the field most associated with social science abroad.

Sure enough, in recent years several events have signaled US government interest in social science expertise, with two in particular capturing the attention of anthropologists. The first was the formation of the US Army's Human Terrain System (HTS), with its explicit focus on anthropology and its deployment of teams pairing civilian social scientists with military personnel to gather in-country data on human geographies. The second was Secretary of Defense Robert Gates's April 2008 speech to the Association of American Universities in which he announced the establishment of the Minerva Program to direct social science research toward national security problems. Such highly publicized marriages of social science knowledge and military funding have only confirmed many anthropologists' suspicions that US military and intelligence activities are actively reshaping anthropology, with potentially disastrous consequences for the discipline and the peoples it studies.

The SAR seminars both occurred within and addressed this fraught context. They had their roots in an airplane conversation between Laura McNamara and SAR President James Brooks after the 2006 Society for Applied Anthropology (SfAA) meetings in Vancouver, Canada. McNamara had just co-chaired a panel on anthropological epistemology, morality, and practice in which a multinational panel of practitioners working in military contexts described the intersection of ethics and practice in their own work lives. Brooks pointed out that anthropologists studying human violence rarely engage with practicing anthropologists working in military contexts and suggested that bringing people from these two areas into dialogue might precipitate new perspectives and insights about the relationship between anthropologists and state entities during times of war. He asked McNamara to work with Neil Whitehead of the University of Wisconsin to convene a short seminar in 2007 that would allow anthropologists who work in or among military personnel to speak with their counterparts who study violence and warfare in human society. The partnership structurally reflected the seminar's goals: McNamara is an organizational anthropologist who has conducted fieldwork among nuclear weapons experts and intelligence analysts in the US government, while Whitehead has spent much of his career studying shamanism, warfare, and violence.

At Brooks's suggestion, the first seminar aimed only at dialogue. It took place in February 2007 and included many of the contributors to this book: Brian Ferguson, professor of anthropology at Rutgers University; David Price, professor of anthropology at St. Martin's College in Washington; Robert Rubinstein, professor of anthropology and international relations at the Maxwell School of Syracuse University; Anne Irwin, chair of civil-military relations at the University of Calgary; and Eric Haanstad, a doctoral candidate from the University of Wisconsin and SAR Weatherhead fellow. These participants represented a wide breadth of present-day anthropological involvement in and around a range of field sites, including relations between US government and academic entities (Price), nuclear weapons experts and intelligence analysts (McNamara), Canadian infantry deployed in Afghanistan (Irwin), Amazonian shamans (Whitehead), the Yanomami (Ferguson), Thai police officers (Haanstad), and UN peacekeepers (Rubinstein). McNamara and Whitehead asked participants to consider a range of themes, including the ethics and practice of fieldwork in groups that engage in violence, the changing relationship between anthropology and institutions of power, anthropological research on human violence, the politics of anthropology, and how national traditions shape distinctive relationships between scholars and governments in different countries. They also asked the participants to consider how and if anthropologists should attempt to effect change in the institutions that they study and to consider the tradeoff between the risks of engagement in ethically fraught environments and the benefits to the discipline from knowledge produced therein.

This first seminar was initially tentative, then tense, and finally honest as the participants learned to engage each other in productive discussions. Rather than focusing on the anthropology of violence in different professional contexts, the first seminar turned out to be a kind of summit among anthropologists with very different ideas about the ethics of engaging the "national security state" (it should be noted that this is a highly US-centric term, as our Canadian colleague Anne Irwin repeatedly pointed out to us), convened during a time of active military conflict. Most participants brought preconceived notions about "them" and "us" to the seminar table. For example, several of the participants had very strong opinions against formal associations between anthropology and the military or intelligence communities and looked suspiciously on the politics and ethics of the seminar participants who had engaged such entities in their work. Likewise, the participants studying government military or intelligence functions arrived with their own biases—for example, about anthropologists who publicly distance themselves from powerful institutions yet fail to critique academia as a center of economic, epistemological, and political authority. These biases came out into the open as we took turns explaining to each other how we came to be the anthropologists we had become and as we questioned and commented on each others' fieldwork, employment decisions, and career trajectories. In doing so we recognized that each of us faced the similar challenge of defining, integrating, and enacting identities as members of a discipline and as members of a democracy; that we faced this challenge in a range of contexts, from academia to government work; and that differences in how we made sense of and put professional identities into practice were sources of friction among several of us in the room (McNamara 2007a).

This theme—the intersection of the personal, the professional, and the political and the tensions this creates for all of us—was productive enough that our group collectively agreed to request support from SAR for a second, more formal seminar organized around the theme of "Scholars, Security, and Citizenship," for which invitees would draft papers, engage in several days of structured discussions, and perhaps generate a book. As a group, we identified four goals for a follow-on seminar: first, we wanted to invite anthropologists from a range of countries to complicate US-centric perspectives on academic-military relations; second, we wanted both academic and practicing anthropologists with connections to a wide range of state and private institutions; third, we wanted participants to report their own experiences with such encounters; and last, we wanted participants who had experience studying violence, warfare, or the military from a variety of perspectives, both within and outside government institutions.

We also identified a set of overarching themes that the seminar would address. Firstly, we decided to reflect on historical intersections between anthropology and the state and to consider how our own personal understandings of these intersections shape our choices in work and research. Secondly, the relationship between personal politics and disciplinary ethos was up for examination: how do personal political commitments impact standards about what constitutes appropriate research, perceptions of intellectual quality, the evaluation of scholarly practice, and the ethics of funding? And finally, we would consider the intersection of our responsibilities as scholars and citizens, in war and in peace.

McNamara and Whitehead also organized the second seminar. Many of the first seminar's participants—including Ferguson, Irwin, McNamara, Price, Rubinstein, and Whitehead—contributed papers to and participated in the second seminar. To this mix we added Clementine Fujimura, a professor of language and culture at the US Naval Academy and one of the few professional anthropologists who teaches US military personnel. We also broadened our view of the relationship between anthropology and the military beyond the boundaries of the United States by including several scholars from outside the country: Nasser Abufarha, a Palestinian anthropologist who studies violence in the Israeli-Palestinian conflict, as well as Eyal Ben-Ari of Hebrew University in Jerusalem and Maren Tomforde of the German Bundeswehr, anthropologists who conduct fieldwork among, respectively, Israeli and German military personnel.

In contrast to the previous seminar, participants were asked to contribute a draft paper for group discussion that would take place over a two-and-a-half-day retreat in Santa Fe. For their papers, the seminarians were asked to consider several interrelated themes. We asserted that cultural anthropology's disciplinary identity is strongly shaped by its colonial history, particularly its ambivalent positioning within the colonial project and the waves of reassessment that anthropology has undergone since the end of the colonial era. We noted anthropology's ongoing political and ethical commitment to what Laura Nader (1972:303) memorably called "the underdog"—those who are not only systematically underrepresented among institutions of power but who are also most vulnerable to exploitation. When cultural anthropologists do "study up,"[2] their work often assumes a form of ethnographic critique aimed at revealing the tensions, cracks, and contradictions in the institutions whose power they take for granted (Marcus 1999:xi).

Inevitably, we argued, these twin commitments to advocacy and critique exist in uneasy tension with anthropological projects that are perceived to align with the goals of powerful institutions: consumer research in emerging markets for multinational corporations, for example, or research among local populations on behalf of military agencies charged with stabilization and reconstruction in conflict zones. At the same time we noted that not all anthropologists experience these tensions in the same way: for example, different national histories with science, politics, and the military have shaped how anthropologists in various countries perceive the relationship between knowledge and power in their own work. Moreover, we recognized that anthropological practice is not determined by institutional settings and wondered how individual anthropologists create their work as they address the myriad expectations of their colleagues, their employers, and their discipline.

Accordingly, we asked our contributors to consider their own practice in the context of myriad disciplinary, political, social, and institutional commitments we all have as human beings. After all, we suggested, how anthropologists balance these commitments in their work lives bears on what each of them considers appropriate research, how they set standards for intellectual quality, and what kind of funding sources are ethically acceptable and practically available. Moreover, all these questions are not only important for anthropologists today but also in training upcoming generations.

In offering these questions for consideration, we gave contributors great leeway in developing their essays. The seminarians were told that they could blend biography and scholarship in whatever balance they felt was appropriate to address the themes at hand. As a result, we ended up with quite a diverse group of essays, from the historical to the ethnographic to the reflective and autobiographical. Some wrote about how the tensions we identified played out in their own careers, while others developed case studies or position papers. These were the basis for the second seminar, which took place in Santa Fe in July 2008. For this seminar, each seminarian acted as a discussant for another seminarian's paper, and we touched on many of the same themes and topics that we had identified in the previous year's shorter seminar.

The discussions were both spirited and collegial until something quite dramatic occurred on the second day: when we raised the possibility of revising the papers for compilation into a book, the seminar broke down rather suddenly over issues of publication, ownership, and institutional affiliation. This conflict only bears mentioning because it is germane to this volume: several of the participants announced that they did not want to publish their essays with contributors perceived as having "military" or "national security" affiliations. Given that the goal of the seminar was to bring anthropologists from multiple perspectives into sustained conversation without attempting to establish or dictate unity on the very contentious problems being discussed, this was a disappointing outcome.

In the end the book project split apart. Several of us agreed to continue working together, and in the spring of 2009 we developed the SAR-sponsored plenary session "Scholars, Security, and Citizenship" at the SfAA meetings in Santa Fe. In the meantime, Whitehead decided to put together a separate volume, while we (McNamara and Rubinstein) took over editorial duties for the remaining seminarians' papers and developed this volume. In doing so we were fortunate to have additional contributions from two people who did not attend the seminar. Danny Hoffman was a resident Weatherhead fellow at SAR at the time we were putting the book together and agreed to contribute a paper based on his fieldwork in Sierra Leone. In addition, we contacted Douglas Fry and asked if he would write a review of his work on violence and culture, and he kindly agreed. Later, our colleague Clementine Fujimura decided to withdraw her paper and redevelop it for a different venue entirely.

Our Contributors

Writing in *War*, Sol Tax (1968:195) observed that "large questions of war and peace require a very broad perspective." Yet because wars generate political polarization, it is difficult during these times to engage in thoughtful reflection on the morally, ethically, and methodologically fraught problem of whether and how anthropologists should engage with the military, intelligence, and diplomatic institutions that comprise such an important part of the modern state. At a time when anthropologists are once again deeply concerned about the use of anthropological knowledge in the context of war, this book aims at such a broad perspective. In organizing this volume we asked contributors to consider different aspects of their experience in studying violence, war, and the state and in doing so to reflect on how they enact their roles as citizens and scholars.

This volume explores the presence of such themes in the lived experience of individual scholars, each of whom has a unique perspective—by virtue of fieldwork, professional affiliation, or personal experience—on the relationship between anthropology and the state-at-war. Although most of the volume's contributors hold academic positions, many have followed somewhat nontraditional career or fieldwork paths. For example, McNamara and Tomforde are employed as government anthropologists in the defense and national security sectors in their countries. Four contributors— Rubinstein, Tomforde, Irwin, and Ben-Ari—have conducted fieldwork among military personnel, both in their home countries and in deployments abroad. Price, Ferguson, and McNamara all rely on primary government documents to develop arguments about the changing relationship between the pen and the sword during times of war. Both Fry and Hoffman's research looks abroad, but their work reflects a decided emphasis on using ethnography and field data as a means of understanding and critiquing the present in their home countries.

Danny Hoffman's experiences in Sierra Leone emphasize the importance of looking beyond issues of immediate political significance to anthropology, such as the Human Terrain System, to identify the many settings in which anthropologists are likely to encounter (or be encountered by) the national security state. While conducting fieldwork with Sierra Leone's Civil Defense Forces (CDF), Hoffman witnessed the establishment of the US African Command (AFRICOM) and saw the early stirrings of a new way of war making in which private contractors to Western governments outsource fighting to local militias. Like that of Catherine Lutz (for example, Lutz 2009), Hoffman's work points to the bureaucratic expansion of empire through a range of organizational channels, not all of which are in the direct control of the governments jockeying for presence in Africa. Moreover, the emphasis on counterinsurgency warfare and the wielding of "soft power" brings social science concerns into uneasy alignment with those of the national security state, creating new contexts in which social science theories, methods, and findings can be drawn into policymaking without the kind of relatively open and traceable engagements implied by the HTS.

Similarly, Laura McNamara's chapter on counterterrorism interrogation practice looks at the emergence of new bureaucratic forms during the Global War on Terror. Many anthropologists were livid about the alleged use of Raphael Patai's ethnography *The Arab Mind* as a source of inspiration for torture techniques documented in Abu Ghraib. In contrast, McNamara emphasizes that interrogation, not just torture, should be of long-term concern to social scientists: not only does it represent a novel amalgamation of criminal justice and military imperatives, but it is largely an unmarked category of state activity whose legal and ethical foundations are taken for granted in comparison to torture. Moreover, her research points to the value of government documents as a valid source of data for ethnographers "studying up," seeking to understand not only how scholarship comes into the service of power, but how individuals within government agencies engage with discourses of national security to produce the new practices of empire.

We know that policymakers and tactical operators do find ethnographic research useful in military decision making, as investments in the HTS and the Minerva initiative demonstrate. David Price's essay reminds us that the direct incorporation of ethnographic research into war-making efforts is neither new nor particularly original, as anthropology is recurrently drawn into formal and informal relationships with military and intelligence entities during times of war. Price reaches back to the war in Vietnam for a comparative case study that examines Gerald Hickey's research with Vietnamese villagers in support of the Strategic Hamlet Program. In Price's view, Hickey's belief that his work was blunting the negative effects of war blinded him to the fact that his work was being conducted in the context of a neocolonial occupation in which ethnographic fieldwork directly informed projects of domination and control. As a contrast to Hickey, Price points to Del Jones, who came to realize during his fieldwork in Chiang Mai that his work on cultural variation in Northern Thailand was of great interest to military planners. Not only did Jones refuse to assist US military efforts in Southeast Asia, but he worked to raise the awareness among anthropologists in the United States that ethnographic research could indeed further the oppression of the indigenous peoples under study.

As an anthropologist employed by the German Federal Ministry of Defense, the Bundeswehr, Maren Tomforde presents an alternative perspective on the history of anthropology and its relationship to the state. As it has embraced its post–cold war mission of international peacekeeping and stability operations, the Bundeswehr has increasingly recognized the importance of social scientists as a source of advice and insight into improving the intercultural skills of military personnel working in foreign countries with international armies. This troubles many German anthropologists who remember the way that ethnographic scholarship was offered and enthusiastically embraced by the National Socialists as justification for their racialized ideology, with disastrous consequences. However, Tomforde is part of a new trend of anthropologists studying military personnel in their home countries, examining how German soldiers adapt to the personal and professional stresses presented by international peacekeeping operations. At a time when the political concerns of American anthropology dominate disciplinary debates about the ethics of engagement, Tomforde reminds us that the United States is not the only country in which a fraught history of scholarly–government relations continues to shape perceptions about the implications of knowledge production for the state.

Like many of the two seminars' participants, R. Brian Ferguson is deeply concerned about programs such as the HTS and the possible effects of national security–directed funding, such as that presented by the Minerva initiative, on anthropology in the United States. Ferguson used his participation in the seminar as an opportunity to consider the multiple ways in which anthropology might become implicated in the security sector: in teaching, through the appropriation of research for military or intelligence purposes, in providing analysts or advisers, or in collecting data or conducting fieldwork on behalf of the state. For Ferguson, some forms of engagement are more troublesome than others—like Franz Boas before him, Ferguson worries about the pursuit of espionage activities under the guise of legitimate field research. Yet most situations are murkier, presenting complex ethical and methodological challenges for scholars in a range of settings. No matter what line of work one chooses, Ferguson points out that politically neutral scholarship is impossible. He argues that anthropologists must remain vigilant regarding the political and social contexts in which they conduct their work—for example, by tracking the orientation and actions of particular presidential administrations—so that they can assess the implications of their research for the people they study and inform themselves before committing to any kind of direct engagement on behalf of the state.

Anne Irwin considers the relationship between journalism and anthropology, using a small controversy over her own fieldwork among Canadian soldiers (she was derogatorily referred to as an "embedded anthropologist" by a number of her Canadian colleagues) as an entry for how knowledge practices and commitments differ between anthropology and journalism. Like Tomforde and Ben-Ari, Irwin reveals how national differences in the evolving relationships among the academy, the military, and the polity challenge the dominant US-centric discourse on the ethics of engagement with military institutions. In Canada the military is not as politically powerful as it is in the United States, but the expanding involvement of Canadian forces in international operations, such as the war in Afghanistan, is drawing public attention to the role of the military in Canadian foreign policy. Enter Christie Blatchford, a journalist who was embedded for a short period of time with the infantry unit that Irwin was observing in Afghanistan. The mechanisms through which Blatchford gained access to the deployed unit, the methods she used to gather information, the events that captured her attention, and the delivery of "the story" contrasted sharply with Irwin's experience, despite the fact that both she and Blatchford had similar roles as participants, observers, and witnesses to the microdynamics of state violence. Like many of the other contributors to this book, Irwin critiques the chauvinism that characterizes much of academia's attitude toward the military, arguing instead that military culture presents fieldwork challenges as complex and fascinating as any other. And like Hoffman, Irwin points out that anthropologists have a unique role as dedicated, long-term witnesses, one that may become increasingly important as news organizations cut budgets for foreign correspondents.

Robert Rubinstein has spent most of the past three decades conducting fieldwork on and writing about the international settings where UN peacekeeping forces are deployed. Like Ferguson and Price, Rubinstein does not believe in the possibility of a purely neutral, disengaged anthropology, particularly in the context of state institutions. However, he goes in a different direction: rather than eschewing all forms of work with the security sector, Rubinstein argues that anthropologists, as citizens and as skilled experts, may have a moral responsibility to engage the very institutions whose conduct they find so reprehensible. Unlike Ferguson, Rubinstein believes that anthropologists need to commit to very long periods of engagement across political administrations if they are to understand and effect change in how their scholarship is perceived and applied. Drawing on his fieldwork and professional experience, Rubinstein argues that by refusing to "go native" and by introducing individual military and intelligence experts to nuanced framings of world events, anthropologists can challenge the taken-for-granted narratives of militarized foreign policy that have dominated US strategic thinking for such a long period of time.

Eyal Ben-Ari's essay turns anthropology's impulse to critique back on the discipline itself, as he points out current debates about fieldwork in military settings evince a particularly American construction of academia, one that uncritically couples ethics and politics, stresses particular forms of scholarly activism, and divides anthropologists who study war and violence into "good" and "bad" camps based on perceived professional and political positioning vis-à-vis military entities. As an Israeli anthropologist who studies military institutions, Ben-Ari is well positioned to describe how political dynamics emanating from the academic centers of the United States shape international standards for assessing the legitimacy of research. Like Ferguson, Ben-Ari is interested in how anthropologists select contexts of engagement; however, Ben-Ari reflects on his own research and professional experience in the Israeli Defense Forces (IDF) to ask how anthropologists can best pursue research in military contexts: to understand the institutional dynamics that legitimize and perpetuate violence, and in doing so, meet their obligations as citizens.

We decided to close this volume with an essay from Douglas Fry, an anthropologist who has spent most of his career carefully gathering data and reviewing evidence related to patterns of violence and warfare across cultures and through historical periods. As Fry points out, the idea that war is somehow a natural state of affairs for humanity is not only poorly supported by available empirical evidence, but is scientifically and politically dangerous. As Fry demonstrates, we tend to find what we are looking for, and assumptions that humans in their natural state are prone to violent forms of conflict resolution creates a distorting lens through which social scientists perceive and interpret human behavior. For citizens, such thinking reinforces the concept that war is somehow inevitable, creating the groundwork for a self-fulfilling prophecy with disastrous consequences for the human beings deployed to fight wars.

As the chapters in this volume demonstrate, there are many ways in which anthropologists engage the national security state. For some, engagement takes the form of protest from a position external to the policies and practices to which they object. For others, particular aspects of the national security state become the objects of study. For still others, the engagement brings them firmly inside the national security state, working to bring their anthropological expertise to support or perhaps attempt to change state policies. The range of ways these engagements take place is quite broad, and a single anthropologist may over the course of a career enact each of these forms.

The broad range of ways in which anthropologists individually and collectively engage the national security state should, of course, be no surprise. One of anthropology's many contributions is the description and understanding of the rich variety of ways that people seek to solve problems of living, both social and physical. We know, too, that in all societies people can act to solve those problems by enacting equally legitimate but potentially contradictory strategies from a broader cultural repertoire (Bateson 1988). It follows, then, that in trying to address the actions of their own political institutions, anthropologists will work in a wide variety of ways, some of which may be mutually contradictory.

One of the contributions made by this collection is the serious exploration of this variety and the presentation of a set of inquiries that seek to theorize these engagements. No matter what form anthropologists' engagement with the national security state takes, it holds many risks for them as individuals and for the discipline. The chapters in this volume discuss many of these risks, though not all of them. For those who engage by standing apart and protesting the state's actions, there is the risk of losing access to funding, if the state should exert its power to keep them from work. For those who engage by studying the institutions of the national security state, the personal risks involve being placed in ethically and morally difficult situations. They may also risk marginalization within their discipline. Anthropologists who work inside the national security state may discover that their scholarly work does not have the effect they intend, or even that it is misused, while professionally they may find themselves misunderstood or demonized within the discipline. Each of these ways of relating to the national security state creates risks for the discipline as well. Perhaps the discipline will be delegitimated and treated as irrelevant by those whose decisions and actions anthropologists would like to affect or access to fieldwork settings will become more difficult and dangerous. No matter what, anthropologists relating to the national security state are faced with a range of difficult personal and professional decisions. In short, any form of engagement with the national security state is likely to be dangerous.

Acknowledgments

We would like to first acknowledge the School for Advanced Research in Santa Fe for its commitment to a project that at times seemed unbearably fraught and for the patience of its staff in helping us bring this manuscript to publication. We would particularly like to thank James Brooks, John Kanter, Catherine Cocks, Lisa Pacheco, Lynn Thompson Baca, Nancy Owen Lewis, and Leslie Shipman for their hospitality (particularly Leslie for the fabulous meals she provided the seminarians). With SAR, the Society for Applied Anthropology co-sponsored a plenary seminar at its 2008 meetings in Santa Fe that gave us a timely opportunity to present our ideas to a broader audience. Two anonymous reviewers provided valuable guidance as we revised this manuscript. We also extend our thanks to the many friends and colleagues over the past few years who have provided input and advice as we developed this volume; you are too many to name, unfortunately, but you know who you are. We are deeply grateful to the excellent scholars who contributed to this volume and who participated in our seminars for their ideas, commentary, occasional hilarity, and refreshing open-mindedness. Lastly, both editors are fortunate to have patient families, spouses, and friends who helped us maintain balance and perspective as we brought this project to fruition. Thank you.

Notes

1. The concept of the "national security state" refers to a state that uses its resources and organizes its activities to support the defense of the state. In the second half of the twentieth century, post–World War II, this led to the elaboration of the "military industrial complex," but it also includes using economic institutions and development activities as security weapons (see, for example, Barnet 1985).

2. Commenting on the tendency for anthropologists to study people and groups who were outside of institutions of power within their societies, or even marginalized from them, Laura Nader pointed out in 1972 that this practice effectively kept anthropology focused on topics that contributed little to the understanding of contemporary problems, and thus from contributing to solving those problems. Nader (1972:303) suggested that to correct this shortcoming anthropologists needed to study up as well as down, writing, "We are not dealing with an either/or proposition; we need simply to realize when it is useful or crucial in terms of the problem to extend the domain of study up, down or sideways."

Dangerous Liaisons

1

The Subcontractor

Counterinsurgency, Militias, and the New Common Ground in Social and Military Science

Danny Hoffman

You have the green light.... You can't just shoot anybody. No vengeance....
But the bad guys...I don't care. Go get them.

> —*Col. Ricky D. Gibbs, 4th Brigade, 1st Infantry Division, US Army,*
> *to Sunni leaders mobilizing community defense units in Rasheed,*
> *Baghdad. Quoted in the* Washington Post, *July 27, 2007*

In the Global War on Terror (GWOT) imaginary, Africa is dangerous. The continent's so-called failed states and ungovernable conflict zones are spaces of unlimited threat. They are the "terra incognita" in which "dark networks" proliferate (Renzi 2006a). Liberia, Somalia, Mauritania, and a host of others appear to combine poverty, religious extremism, ethnic nationalism, weak governance, and vast natural resource wealth in ways that observers find dangerously unacceptable to global security. Yet US and European security sector strategists concerned about Africa labor in the shadow of the 1993 debacle of US operations in Somalia and in a policy environment with little understanding of African affairs and little appetite for heavy investment in the continent. Military planners must innovate when it comes to Africa and its threats—and they must do it on the cheap.

Witness AFRICOM. With little fanfare, the US military's Africa Command became fully operational on October 1, 2008. For the first time, AFRICOM makes sub-Saharan Africa the exclusive focus of an entire apparatus of US military services. But of the six regions that make up the military's unified command structure, AFRICOM is unique. It hosts relatively few US troops and its focus is "civilian-military partnerships."[1] Half of AFRICOM's staff is civilian, not military. One of its two deputy commanders is a State Department officer. Its mission is a complex mix of training support, disaster and humanitarian relief efforts, development assistance, and economic projects. "Bases? Garrisons? It's not about that," said Gen. William Ward, the new AFRICOM commander, in an interview at the operational launch. "We are trying to prevent conflict, as opposed to having to react to a conflict" (Shankar 2008:10; see also McMichael [2008]). AFRICOM, it would seem, is a bold experiment. But it is one that military leaders believe "could change how the American government does business around the globe" (Bennet 2008).

I begin this chapter with Africa and with the largely unnoticed inauguration of AFRICOM because it illustrates an important absence in discussions about the relationship between social science and the global security sector today. For the past few years, that conversation has been dominated by military programs like the Human Terrain System (HTS) and by concerns over mercenary anthropology in the wars in Afghanistan and Iraq. The emphasis is on embedded scholars and the way the military seeks to employ academics for strategic cultural insights. As important as those debates are, they overshadow more ambiguous contexts in which social scientists encounter the security sector. What these debates miss is that the military has in recent years grown more amorphous and harder to locate. So too have the field sites that are in or out of its purview.

In this chapter I argue that changes in US military philosophy and structure make it more likely that in the future, scholarly and military research will overlap at the level of the subcontractor. What I mean by this is that field researchers are most likely to find themselves in circumstances in which the labor of war and the knowledge production about war have been outsourced. Counterinsurgency (COIN) operations are now central to the US military mission worldwide, a development with profound ramifications for local communities and for community-based social sciences. COIN strategy increasingly seeks to mobilize local populations to provide for their own security or to assist regular troops in doing so. This greatly expands the number of social scientists, particularly anthropologists, whose work will overlap with US and other security apparatuses and shifts the kinds of demands that will be placed on scholarly knowledge. Overtly "helping the military win" is the extreme case of social scientists' relationship to military science. But it is one that doesn't necessarily address the practical, theoretical, and ethical challenges most ethnographers face when they come into contact with, or are asked to serve as, the subcontractors of war.

Here I take the proliferation of militias in the recent conflict in West Africa's Mano River region as emblematic of the future overlap between social and military science. In Sierra Leone and Liberia local community defense forces received considerable training, materiel, and logistical support from a range of international actors interested in the outcome of the war but unwilling or unable to commit conventional state or multinational combat forces. This was an outsourced war. The result was the militarization of an entire region. In a profound reorganization of the social, economic, and political landscape, young men were made available for rapid assembly and deployment wherever and whenever necessary, fighting as part-time combatants against a highly decentralized, networked enemy.

This mode of outsourcing violence to local communities is increasingly important to how US military thinkers approach global security. Although expanded greatly as a result of US president George W. Bush's poorly planned wars in Afghanistan and Iraq, the strategy of devolving security to local actors seems also to be central to the post-Bush "soft power" strategy of the United States. For social scientists, this means the figure of the embedded professional researcher grows obsolete even as programs like the Human Terrain System are in their infancy. The future promises less demand for the kind of "culture knowledge" that an embedded researcher can provide and fewer of the large deployments of combat troops that gave rise to Human Terrain Teams (HTT) in Afghanistan and Iraq. On one hand, this avoids some of the more pressing contemporary debates over the propriety of working "for" the military. On the other, it presents a different set of quandaries—and possibilities—for what it means to do politically committed and ethical fieldwork.

THE ALREADY OBSOLETE EMBEDDED ANTHROPOLOGIST

"Something mysterious is going on inside the US Department of Defense," writes Montgomery McFate (2005:24a), an anthropologist working with the US military. Top US military officials such as Army Maj. Gen. Robert Scales, Defense Secretary Robert Gates, and Central Command Chief Gen. David Petraeus have begun to argue for a new emphasis within the military on cultural understanding—or what one author calls "ethnographic intelligence" (Renzi 2006a). In a survey of US military relations with local social actors in Iraq, Lt. Col. Michael Eisenstadt (2007:174) writes that "cultural knowledge is the ultimate in force protection."[2] More poetically, a *Military Review* article on HTS opens: "Conducting military operations in a low-intensity conflict without ethnographic and cultural intelligence is like building a house without using your thumbs" (Kipp et al. 2006:1). This is indeed a radical shift. For decades the preoccupation within the military has been technological innovation and the hard sciences. But if the war in Vietnam put a damper on military theorists' interest in foreign cultures, the war in Iraq has rekindled it (M. McFate 2005a).

The Human Terrain System is the most visible exemplar of this cultural turn, putting professional anthropologists at the heart of the paradigm shift. Within the discipline HTS has been the focus of debates over how scholars relate to government security forces at this historical moment. (As Ben-Ari points out in this volume, these are particularly *American* debates, due not only to the hegemony of the US military but also to the hegemony of the US academy.) The program embeds professional ethnographers in small teams (the HTTs) of mixed civilian/military personnel to collect data on the ground in Afghanistan and Iraq (see Ferguson, this volume; González 2009a; and Kipp et al. 2006 for more detailed descriptions of the HTS program). The underlying principle is that for US military forces, understanding the cultural contexts of an area of operations pays off in multiple ways. In contrast to the "drain the swamp"[3] approach to counterinsurgency that has dominated military thinking, the new culturalists argue that understanding local norms generates better intelligence, wins hearts and minds, and makes US combat operations more effective and more precise.

The narrow definition of culture at work here and the usefulness of various forms of cultural knowledge have been the subjects of a great deal of commentary, particularly as they relate to HTS and to the new *U.S. Army/Marine Corps Counterinsurgency Field Manual* (see González 2007b, 2008b; M. McFate 2007; M. McFate and Fondacaro 2008; Price 2007). The ethics of HTS work has been even more fiercely contested. That participation in HTS violates the American Anthropological Association (AAA) code of ethics seems to be the view of an overwhelming majority of AAA members, though a vocal minority has argued that the HTS ultimately benefits "researched" communities by reducing the lethality of military operations. The fact that at least some members of HTTs are armed has generated profound discomfort and raises the question of whether HTS ethnographic research can be conducted with subjects' informed consent. Even when unarmed, the HTTs' military uniforms and armed escorts have led many scholars to question whether future researchers will be negatively affected as social science work in general is associated with military operations.

These are extremely important debates. There is no doubt that the consequences are serious for scholars throughout the social sciences, perhaps most notably in anthropology. The outcome of this disciplinary self-examination stands to reshape not only how ethnographic research is done and by whom, but how it is taught and how it is disseminated.

Nevertheless, it is a debate that has been defined largely by the exceptional case. Although the numbers are hard to pin down, the HTS at present involves very few personnel in very specific circumstances.[4] As a number of contributors to this volume point out, the classroom, rather than the front lines, is a much more likely place for academy-based anthropologists to encounter security personnel.

More importantly, given its current configuration, it seems unlikely that the HTS is a sustainable program. Despite the fact that the program is in its infancy at the time of this writing (it is still referred to as a "proof of concept" program on its website), despite the fact that its funding has increased, and despite the fact that it seems so perfectly in tune with the military leadership's new appreciation for culture, it is a program that is ineffective—and strangely anachronistic.

Embedded anthropologists have to date been poorly trained and are often much less knowledgeable about the communities in which they work than are the soldiers who have been stationed there for considerably longer (Ephron and Spring 2008). Serious questions have been raised about early glowing reports of massive reductions in violence and improved relations with local communities (Rohde 2007). What's more, the various armed services are expanding their own capacity for cultural training. Add the backlash from the AAA and other professional organizations, and one can guess that in the future the military will rely on its own personnel to do on-the-ground ethnography rather than bringing in professional civilian ethnographers.

Indeed, it is instructive to read the counterinsurgency literature in military journals like *Military Review* and note their lack of emphasis on civilian researchers in their calls for rethinking counterinsurgency warfare. In his article on the need for ethnographic intelligence, for example, Lt. Col. Fred Renzi (2006a) elaborates a proposal for ethnographers and culture analysts based out of US embassies but focuses exclusively on training US military personnel for this task. In his analysis of "indirect" military action in the Philippines, Col. Gregory Wilson (2006) writes of special forces operations in which small military units trained in local languages and cultural practices (and without embedded civilian ethnographers) surveyed local sociopolitical environments as they supported the Armed Forces of the Philippines in counterinsurgency measures. US Marine Corps Maj. Ben Connable (2009), in a forceful critique of the HTS program, points out that the US military already trains personnel for the tasks envisioned by HTS and does so in a more organic and sustainable way (see also Selmeski 2007). The fact that the anthropologists most vocal in support of the HTS program and military culture training in general are largely teaching in the service academies, and not training civilian anthropologists, suggests that the military services will be looking inward rather than outward for future expertise.[5]

But what makes the HTS program even more peripheral to the field of encounter between scholars and the security sector is the changing nature of war and the military. There is another trajectory for the US military's culturalist turn that does not lead to HTS as its logical conclusion and that is more in keeping with other trends in military science. And that trend is toward deploying local surrogate forces to do the work of security and war.

A REVOLUTION IN MILITARY AFFAIRS

The large troop deployments that characterized the wars in Iraq and Afghanistan are not the future of American war. Despite the criticism of US Secretary of Defense Donald Rumsfeld's minimalist strategy for the Iraq occupation, there is an ever greater emphasis put on networks, swarming, and indirect and counterinsurgency warfare over the conventional models of massive, centralized, and unilateral military operations. The so-called Revolution in Military Affairs (RMA) places a premium on high-technology weapons and a smaller, more flexible, and decentralized military. Andrew Latham (2002:240) summarizes RMA thinking:

> Simply stated, proponents maintain that as the RMA unfolds, "God" will no longer be on the side of the "big battalions." Rather, military advantage will more likely accrue to those who restructure their military forces around rapidly expanding reconfigurable "virtual task forces" comprising small "agile units" that can be quickly created, dissolved and recombined as specific missions and battlefield dynamics require.

Combining high-tech weaponry with productive human relationships with "locals" is intended to reduce the need for massive numbers of US troops and heavy materiel. While there is a great deal of discussion about what this more flexible military might look like, there seems to be little doubt that the nature of war fighting is changing. COIN operations, networked warfare, fourth-generation warfare—all of these new approaches to combat suggest that the US military is increasingly shying away from a model in which its mission is to drop massively into "terra incognita" and effectively deploy there—a model for which the HTS system is designed to supply quick, reliable, comparable, and compoundable data.

Instead, "the mission" is increasingly to deploy indirectly, working with and through more knowledgeable and better positioned surrogate forces and doing so in a way that complicates the war/peace divide. In his article in *Military Review*, Wilson (2006) argued that in a successful counterinsurgency operation, small units of American special forces should work in peacetime and "invisibly" through local forces. "Therefore, the US WOT [War on Terrorism] strategy should emphasize working directly 'through, by, and with' indigenous forces and building their capacity to conduct effective operations against common enemies" (Wilson 2006:38).[6] The trend is toward finding local partners and outsourcing the labor of war.

This is not, of course, entirely new in military history. British and French forces were bolstered by local fighters in their colonial territories, and the US military has over the years provided more or less clandestine support to local factions around the globe. What marks this moment as a revolution in US military affairs is the scale of such outsourcing; its erasure of the war/peace divide so that COIN is fought "across the political, social, and military spectrums" (Hammes 1994:35); and its centrality to military doctrine. The language of the most recent US Department of Defense *Quadrennial Defense Review Report (QDRR)* echoes Wilson's—and makes it the "official" view of the US military:

> Maintaining a long-term, low-visibility presence in many areas of the world where U.S. forces do not traditionally operate will be required. Building and leveraging partner capacity will also be an absolute essential part of this approach, and the employment of surrogates will be a necessary method for achieving many goals. Working indirectly with and through others, and thereby denying popular support to the enemy, will help to transform the character of conflict. In many cases, U.S. partners will have greater local knowledge and legitimacy with their own people and can thereby more effectively fight terrorist networks. [United States Department of Defense 2006c:23]

Two points are crucial to note. Firstly, the outsourcing of security envisioned in what Martin Shaw (2005) calls "the new Western way of war" is partly predicated on the idea that local forces are better able to understand appropriate cultural logics of violence. For example, John Arquilla (2003), a professor of defense analysis at the Naval Postgraduate School and one of the chief theorists of netwar (networked warfare), has argued that the US military should adopt the strategy of recruiting local "pseudo-gangs" that the British used against anticolonial movements like the Mau Mau insurgency in Kenya.[7] Such surrogate forces, the argument goes, are effective because they fight the way the enemy fights. This mirroring approach to counterinsurgency is rendered as military doctrine in the *U.S. Army/Marine Corps Counterinsurgency Field Manual*:

> By mid-tour, U.S. forces should be working closely with local forces, training or supporting them and building an indigenous security capability. The natural tendency is to create forces in a U.S. image. This is a mistake. Instead, local HN [host nation] forces need to mirror the enemy's capabilities and seek to supplant the insurgent's role.[8] [United States Army and Marine Corps 2007:298–299]

Local forces, according to the more radical strains of this thinking, are not only better culturally equipped but are free of the legal or moral constraints that prevent the US military from effectively combating insurgent forces. This has become something of a cause for the most conservative (but influential) voices in security analysis since 2001. Writers like Michael Rubin of the American Enterprise Institute, journalist and theorist Robert Kaplan, and Richard Perle, head of the Defense Policy Board, argue that it is the nature of asymmetrical warfare as waged by Al-Qaeda and other networks to "augment their power relative to Western countries simply by eschewing legal responsibilities" (Rubin 2007:4; see also Kaplan 2003). Bound by a commitment to the United Nations, the Geneva Conventions, and other international protocols for the conduct of war, the US and allied state armies, these theorists argue, are hampered in their ability to defeat non-state armies. Local surrogate forces, by contrast, face no such restrictions and are therefore considerably more effective (not to mention cheaper). One consequence of this reliance on the local knowledge of surrogate forces is that the kind of cultural knowledge embedded civilian ethnographers can supply is unnecessary. It is redundant at best. At worst it is a liability.

The second key point I wish to emphasize here is that the local partners in question might be, but are not necessarily, the official militaries of recognized states. Although Wilson's case study is on the Armed Forces of the Philippines, it is worth noting that he repeatedly speaks of alliances with "indigenous or surrogate" forces rather than with national militaries. The same holds true for the 2006 *QDRR* and the *Counterinsurgency Field Manual*. In fact, the abstract language of partnerships, surrogates, and indigeneity appears throughout both official military publications and the language of security sector strategists and observers. This is not terribly surprising, given that the US government views the security services of a number of so-called rogue nations and failed states as complicit in the operations of non-state networks like Al-Qaeda. The upshot is that a great deal of the investment of US military resources is currently dedicated to the cultivation of local forces, with no a priori assumption that the army of the state is the force most suitable for that aid.

What this amounts to in cases where the official state army is not the most reliable or desirable partner for the US military is the militarization of other sociopolitical formations, or the creation of new, militarized sodalities. As Renzi (2006a:16–17) puts it, drawing from Anna Simons, the concern of military culturalists is increasingly with indigenous modes of mobilization.

The Awakening movement in Iraq is the most high profile recent exemplar. Begun in the summer of 2005 in Anbar province, Awakening groups amounted to the arming of local militias to patrol neighborhoods, guard sensitive infrastructure, and hunt insurgent fighters and cells. US military personnel in Iraq have referred to Awakening units as "security contractors" and even as "little Iraqi Blackwaters" (the private security company infamous for the September 2007 massacre at Nisour Square in Baghdad) (see Tyson 2007). By the end of 2007 there were estimated to be between 65,000 and 80,000 members of such ad hoc militarized formations in Iraq (Rubin and Cave 2007). Most often these Awakening units are organized along ethnic or "tribal" lines, or what amounts to the arming of sectarian factions to fight other ethnically affiliated insurgent groups. In his summary of the lessons learned from the US military's engagement with Iraq's social structures, Lieutenant Colonel Eisenstadt (2007:29) writes that if Iraq is ever stabilized, it will be in large measure due to the "leveraging of Iraq's tribes and tribal networks" in mobilizations such as the Anbar Awakening.

There is every reason to think that these mobilizations, working in conjunction with or on behalf of small units of US security operatives, will be the primary actors in COIN operations of the future. Understanding the subcontracted mode of warfare represented by the Awakening movement will be critical to understanding the foreseeable future of global security— and the new common ground of social and military science.

I turn now to another example of such community mobilizations, an unlikely one to be sure, but nevertheless a case study capable of shedding light on the mechanisms by which social networks become militarized and the consequences for scholars and strategists when they do.

DANNY HOFFMAN

A LABORATORY OF THE FUTURE

The war in Sierra Leone officially began on March 27, 1991, with a small invasion force crossing the eastern border with Liberia. Though it launched its campaign with only a small contingent of Sierra Leonean dissidents and regional mercenaries, the Revolutionary United Front (RUF) inaugurated a decade of violence. For a war in a small country seemingly so peripheral to world politics and the global economy, the conflict in Sierra Leone involved an incredible array of international actors and networks.

Most obvious was the RUF's relationship to the National Patriotic Front of Liberia (NPFL), a rebel force headed by Charles Taylor. Taylor and other NPFL leaders, along with a handful of the RUF leadership, were part of an amorphous cadre of West African dissidents, and European and Lebanese businessmen who circulated throughout the region during the 1980s. These were individuals and institutions for whom the war on both sides of the Sierra Leone–Liberia border created opportunities to profit from the unregulated trade in diamonds, timber, rubber, and gold. The conflicts in Sierra Leone and Liberia were arguably the first of the post–cold war "new wars" or "resource wars," conflicts that redefined the nature of warfare to include the violent activities of warlords and quasi-criminal, transnational networks.[9]

The Mano River War (a term that encompasses the fighting in both Sierra Leone and Liberia) was also unique for the major role played by an African armed intervention force. The Economic Community of West African States Cease-fire Monitoring Group (ECOMOG) was a largely Nigerian peacekeeping force deployed first in Liberia and then in Sierra Leone. With the United Nations, the United States, and European countries unwilling to deploy their own forces as peacekeepers or peace enforcers until very late in the conflict, Nigeria spearheaded the first regional intervention force after the cold war, to which the United Nations agreed to be a secondary, supporting partner. As Herbert Howe (2001:131) notes in his analysis of ECOMOG, it was a move that calls into question the very meaning of sovereignty in Africa—but one that has been repeated by the African coalition intervening in Darfur and will likely continue under AFRICOM.

The domestic partners that these international forces found on the ground are the most significant for my purposes here. The *kamajoisia*, or Kamajors (the Anglicized and increasingly standardized name for mobilizations of kamajoisia), were a decentralized group of grassroots civil defense units that appeared in the early 1990s in southeastern Sierra Leone. Prior to the war the kamajoisia were specialized hunters in Mende

12

villages capable of harnessing occult forces to hunt large game and to protect communities from both natural and supernatural threats of the forest. They were also the only figures under customary chiefdom law authorized to carry firearms. As the war progressed in Sierra Leone and it became clear that the state army was unable, and in many cases unwilling, to protect rural communities from violent attacks, the Kamajors were the key figures around which young men mobilized to defend rural communities. Conducting patrols, ambushes, and intelligence gathering operations, the Kamajors rapidly expanded their numbers across the southeast, waging a low-intensity war against the rebels and often against the untrustworthy Republic of Sierra Leone Armed Forces. As it gained popularity, participation in the Kamajors replaced the initiations that previously marked the passage from childhood to adulthood for some rural Mende males. In many areas the Kamajors' security presence was crucial to the conduct of trade, farming, water collection—the everyday modalities of village life in West Africa.

The nature of the Kamajors began to change in 1995. Though they received some support from the Sierra Leonean government from the earliest days, that support changed dramatically when the government hired a private military company, the South African Executive Outcomes (EO), to train the Sierra Leonean army and to assist in driving the rebels away from key sites. Finding the army a less than reliable partner, EO began training the Kamajors and offering them logistical assistance in their war with the RUF.

When a new democratically elected government was overthrown in 1997 by the state army, the Kamajors became an even more important factor in the war. As the primary domestic resistance to the military junta, their numbers rapidly expanded.[10] Kamajors around the country coordinated their activities—and received materiel—from the Nigerian ECOMOG forces. Now called the Civil Defense Forces (CDF), the irregular forces served as trackers, surrogate gunners, intelligence gatherers, and in many cases the forward operating units for ECOMOG and for a handful of former EO personnel who stayed on after its contract expired. Those forces were in turn supported and advised by US security contractors like Pacific Architects and Engineers (PAE) and by the military affairs officers at US and European embassies in the region. When the junta was overthrown a year later, the CDF was the government's only functioning security apparatus, despite its irregular status.

The CDF was officially disbanded at the end of the war in January 2002. By that time British forces and UN peacekeepers had deployed around the country and taken on the task of training the new Sierra Leone Army, a force that included ex-combatants from both the CDF and the rebels. Talk of a territorial defense force that would institutionalize the CDF militias came to nothing, in large part due to fears that the CDF would overthrow the government it previously fought to restore. A poorly designed and executed disarmament program left thousands of former CDF fighters displaced and without work. Large numbers of demobilized fighters moved across the border with Liberia to work as mercenaries on that front of the war or labored in the violent and unregulated diamond mines of the east. In the former case, these mobile warriors were armed through US military assistance supplied by the Guinean government and then forwarded to the rebels. Many more ex-combatants deployed from rural communities to the cities to protect urban areas during the war were abandoned there. These young men lacked the capital—financial and social—to return to their villages. They currently live a precarious existence in the country's urban centers, "available" for recruitment by a diverse array of political and economic actors interested in utilizing their violence (see Christensen and Utas 2008; Hoffman 2007a). This highly mobile population of militarized and marginalized young men poses the greatest threat to regional stability in a highly volatile region.

Beginning in 2000 I conducted ethnographic fieldwork with CDF fighters in Sierra Leone, Guinea, and Liberia. Much of this work consisted of interviews about earlier mobilizations and the cultural meanings of violence, masculinity, and the responsibilities of rural men to protect their communities. But perhaps even more important for what I present here, this research also involved living with combatants intermittently over an eight-year period as they cycled through regional conflict zones and various forms of labor. I spent considerable time in the primary CDF barracks in Freetown watching groups of young men navigate the impossible terrain of Sierra Leone's shattered economy, often by participating in networks of armed gangs that relied on the same patterns of mobilization that organized them as fighters. As the war ended in Sierra Leone, an underground railroad recruited experienced fighters as mercenary labor for a new Liberian rebel movement; moving with these young men across multiple international borders allowed for a firsthand look at how youth who began fighting with a community defense militia quickly became part of a violent regional labor pool. Researching the changing nature of violent deployment as a participant/observer made it clear just how easily these same young men could be made available to Sierra Leonean politicians and international commercial interests for the often violent work of political campaigning or digging diamonds in the region's quasi-legal resource trade.[11]

What this ethnographic research suggests is that, though it seems removed from the center of the post-9/11 geopolitical world, Sierra Leone's history is a laboratory of the future. The Kamajors/CDF are exactly the kind of indigenous force envisioned as partners in the current strategic thinking of US military planners and commentators. They were without question the faction most "loyal" to the democratically elected (and US-friendly) government after 1996—certainly more so than the state army, which was notoriously corrupt and widely known to be colluding with the rebels.[12] As key social actors in the local cultural landscape, they had the respect and support of local communities. The "Kamajor" was an already recognizable figure, literally and figuratively, whose role it was to protect villages from outside threats. They were a logical choice around which to base a counterinsurgency strategy, well positioned to act on the kind of "ethnographic intelligence" seen as key to the new way of war. What's more, the Kamajors/CDF could by definition "mirror the enemy's capabilities" (in the language of the army counterinsurgency manual): everything from their occult powers to their particular modes of violence were crafted in response to the perceived threats posed by the RUF and the army.

Perhaps even more important, the Kamajors/CDF were structured along exactly the lines that the network theorists of war envision as most effective for counterinsurgency operations. The militia combined its "ethnographic intelligence" with a decentralized organization that allowed it to mobilize quickly wherever necessary. A truly grassroots organization, it materialized as needed throughout the country in response to specific threats. Though the CDF became more institutionalized as the war went on, local units never lost the capability to act independently, move quickly, and adjust themselves to rapidly changing circumstances and new threats. As a community-based outfit structured according to an existing social logic, the CDF could be wherever it needed to be. What the CDF amounted to was the militarization of everyday life and local communities such that they could be quickly mobilized and deployed as necessary in the interest of security.

In 2003 three members of the CDF were indicted by the UN-backed Special Court for war crimes in Sierra Leone.[13] Although it was widely acknowledged by human rights groups to have committed fewer abuses than other parties to the conflict, Kamajors/CDF units unquestionably enlisted child soldiers, executed prisoners of war and civilians, and, at the later stages, threatened to become a private army for local politicians. To paraphrase Herbert Howe (2001), the CDF offered a highly ambiguous order—a force on the right side of history that played a key role in defending a democratically elected government and protecting civilian lives, but a force that nevertheless threatened the very stability it sought to ensure.

The Sierra Leone case is an interesting historical study for places like Iraq and Afghanistan, a point to which I will return below. But it is important to note that initiatives like AFRICOM and other trends in the reorganization of global security are laying the groundwork for continued mobilizations of exactly this kind. AFRICOM is part of a more generic discourse on African security that would like to see so-called African solutions to African problems. In other words, the kind of regional peacekeeping and peace enforcing operations epitomized by ECOMOG and by the African Union forces in Darfur are exactly the model being pushed to deal with future conflict zones—regional forces and ad hoc coalitions of the willing, with minimal advising and financial and logistical support from the United States, the United Nations, or contracted private security companies. If past experience is anything to judge by, these forces will not receive the levels of support necessary to operate effectively even as the demands on them grow. The upshot is that they will have to work with local surrogate forces like the Kamajors. In fact, since it is in keeping with the US military's culturalist turn to work with local surrogates, it is easy to imagine AFRICOM's trainers and security advisors encouraging its African partner forces to do just that. Jeremy Keenan (2008:20), in his review of AFRICOM's operational status, writes that "the indications are that AFRICOM's mission will be outsourced to 'contractors,'" notably private military companies (see also S. McFate 2008:118–119). No doubt he is correct, but it is the subcontractors of war like the Kamajors and the CDF who will likely do most of the fighting.

WHAT ROLE THE ANTHROPOLOGIST?

As US and other security forces expand their sphere of operations, as the groundwork is laid for peacetime collection of "ethnographic intelligence," and as indigenous mechanisms of mobilization become of greater interest to security services, many more anthropologists will find themselves working in areas of concern to military science or overlapping with actual areas of operation. Researchers conducting fieldwork on violence, civil conflict, masculinity, nationalism, or the "everyday" of conflict and postconflict zones will increasingly find themselves working in situations with ambiguous ties to the US security sector, but so too will researchers working on less immediately obvious issues or in less high visibility field sites. The US Army counterinsurgency manual proviso to "engage the women, be cautious around the children" gives some indication of just how expansive the culturalist imaginary in military thinking really is.[14] If the future terrain of war is the mobilization of social networks and the militarization of everyday life, then the separate domains of military and social science begin to converge. This overlap potentially brings a much greater range of anthropologists into dialogue with the military than simply those who chose to work "for" it. The question is how?

The anthropologist as witness is an idea that has gained considerable traction in recent years as an ethically and politically responsible position. Bearing witness, Keenan (2008:20) writes in regard to the impact of AFRICOM operations across Africa, is a duty for anthropologists working on the continent and the primary contribution anthropologists can make "to the discipline and to the peoples of Africa." Given the record of US covert operations in North Africa that he documents, Keenan makes a strong case. At issue here is the violation of US laws, laws of sovereign states in the region, and international conventions governing warfare and state sovereignty. Keenan describes a number of incidents in which the US military in collaboration with the highly suspect state security apparatuses in Algeria have staged acts of destabilization in the Sahel that have contributed to a series of regional rebellions.

Again, if some part of the military intelligentsia is advocating for the circumvention of US and international laws as a strategy to wage the Global War on Terror (or, in the post-GWOT language of the Obama administration, to wield "soft power"), then it seems obvious that social scientists—both as social scientists and as citizens—are ethically obligated to make those abuses public. And as media outlets around the world have downsized their operations, particularly in Africa, anthropologists may be among the last cohort of observers capable of documenting such flagrant abuses.[15] Researchers with extensive experience on the ground are uniquely positioned to critically examine official claims made about COIN operations or anti-terror measures and bear a responsibility to go public when those measures are falsely represented and illegal. And there is every reason to assume that such boundaries are now regularly crossed.[16] When anthropologists take on this role, however, they would do well to follow the model of investigative journalism in at least one respect. It is possible to bear witness, document, and make public abuses by structures of power without concluding that such witnessing can only be done by two inherently adversarial camps. Investigative journalism as a profession (or as a discipline) is not by definition "antimilitary," even if some part of its mandate is to expose abuses by the military or other organs of state power. The middle ground between embeddedness and adversary is one that journalists continuously wrestle with (and more so now than ever), but it remains the ideal and is maintained with some degree of success (for another perspective on this issue, see Anne Irwin's discussion in chapter 6, this volume). Social scientists can choose to occupy a similarly nuanced space. It is worth under-scoring that this is not a call for middle-of-the-road politics. I believe anthropologists in particular have a responsibility to advocate for the progressive, even radical politics that has been largely absent from public discourse in the United States. But this begins by writing and advocating in a way that targets *specific* abuses and does so with the necessary documentation to avoid unsupportable generalizations.

And it calls for recognizing that the military and security services are not monolithic structures. There are cracks, fissures, and disagreements within these bodies where a reasoned critique can find purchase. (Connable's *Military Review* critique of the HTS program [2009] and Brian Selmeski's 2007 paper for the Royal Military College of Canada on cultural competency demonstrate just how divergent opinions can be within the military on questions of culture and the "human terrain.") Therein lies an opportunity for those of us working in contexts in which local communities are enlisted by the US security services or their counterparts to contribute to their own security. Accounts of the Awakening movement in Iraq have made it abundantly clear that even within the military (if not in the more extreme views of hawkish, neoconservative nonmilitary analysts), there is a great deal of ambivalence about programs to militarize local communities as security contractors. "It remains to be seen," writes Eisenstadt (2007:170) in his survey of the military's use of tribal structures in Iraq, "whether the Anbar Awakening can hold together…or whether coalition efforts to work with the tribes and arm tribal militias are in fact paving the way for an even more violent civil war." The memory of Afghanistan, in which US covert efforts to arm anti-Soviet forces led to the formations that became the Taliban, looms large in the writings of many security theorists.

The current circumstances of militarization are very different from Afghanistan in the 1980s. But there is an audience within the security forces interested in the long-term consequences of outsourcing security. And social scientists are uniquely positioned to explore the broad and pressing consequences of the militarization of local communities and existing social networks. For example, militarization as a social preoccupation with war (Gusterson 2007:156) or the crafting of national narratives around military activity (Lutz 2002) are two ways to define militarization.

And they seem to be most at work in current military theory. Commanders in the US military are advised in the *Counterinsurgency Field Manual* to "find a single narrative that emphasizes the inevitability and rightness of the COIN operation's success" (United States Army and Marine Corps 2007:298).

This narrative form of militarization is clearly evident in efforts to mobilize Iraqi neighborhoods to take charge of their own security in Baghdad or to guard the nation's future by forming irregular militias to secure oil pipelines. Sunni leaders in Iraq are urged to take responsibility for the nation's future by gathering together youth for security patrols, and appeals are made to both the national and masculine pride of community leaders in standing up to insurgents. What the conventional wisdom on militarization as a master narrative fails to capture is that militarizing communities in much of the world leads to a fundamental reorganization of youth, labor, violence, and social hierarchies. What we learn from the Sierra Leone example, and countless others more familiar to social scientists than to most other witnesses, is that these mobilizations are not easily demobilized. More often they become critical and often dangerous players in the mode of popular politics that governs much of the world today (Chatterjee 2004). Providing payment and logistical support to marginal young men to act as security guards or militia fighters is an act of employment (not only deployment) that cannot simply be revoked in a state with little economic opportunity for youth. In an environment in which masculinity and citizenship are tied to the exercise of violence it can be enormously difficult to simply disband armed cohorts. And when politics is governed by a logic of interest groups competing for limited resources of the state, local communities with access to the means of violence are unlikely to give them up just because foreign forces declare *their* mission accomplished. All of this was true of the CDF in Sierra Leone as it has been and will continue to be elsewhere. Anthropologists with an interest in the long view of social organization and the micropolitics of local communities can fill in a great deal of the detail as to how this happens. And they can do so in dialogue with at least some military leaders who voice unease over whether outsourcing to local surrogates will lead to "an even more violent civil war," as Eisenstadt wrote of the Awakening in Iraq.

In those situations where local militias have been mobilized under the auspices of external forces, it is imperative that social scientists participate in demobilization planning. "DDRs" (Disarmament, Demobilization, and Reintegration programs) have become a subspecialty within the world of postconflict development assistance. There is a conventional wisdom as to how to conduct DDRs, and the same formulas are replicated in case after case. In Sierra Leone, Liberia, and then in Côte d'Ivoire, the United Nations, with a great deal of support from the United States, the United Kingdom, and the World Bank, repeated the same failed process in each country. The only significant change in design between these three programs was an increase in the amount ex-combatants were paid for turning in weapons—a strategy that led to a massive influx of weaponry to Côte d'Ivoire by the time the DDR train reached that country. In every instance the "reintegration" component in disarmament planning has been given short shrift. International military observers on the ground in Sierra Leone in 2001 were open about the fact that from a military point of view, removing weapons from circulation was the only real priority in the DDR exercise, a fact made glaringly obvious by the poor job training and lack of follow-up for placing ex-combatants into stable postconflict environments.

What the culturalist turn in military thinking should produce is an understanding that demobilization of irregular militias is a social project more than a military project. Where reintegration worked best in Sierra Leone after the war was outside the official DDR process, when community leaders set the terms of return for ex-fighters and when those youth who did return to their home communities did so with something meaningful to contribute. From that perspective, "security" in a postconflict environment is divorced from the demobilization component of a DDR and requires an entirely different base of knowledge.

This is true when the goal is to disband militias entirely, but it is also true in contexts in which the goal is to transition informal security contractors into the formal police or military services, as is the case in much of Iraq with the Awakening movement. "Wild success," according to one US officer in Baghdad, "is these guys being integrated into honest-to-God, badge-holding cops. That would be a magnificent sign" (Tyson 2007). Yet as Sean McFate noted in 2007, there is virtually no academic or policy literature on the process of vetting personnel for security sector jobs in postconflict conditions—a glaring absence. Ascertaining who among an ex-combatant populace is of the "proper character" (S. McFate 2007:79) to transition from irregular combatant to security sector agent requires a depth of local knowledge. It requires sensitivity to the operations of power and authority and to local conceptions of legitimate and illegitimate violence. The yardsticks by which military strategists judge parties to a violent conflict may not—indeed probably are not—those most useful for establishing who should participate in a postconflict security force. Working with the US or other militaries in such a planning capacity for postconflict programs is a far cry from the kind of cultural knowledge production envisioned by the HTS; and while it may not be ethically unambiguous, it cannot justifiably be thought of as "mercenary anthropology."

Anthropologists working on these issues are in a unique position. They can speak in a way that is both ethically responsible to the communities in which they work and does not require sacrificing the theoretical gains of the discipline to preach a dumbed-down version of culture. The knowledge that matters in these circumstances is not the bits and pieces of cultural data envisioned by the HTS and its supporters. It is a more nuanced and theoretically sophisticated understanding of process and global forces. It includes analyses of commodity chains, flows of late capital, and the legacies of colonialism. It is not ethnographic intelligence but anthropological theory that is most useful in understanding the future effects of outsourcing war.

THE NEW APPLICATION OF THEORY

As military interest in "open source" ethnographic knowledge continues to grow, it will be less and less relevant whether anthropologists choose to speak their truths directly to military or intelligence personnel. More important will be that anthropologists are not restricted in their ability to conduct research in conflict zones and that their knowledge is put into circulation. No doubt there will be opportunities for those who choose to conduct classified research under security service auspices, but that model of knowledge production will remain much less significant than the work of anthropologists as teachers and the anthropological material in academic journals and popular media that are now required reading for military culturalists. (One has only to look at the footnotes to Eisenstadt's 2007 "Iraq: Tribal Engagement Lessons Learned" to recognize that it is as well sourced in the anthropological literature as many graduate level papers.) This is not necessarily something that anthropologists should shy away from. The key intervention in the future is not a laundry list of cultural traits or ethnographic details that might jeopardize those with whom social scientists work in the field. The real contribution is a theoretical one, an understanding of how violence works as a social force, the consequences of mobilization and militarization, and what it means to employ social formations for violent ends.

Here, ironically, we may yet see the revalorization of theory, or at least the end of the pointless "applied" versus "theoretical" divide. This has been one of the undercurrents of much of the debate over HTS and the relative positioning of social scientists within the academy versus those working directly within military institutions. Both Montgomery McFate and Anna Simons, anthropologists working directly with the armed forces, have drawn a contrast between the abstract "long winded discussions on 'capitalism' and 'colonialism'" of professional academics and the "more pressing tasks" faced by those engaged in military affairs (M. McFate 2007:20; see also M. McFate 2005a; Simons and Lutz 2002). But in an era when the Israeli Defense Force is reading the French psychoanalytic Marxist philosophers Gilles Deleuze and Félix Guattari for strategy insights (Weizman 2006) this distinction is silly. It creates an entertaining debate but one that obscures a more important point. The vision of cultural knowledge (or ethnographic intelligence) as bits and pieces of useful data that underlies the HTS is not where military and social science really meet. The more productive—and less ethically fraught—common ground is the realm of theory. This is the terrain we should investigate by exploring what happens when existent social networks become the militarized subcontractors of war, and what we, the subcontractors of knowledge production, can do about it.

Notes

1. Robert M. Gates, US Secretary of Defense, quoted in Shankar 2008:10. See also the "About AFRICOM" section of the command's website, http://www.africom.mil /AboutAFRICOM.asp (accessed October 9, 2008). Additional background and commentary on AFRICOM can be found in Besteman 2008, 2009; Keenan 2008, and S. McFate 2008.

2. Eisenstadt is the director of the Military and Security Studies Program at the Washington Institute for Near East Policy. He was involved in the planning of Operation Iraqi Freedom and served as an advisor to the Iraq Study Group.

3. This is the approach that prevailed during the US involvement in Vietnam, for example, where it was assumed that terrorizing communities, or simply destroying them, would undermine support for the enemy. See Kipp et al. 2006:2–3.

4. The AAA's Commission on the Engagement of Anthropology with the US Security and Intelligence Committee (CEAUSSIC) report of October 14, 2009, states that as of April 2009, only six HTS employees hold PhDs in anthropology. Five more possess MAs in the discipline. These figures come directly from HTS. As the report indicates, however, the number of HTS personnel has fluctuated since 2007, and the particular specialties of HTS personnel are not always reported.

5. Indeed, the CEAUSSIC report points out that in the summer of 2009 the number of HTS contractors dropped as these positions were shifted to government jobs.

6. Colonel Wilson, according to his biography in *Military Review*, "recently completed an Army War College Fellowship in irregular warfare and counterterrorism with the Defense Analysis Department at the Naval Postgraduate School in Monterey, California. He is currently serving as the operations director for Special Operations Command South in Homestead, Florida" (Wilson 2006:38). This makes Colonel Wilson a significant figure in both crafting and implanting US counterinsurgency philosophy.

7. This passage from Arquilla's editorial is also discussed in Hersh 2005 and critiqued in Elkins 2005.

8. The manual goes on to state: "This does not mean that they should be irregular in the sense of being brutal or outside proper control" (United States Army and Marine Corps 2007:299), though it is not clear where that line of brutality is to be drawn or what being "under proper control" means if the force is not operating "in a U.S. image."

9. Renzi (2006a:18–19), writing in *Military Review,* somewhat simplistically calls Taylor and his contacts a "blood diamond cartel" and identifies them as one of his three case studies in "dark networks," along with Al-Qaeda and drug-trafficking syndicates. More detailed histories of the war in Sierra Leone and Liberia can be found in Ellis 1999, Gberie 2005, Keen 2005, and Richards 1996.

10. There is no reliable data as to how many Kamajors there actually were. Mendes in rural areas of Sierra Leone often claim that every adult male was a Kamajor. Sam Hinga Norman, the leader of the Kamajors, put the number at 99,000, an estimate that is much too high. Some 37,000 combatants registered as Kamajors during the disarmament campaign, a number that is suspect given the way the disarmament was conducted. One of the complicating factors in arriving at an accurate census for the Kamajors is that many men mobilized only for a short time when their communities were under attack, while others became more active and mobile and fought throughout the war. Both types of combatants self-identify as Kamajors.

11. This research is detailed further in Hoffman 2004a, 2007a, 2007b.

12. And, as subsequent investigations have shown, with Al-Qaeda, for whom Charles Taylor and his allies in the RUF and the Sierra Leone Army were trading diamonds. See Farah 2004.

13. In 2006 I served as an expert witness on behalf of one of the CDF accused, Moinina Fofana. I was at the time and remain highly critical of the Special Court indictments of the CDF, primarily on the grounds that it is a mistake to think of mobilizations like the CDF as "armies" organized and regulated by military chains of command (see Hoffman 2007b). On the human rights record of the CDF and local understandings of the laws of war, see Ferme and Hoffman 2004.

14. "[I]n traditional societies, women are hugely influential in forming the social networks that insurgents use for support. When women support COIN efforts, families support COIN efforts....Homesick troops want to drop their guard with kids. But insurgents are watching. They notice any friendships between troops and children. They may either harm the children as punishment or use them as agents" (United States Army and Marine Corps 2007:296–297).

15. This is an argument I have made in more detail in Hoffman 2003, 2004b.

16. A 2005 article in the *New Yorker* by Seymour Hersh describes the structural realignment of US security services that facilitates a great deal more "black operations" by the Pentagon without congressional oversight. Such institutional change has implications that will last beyond the end of the George W. Bush administration under which it began.

2

"Torture Is for the Incompetent"

Toward the Ethnography of Interrogation

Laura A. McNamara

President George W. Bush declared a War on Terror on September 20, 2001. Seven years, four months, and two days later, on January 22, 2009, a newly inaugurated President Barack Obama signed three executive orders related to detention and interrogation operations conducted as part of intelligence, military, or counterterrorism efforts in the United States and abroad (Obama 2009b; Obama 2009c; Obama 2009d). The move was hailed as a sentinel shift in US foreign and domestic counterterrorism policy: the *Washington Post* declared that Obama had ended the Global War on Terror (GWOT) with a few strokes of his presidential pen, while the *Los Angeles Times* more measuredly observed that Obama had started to "dismantle the most widely condemned components of the Bush administration's war on terrorism" (Miller and Barnes 2009:1; see also Priest 2009). Symbolic change accompanied substantive decisions: pundits, activists, even politically conservative national security experts had long criticized Bush's rhetorical catchphrase, the "Global War on Terror," for being overly vague, ideological, or inflammatory—not to mention grammatically dubious.[1] Within a few weeks of the inauguration *Newsweek* reported that the new Obama administration was seeking language to replace the "signature phrase[s] of the Bush presidency," as a way of signaling the distance between Obama's administration and the controversial tactics, policies, and practices of his predecessor (Isikoff and Hosenball 2009). By March 2009 the bureaucratically opaque "overseas contingency operations" had emerged as a preferred expression to describe counterterrorism efforts abroad (Burkeman 2009; FOXNews.com 2009; Wilson and Kamen 2009).

In its first two months in office the Obama administration seemed well on its way to undoing seven years' worth of legal, rhetorical, and institutional frameworks the Bush administration had wrought in the Global War on Terror. Yet this seemingly abrupt *volte-face* is perhaps less dramatic than the *Washington Post, Los Angeles Times, Newsweek,* or even the Obama administration might have it. For one thing, dismantlement of many Bush-era GWOT initiatives was already underway: facing public outrage about the overextension of presidential power, not to mention a stinging defeat in the Supreme Court (which ruled 5–4 in the 2006 *Hamdan v. Rumsfeld* case that, yes, the Geneva Conventions do indeed apply to enemy combatants), the Bush administration was backpedaling on many of the policies and institutions that it established in the wake of 9/11.[2]

Secondly, the Global War on Terror catalyzed the formation of new institutions, policies, and practices at the federal, state, and local levels of government in the United States: the Department of Homeland Security (DHS) and the National Counter Terrorism Center (NCTC) are prominent examples, while the Criminal Investigation Task Force (CITF) is perhaps less recognizable (Norwitz 2005; Powlen 2007). Some of these will certainly disappear, that is, institutions that formed to support Guantánamo Bay, Cuba, detention operations may be dissolved if the base reverts to its previous logistics mission, while reconsideration of the legal memoranda that opened the door to torture is underway. However, other changes may be more permanent, possibly for as long as the United States continues to pursue counterterrorism initiatives, whether on its own soil or abroad. Indeed, while Obama's orders accelerated the dismantlement that began under the Bush administration, particularly in regards to Guantánamo, the orders also left room for continuity in regard to legal positioning, counterterrorism operations, and even the application of harsh interrogation tactics and secret renditions.[3]

Rather than assume that a change in administration, language, or policy signals a cessation to the Global War on Terror, we might look instead for indications of its endurance. After all, as long as the United States faces a risk of terrorism attacks, at home or abroad, the federal government is unlikely to put a full stop to its counterterrorism operations. Given how dramatically US counterterrorism operations have expanded since 2001, we can expect that at least some of the institutions, policies, and practices that emerged under the Bush administration will continue into the indefinite future.

Counterterrorism interrogation is one institution that is likely to endure for a long time and therefore merits our sustained inquiry. As recently as January 2009 Amnesty International called "on the new [Obama] administration to categorically reject the notion that any additional special techniques or methods beyond the *Army Field Manual* are needed. Torture or abuses in any form are neither acceptable nor necessary in protecting the United States" (Amnesty International 2009). Such declarations presume that noncoercive interrogation is an ethically and practically viable alternative to so-called enhanced techniques. Yet scholars have raised significant social, legal, and ethical questions about the role of interrogation in the US criminal justice system, and it is worth asking how that critique might extend to new practices of interrogation involving enemy combatants captured and detained by the United States in the Global War on Terror.

Accordingly, in this chapter I describe how I became interested in counterterrorism interrogation and offer three intertwining themes of anthropologically grounded critique in which I examine interrogation as an epistemic culture, the emergence of "culture" as a salient theme in interrogation practice, and the interrogation encounter as a complex discursive event. However, I am also interested in questions of how anthropologists can develop methods, data, and positioning to produce valid assessments of powerful institutions. In 1972 Laura Nader (1972:301) urged indignant anthropologists to "study up" by focusing on institutional elites, but allowed that such projects faced significant challenges of access, attitude, ethics, and methodology. Here, I hope to demonstrate the value of anthropologically nontraditional sources of data, such as public archives of government documents, to develop an empirically grounded yet anthropologically faithful critique of the state-at-war.

AN ANTHROPOLOGIST ENCOUNTERS AN ARCHIVE

Interrogation is a domain of research and practice that belongs largely to psychologists, criminal justice practitioners, and legal scholars. With a few exceptions—Lesley Gill (2004, 2005) writing about interrogation training at the School of the Americas and Marshall Sahlins's (1966) twenty-four hours in Vietnam with US interrogators Mr. X and Captain Y—anthropologists do not typically study or write about interrogation. It is certainly not my primary area of study. I am not a legal anthropologist or a Middle East studies expert; nor am I a student of terrorism, insurgency, warfare, or

Islamic extremism. Instead, I have spent the past decade working in government research facilities oriented toward national security science and technology. I wrote my dissertation about knowledge loss among nuclear weapons experts at Los Alamos National Lab, and these days I spend most of my time studying "sideways" (to paraphrase Laura Nader), examining the organizational dynamics of the computational informatics revolution in the US intelligence community. My research on interrogation is a personal project, something I pursue intermittently with my own time and resources.

In some sense, however, my professional affiliation with the national security community did spur my interest in interrogation practice. As most anthropologists are acutely aware, the Department of Defense (DoD) and the US Intelligence Community (which itself comprises more than a dozen civilian departments and agencies, in addition to the military elements) are courting social scientists to help guide tactical and strategic thinking in a number of critical areas, from insurgency warfare to religious radicalization to terrorism (for example, Gates 2008). Although my work focuses strictly on organizational studies in US government bureaucracies, my professional identity as an anthropologist means that I am frequently asked to comment on whether anthropology might help military and civilian decision makers make better sense of the conflict dynamics they are facing. These conversations inevitably touch on anthropology's fractious history with projects of empire. Along the way I have learned that the ethical scandals so easily recalled by anthropologists are tiny motes in the collective memory of US military and intelligence personnel. Most policy and decision makers sincerely believe that the present benefits of cultural awareness outweigh the hazards of ignorance and are largely unaware of anthropology's complicated disciplinary history in this regard, even as recently as Vietnam (see David Price, this volume). In that regard, I initially approached the Abu Ghraib scandal as a present-day case study that would help me explain to government colleagues why anthropologists eschew involvement with intelligence and military endeavors.

The Abu Ghraib scandal broke in April 2004, when the CBS television newsmagazine *Sixty Minutes II* ran a story about naked, hooded detainees being humiliated by young military personnel from the US Army Reserve's 320th Military Police Battalion, part of the 800th Military Police Brigade under the command of Brig. Gen. Janis L. Karpinski.[4] The scandal became specifically disconcerting for social scientists, particularly psychologists and anthropologists, when the *New Yorker* published three articles written by Pulitzer-prize winning journalist Seymour Hersh (2004a, 2004b, 2004c) alleging that Abu Ghraib torture was a deliberate psychological/ cultural strategy on the part of DoD and intelligence officials to get information from enemy combatants and prisoners of war. In the final article in the series, "The Gray Zone," Hersh (2004c) implied that Raphael Patai's 1973 ethnography *The Arab Mind* provided input for policymakers formulating a secret coercive interrogation strategy that relied on sexual humiliation and blackmail of Arab detainees. Hersh (2004d) repeated the allegation almost verbatim in his 2004 book on the subject, *Chain of Command.*

As an American citizen who opposed the invasion of Iraq, I was disgusted and angry at what American soldiers had done to human beings in their custody. As an anthropologist, I was dismayed that high-level decision makers had apparently put scholarship to such ends. Many anthropologists were similarly dismayed and angry. Hersh's paragraphs evoked what Jane Cowan (2006:11) describes as the discipline's "pronounced ethical streak— our collective self-image as advocates of the less powerful, our egalitarian commitments, and the political vision implicit in any critical analytical approach." In Hersh's narrative anthropologists saw themselves in the position that Elaine Scarry (1985) describes for doctors and lawyers in the torture chamber: as members of a horrifically inverted social institution whose expertise is pirated, deconstructed, and implemented in the state-sanctioned production of suffering. Just as the Abu Ghraib photos served as a grim reminder that torture can occur in even the most democratic of Western democracies (Conroy 2000; Zimbardo 2007), Hersh's articles were seen by many anthropologists as cautionary tales about the dangers of blindly handing over ethnographic products to the national security state (for example, Abu El-Haj 2005; Caton 2006; Fluehr-Lobban 2006), a theme that both Maren Tomforde and David Price discuss in greater detail in their contributions to this volume. At the American Anthropological Association's business meeting in San Jose in December 2006, a rare quorum voted to adopt twin resolutions condemning both the war in Iraq and the use of anthropological works in torture (American Anthropological Association 2008).

In late 2005 I decided to write a brief position paper about the role of anthropological scholarship at Abu Ghraib, one that I could circulate among my intelligence community colleagues to illustrate the clash between anthropological ethics and GWOT operational imperatives. Since I expected to publish this as an internal white paper, or perhaps even an article, I felt that the document needed to be grounded in primary references. Accordingly, using Hersh's account as a starting point, I began trolling the Internet to gather source material.

My project was well timed. Since 2003 the DoD has conducted more than a dozen official investigations into the events at Abu Ghraib, producing a series of reports with tens of thousands of pages of supporting documentation detailing military detention and interrogation operations in Guantánamo, Afghanistan, and Iraq, the best known of which is the *Taguba Report* (Taguba 2004a, 2004b). Many of these are publicly available. In 2004 the American Civil Liberties Union (ACLU) led a coalition of human rights and legal activist groups in successfully suing to demand the immediate processing and release of documents related to the treatment of detainees in the Global War on Terror. By September 2005 the ACLU had posted the first installment of documents released under the conditions of the lawsuit. By 2007, when I began drafting the background materials for this chapter, the ACLU's torture Freedom of Information Act (FOIA) website provided access to more than one hundred thousand pages of official documentation from US military, intelligence, and law enforcement communities.[5]

As I have written previously (McNamara 2007b), in the course of reading approximately ten thousand pages of this documentation, I began to doubt that Raphael Patai's book was the guiding source for torture techniques in Abu Ghraib. Yes, the book did appear and remains on several DoD reading lists, including one that was apparently used in training interrogators in the wake of the Abu Ghraib scandal (Lagouranis and Mikaelian 2007). However, several years' worth of investigations and hearings have revealed a DoD countermeasures training program known as SERE (for Survival, Evasion, Resistance, and Escape, pronounced "seer") as the origination point for the coercive techniques that surfaced in the Abu Ghraib photos (Jaffer and Singh 2007; United States Department of Defense 2005b).[6]

Moreover, as I reviewed this documentation, it struck me that combing through primary documents for evidence of people reading *The Arab Mind* was a rather narrow sort of scholarship, what my friend Gregory Starrett (2004) described as a "largely pointless game of *cherchez le livre*." The materials I was reviewing did not reveal evidence that agents of the state were using anthropological knowledge to develop new ways of torturing Iraqi and Afghan males. However, they did reveal a complex chain of communications and events through which techniques derived from the SERE program were first promoted for restricted use in Guantánamo but quickly migrated to other theaters as military interrogators carried practices and policies across two continents to Afghanistan and Iraq. In addition, I saw evidence of a complex institutional response to the Abu Ghraib scandal in which multiple agencies reasserted the importance of professional interrogation practice in getting reliable and timely information from detainees in US custody. This made me wonder about the norms of professional interrogation and what might be involved in translating professional interrogation practice from mainstream criminal justice into the evolving context of counterterrorism interrogation. Along the way I came across a set of interrogation transcriptions of US government personnel questioning inmates in Guantánamo Bay that provide some insight into what the interrogation encounter actually looks like.

Thus in the remainder of this chapter I describe the three intertwining ways in which I have come to frame the intersection of interrogation and culture. I borrow from science and organizational studies to frame interrogation as an epistemic culture with roots in the police reform movements of the twentieth-century United States (Knorr-Cetina 1999). I also describe how interrogators in military and civilian agencies have been working since 2001 to identify, develop, and formalize culturally appropriate interrogation techniques. In this process they are drawing from their own experience, funding new research on topics like cross-cultural deception detection, and reading widely about language and culture in the Muslim world; and if there is any place where anthropological scholarship is most likely to have a following among interrogators, it is here. Lastly, we know that enemy combatants held in US military detention facilities like Guantánamo experience extreme psychological, social, and cultural disjuncture (Begg 2006); importantly, the firsthand "grunt lit" (Brown and Lutz 2007) accounts of US interrogators indicate that the experience is disorienting for soldiers as well, albeit in different ways and for quite different reasons (Lagouranis and Mikaelian 2007; Mackey and Miller 2004; Metcalf 2001; Saar and Novak 2005). Ultimately, interrogation becomes a critical ethnographic site in which we can learn "how our ideas of 'us' and 'them' play out in conflictive settings" (Whitehead 2005).

INTERROGATION AS AN EPISTEMIC AND PROFESSIONAL CULTURE

Modern interrogation is a process of investigatory questioning through which government officials (police, military personnel, intelligence officers, or their designated representatives) attempt to elicit and document information related to a matter of interest to the state from a person or persons assumed to hold that information (Intelligence Science Board 2006; Leo 2008). Yet framing interrogation solely as a legal-juridical institution belies a rich and complicated history. It is more productive to approach interrogation as an epistemic culture comprising history, identities, objectives, artifacts, techniques, technologies, and people who are collectively engaged in producing, promulgating, and validating a specific form of power-knowledge. It is also a profession that is maintained and has evolved and extended across generations of interrogators in specific communities of practice, including local, state, and federal police agencies; the military; and the intelligence community (Foucault 1970, 1980; Knorr-Cetina 1999; Lave 1988; Lave and Wenger 1991; Wenger 1998).

The epistemic culture of modern interrogation is rooted in the Western Christian confessional tradition (Otis 2006). In the mid-thirteenth century both Dominican and Franciscan friars produced short handbooks intended to "aid [priests] by explaining how to interrogate the penitent,...how to guide the penitent through his or her examination of conscience, how to illuminate motives and circumstances, and thus how to evaluate the magnitude of an offense, and how to overcome obstacles to a good confession" (Otis 2006:xvii). Inquisitor General of Aragon Nicholas Eymerich described a series of techniques that Catholic inquisitors should use to elicit the truth from evasive suspects and described "ten ways in which heretics seek to hide their errors" during an interrogation (Otis 2006:xvii). These handbooks were precursors to the Inquisition manuals used by church investigators and judges in prosecuting alleged witches throughout Europe and North America in the seventeenth and eighteenth centuries (see, for example, Given 2001). Given this history, it is not surprising that the relationship between interrogation and torture is a complex and tangled one. Indeed, many of the principles codified during the Inquisition extended into secular state interrogation practice in the eighteenth and nineteenth centuries, and even into the twentieth-century United States (see Otis 2006:xvi–xvii).

With the consolidation of the secular state in the late eighteenth and nineteenth centuries, "the rules about the use of pain to elicit information were consistently tightened to protect individual rights and liberties within the domestic law enforcement community" (Otis 2006:xvii–xviii). The police reform movement in the Depression-era United States marked a significant watershed in the development of modern interrogation practice. Prior to the 1930s it was common for police to use the "third degree" to wring confessions from suspects. However, when public outcry over police brutality "began to cast doubt on the legitimacy of criminal justice in America" (Leo 2008:63), elected officials and administrators responded with efforts to reform and professionalize police activities, developing policies, laws, and practices regulating how information was elicited from suspects. Reform efforts that started in the 1930s were redoubled in the 1950s with the rise of scientism in postwar American culture and the emergence of the national security state under the Truman and Eisenhower administrations. Under J. Edgar Hoover the Federal Bureau of Investigation (FBI) led the way in developing scientific investigation methods, including research into the psychology of confession, techniques to induce information from suspects, and the development of the polygraph, the most recognizable artifact of interrogation culture (Leo 1992, 2008; Leo and Skolnick 1992). Today, the normative rejection of blunt coercion and the embrace of psychological techniques to educe information are two major hallmarks of modern interrogation in the United States.

This long reform movement also marked the emergence of interrogation as a form of professional activity, albeit a complex and multisited one. These days, one can broadly identify three forms of interrogation practice: domestic criminal justice, military, and intelligence. Each pursues a similar yet distinct set of objectives within its own particular institutional and legal frameworks. Domestic criminal justice interrogators tend to work in local, state, and federal law enforcement institutions, and their work is oriented toward building a body of legally admissible evidence for a court case and is governed by the US Constitution (specifically the Fifth Amendment). In contrast, military interrogation is regulated by the Geneva Conventions, the Uniform Code of Military Justice, and the Detainee Treatment Act of 2005 (Leo 2008; United States Army 1992; United States Department of Defense 2006b:7). Although the military has its own criminal justice functions (for example, the US Army's Criminal Investigation Command and the prosecution of enemy combatants in military tribunals), military interrogation has historically focused on battle information, emphasizing "situational awareness" on the battlefield (United States Department of Defense 2006b:13). Similarly, intelligence interrogation has historically emphasized collection requirements for national security priorities. Ostensibly, the same laws of war and international treaties should govern intelligence interrogation, but US intelligence agencies have historically been given greater legal and operational leeway in developing and promulgating their own interrogation practices (McCoy 2006; Otis 2006:xiii).

Within these various institutions, however, exist a range of formal training programs for novice interrogators that play an important role in socializing new members in the norms and practices that mark particular institutional cultures. For example, the FBI conducts training in Quantico, Virginia; novices receive twenty weeks of intense training in a range of disciplines, including witness interviews and techniques for interrogating suspects. The FBI also conducts its own research to improve existing and develop new interview and interrogation techniques and provides training to local and state law enforcement professionals at its own training academies and through field offices around the country. In contrast, the DoD runs its own interrogation training programs. A major training center is the US Army's Military Intelligence Center in Fort Huachuca, Arizona, where "Human Intelligence" (HUMINT) collectors go through a three-month intensive interrogation course that includes guidance on warfare-specific topics, including the Geneva Conventions and obtaining tactical information from enemy prisoners of war (United States Army 1992; United States Army Intelligence Center 1997; United States Department of Defense 2006b). Training conventions for civilian intelligence operatives are less clear; however, one assumes that civilian government intelligence agencies such as the Central Intelligence Agency (CIA) provide interrogation training at their own facilities. Moreover, it is highly likely that federal agencies in all three areas—criminal justice, military, intelligence—send personnel to each others' training programs, depending on the requirements of their job assignments.

Despite these differences, if there is one principle that marks interrogation as a modern profession, it is the normative *rejection* of physical force. In fact, the quotation in the title of this chapter comes from a telephone conversation I had in the spring of 2008 with a retired DoD interrogator. Like many civilian DoD interrogators, he had spent years working with local, state, and federal criminal justice agencies. The Global War on Terror had taken him first to Afghanistan and then to Guantánamo Bay, where he was a senior member of the DoD's Criminal Investigation Task Force. At the time I spoke with him he had retired from the CITF and was working for a private government contractor. "People who don't know what they're doing resort to force," he told me. "Torture is for the incompetent. Interrogation is for professionals."

The extent to which this norm is put into practice varies tremendously. These days, most professional interrogators get some training in the psychologically based interrogation approaches that form the basis of criminal justice approaches. Perhaps the best known of these is the Reid Technique, which was developed in the 1940s and formalized in 1962 as an instructional manual that remains in publication today (Inbau et al. 2001:ix). It is widely used in the US criminal justice system and includes a nine-stage interrogation process through which investigators question suspects using behavioral, interviewing, and psychological techniques aimed at drawing out and developing a full confession.[7]

Nevertheless, abuse does happen, as reports from multiple sites in the Global War on Terror have so viscerally demonstrated. As psychologist Philip Zimbardo (2007) pointed out many years ago, torture is about dehumanization, power, and control; and in settings that allow its emergence, cruelty will make its presence felt in the absence of any perceived need for information extraction. Thus, physical abuse of prisoners does occur in the US criminal justice system (Conroy 2000), despite the fact that the culture of criminal justice interrogation normatively rejects physical coercion. Moreover, the US intelligence community has a long history of research into the development and promulgation of coercive techniques such as hypnotism, sensory deprivation, and blunt force (United States Central Intelligence Agency 1963, 1983). During the cold war, concerns about Soviet and Chinese "mind control" techniques spurred secret government research into the psychology and physiology of interrogation. Much of this work emphasized defensive countermeasures that would enable captured US servicemen to survive questioning at the hands of communist interrogators. However, other programs were more offensive in nature. For example, the army developed *Field Manual 34-52*, which provided soldiers with sets of topics and questions designed to get tactical information from captured prisoners of war. More secretive was the CIA's MKULTRA program, which explored the efficacy of hypnosis, sensory deprivation, and mind-altering drugs on human subjects. Such work formed much of the basis for the *KUBARK* manual that remained in publication through the late 1980s and was only declassified in 1997 (Fein 2006). As Otis (2006:xiii) points out rather chillingly, many of the principles in the thirteenth-century Eymerich guidance were present in KUBARK.

Even in the absence of force, some scholars argue that interrogation as practiced in the US criminal justice system is fundamentally problematic, if only because noncoercive techniques rely on manipulation and persuasion to convince suspects to release information that they might not offer voluntarily. This is, unsurprisingly, an unpopular perspective among professional interrogators, though legal scholar Richard Leo (2008:6) makes a good point when he argues that "American police interrogation is strategically manipulative and deceptive because it occurs in the context of a fundamental contradiction" between the interests of the individual and the interests of the state. For Leo, the contradiction is a systemic one: we demand that our criminal justice system be fair, transparent, and humane; however, Americans want police to "solve crimes at high rates in order to apprehend the bad guys," and we have laws that permit, even authorize, interrogators to use techniques that can "distort a suspect's perceptions and lead him to make incriminating statements against his self-interest" (Leo 2008:3). Insofar as interrogation techniques persuade individuals to make decisions that may not be in their legal, social, or psychological best interest, such contradictions may be at play in military and intelligence settings as well.

Interrogation in the Global War on Terror

The Global War on Terror is complicating the already complex terrain of American interrogation practice in at least two ways. Firstly, the prosecution of the war has challenged many of the explicit and implicit boundaries among domestic criminal justice, military, and intelligence interrogation. Conventional cold war, territorially focused military arrangements are inadequate for a transnational battlefield in which threats that originate in ideological and social movements gain support from both government and private financial and material suppliers, and realize themselves in surprise attacks on institutional symbols rather than strategic geographies. As the US government attempts to trace the lines of terrorism and extremism, the Global War on Terror assumes the contours of a massive law enforcement operation, with multiple parallel investigations to discover and apprehend individuals involved in the generation, planning, and execution of terrorist events. Indeed, the Global War on Terror is the most advanced hybridization of the legal and military realms to date (Dunlap Jr. 2001, 2007, 2009).

Not only does this bring interrogators from military, criminal justice, and intelligence interrogation into contact with each other, but the blending of interrogation functions in the Global War on Terror is problematic because the objectives of criminal justice, military, and intelligence interrogation are inherently contradictory. Guantánamo investigator Jeffrey Norwitz (2005:80) points out that

> Testimony and evidence are intended for criminal court prosecution and judicial scrutiny, while classified intelligence is purposely limited to protect sources and methods from compromise.... More irreconcilable, however, is the method by which each community questions people for information, not whether the information is sensitive. Criminalists expect to be held accountable for how they obtain information, [and] interview methods by law-enforcement officials must never shock the conscience of the court or the American public. Interrogations for intelligence purposes have a completely different set of criteria, none of which is ever seen in a courtroom.

How this blending of functions plays out in the real-world setting of interrogation is difficult to tell, although the "grunt" accounts (Brown and Lutz 2007) of military personnel indicate that different agencies have brought different techniques and approaches to bear on detainees in the Global War on Terror. Guantánamo interrogator Eric Saar, for example, contrasts the harsh techniques of military personnel to the incentive approach of interrogators from an "Other Government Agency," or OGA, which offered cooperative detainees a "comfy couch, cigarettes, treats from McDonalds," and even pornography (Saar and Novak 2005:180). After working with an OGA interrogator, Saar writes, "I had been clued into at least one reason why OGA and military interrogators barely spoke to each other" (Saar and Novak 2005:174).

It is worth pointing out that in the realm of counterterrorism, interrogation is not just aimed at prosecuting suspects for known terrorism plots but also has a forecasting role, insofar as information from GWOT suspects is seen as necessary for identifying and preventing incipient plots (Otis 2006:viii). This is largely due to public expectations that the US government will find a way to connect the proverbial dots and stop the next 9/11-type of event. As a result, interrogation is likely to remain a critically important element of the Global War on Terror. In fact, the United States has already apprehended and detained thousands of people in multiple geographical locations and conducted literally tens of thousands of interrogations—by April 2006, twenty-four thousand interrogations had taken place at Guantánamo alone (United States Department of Defense 2005a).

Culture in GWOT Interrogation

The fact that so much of this activity revolves around suspects from overseas, and particularly foreign nationals of Middle Eastern/Muslim/Afghan/Iraqi descent (Brown 2008), creates a second complicating dynamic. Prior to Abu Ghraib, expertise in conducting interrogations with terrorism suspects from overseas was limited to small pockets in the federal government—for example, the FBI's counterterrorism units—while neither the military nor intelligence communities had put much effort into developing interrogation practices and techniques appropriate for the post-Soviet era (Otis 2006:vii). In response, interrogators in multiple federal, state, and local institutions have been working to identify and develop new methods for conducting counterterrorism interrogations, particularly with non-Western detainees. Of particular interest in this regard is the development of what might be termed "culturally aware interrogation techniques," approaches that attempt to bring Middle Eastern/Muslim/Afghan/Iraqi cultural nuance to well-established interrogation approaches such as the Reid Technique. This emerged as a key theme not only in my review of the FOIA documentation from the ACLU's collection but also as I explored some of the more recent literature on the psychology of deception detection. Below I review three ways in which this novel concern with "culture" is manifest.

First, in the wake of the 9/11 attacks agencies that did have experience dealing with terrorism suspects quickly worked to consolidate and codify approaches that seemed effective and to develop mechanisms for sharing these with other agencies. For example, in 2003 the FBI's Behavioral Analysis Unit (BAU) hosted a workshop entitled "Interview and Interrogation of Extremists: Working Group" to "bring together personnel with background in terrorist investigations and incorporate this information into a practical guide for...controlled environments such as Guantánamo Bay." The workshop brought together a group of FBI special agents who "have been particularly successful in obtaining information from terrorists and their associates" and focused on such issues as "the need to better understand not only the mindset of those terrorists, but also the cultural, political and economic influences which may have contributed to their decision to align themselves with extremist causes. More important, BAU I [Behavioral Analysis Unit One] is interested in learning how we can better elicit information from these individuals either as sources, subjects, suspects, witnesses or victims" (United States Department of Justice 2003). The workshop's findings would be used to create new training programs and manuals for counterterrorism interrogators.

Second, federal counterterrorism institutions identified "culture" as a major obstacle to educing information and detecting deception. As a review conducted by the Intelligence Science Board pointed out, "Research on persuasion, influence, compliance and resistance has focused primarily on persons from Western cultures, and the results and insights may not apply equally or evenly across all cultures" (Borum 2006:17). To address this knowledge gap, the federal government has invested money in this area of research. Since the 9/11 attacks, researchers in a range of fields—from psychology to linguistics to computer science—have been exploring cultural and linguistic differences in the manifestation of deception, with an eye toward developing new techniques to improve the ability of investigators to discern when an informant is lying (Sabourin 2007; Zhou and Lutterbie 2005). This research is quite diverse, including narrative analysis (Gerwehr 2007), brain mapping using functional magnetic resonance imaging (Mohamed et al. 2006), and psychology studies in which, for example, researchers play videotapes of individuals from several different countries making true and false statements in several different languages; they then play these tapes to observers from these countries to assess if language and culture influence an individual's judgment about whether or not someone is telling the truth (see http://www.cossa.org/seminarseries/detectingdeception.htm; Bond and De Paulo 2006).

Finally, this interest in culture is making its way into the canons that guide interrogation practice. For example, in the wake of the Abu Ghraib scandal, the army rewrote its entire approach to interrogation. *Field Manual 2-22.3* emphasizes the importance of cultural sensitivity and respect roughly two dozen times. However, the manual goes well beyond recognizing "social taboos, desired behaviors, customs and courtesies," requiring that HUMINT collectors understand "basic [human] behavioral principles...and how these are manifested in the area and culture in which [they are] operating" (United States Department of Defense 2006b:1.13).

Even more interesting is the fact that professional interrogators who were disgusted with abuse in US GWOT facilities began to develop their own approaches to addressing cultural differences in the interrogation chamber. This brings me to a conversation I had with a man calling himself Abu'l Haq al-Amriki, a pen name used by a retired US federal civilian interrogator, a white male in his midfifties who has an extensive background in law enforcement, psychology, and interrogation. At Guantánamo he had fought against the use of SERE methods in the interrogation chamber, and he and his colleagues (many trained in criminal justice interrogation) decided to develop their own relationship-building methods that tried to take into account what he called the "cultural nuances" of the detainee's background. According to al-Amriki, they were far more successful than their military or intelligence counterparts using more coercive techniques.

At the time I spoke with him, al-Amriki had left the DoD and was working for a private consulting company in the Washington DC area, where he was using his own experience to provide training and guidance to civilian and military interrogators. In August 2008 he sent me a copy of a sixty-one-page interrogation manual he had been working on since June 2005 in which he had documented his approach to interviewing Muslim extremists. Al-Amriki explained to me that he read widely in the social science literature to ground his approaches to interrogation, and indeed, his manual drew on a number of sources from history, political science, and anthropology, including—yes—*The Arab Mind*. Al-Amriki was interested in talking to me because I am an anthropologist. He explained to me that he sincerely believed that anthropological research could play an important role in the development of humane, cross-culturally valid interrogation techniques for the Global War on Terror and that he planned to continue promulgating what he considered culturally sensitive, historically informed, humane, and effective interrogation techniques across the counterterrorism community.

THE INTERROGATION ENCOUNTER: THE GUANTÁNAMO TRANSCRIPTIONS

A handful of conversations with interrogators who are promoting humane and culturally sensitive techniques have led me to wonder what happens in such a noncoercive interrogation session. In this regard, one small section of the ACLU's torture FOIA library is particularly interesting: namely, a small collection of roughly sixty FBI interrogation "transcriptions" (the FBI's term, not mine) moderately to heavily redacted documenting exchanges between teams of interrogators and prisoners at Guantánamo Bay between April 2002 and July 2003. In this section I describe the challenges of working with redacted interrogation transcriptions, then present the results of a thematic analysis of the FBI Guantánamo transcriptions.

The FBI Guantánamo transcriptions are available at the Minnesota Human Rights Library website and is a subset of the larger FOIA collection maintained by the ACLU. The Minnesota collection contains documents that focus on medical operations in detention facilities in the Global War on Terror and was organized by Steven Miles (2006, 2007a, 2007b), a medical and bioethics professor at the University of Minnesota who has written extensively about the involvement of medical personnel in human rights abuses. The transcriptions clearly originate with the FBI. However, the agency that released this particular set could be the DoD or the FBI, as header and footer markings indicate these transcriptions may have been used as evidence in either a DoD or Department of Justice inquiry into operations at Guantánamo.

These transcriptions require some methodological comment. For one thing, they are not transcriptions in any traditional sense. Each entry consists of a few pages of official narrative that recounts a single interrogation event. The participants include the prisoner, one or two interrogators, and a linguist or a native language speaker acting as an interpreter. The interrogation teams consist of personnel from the DoD and one or more special agents (SA) from the FBI; the prisoners seem to be mostly Afghan, Saudi, or Pakistani detainees picked up by the Afghan Northern Alliance or American forces in the early days after the Afghan invasion. The transcription narrative is written in third person; the exact questions of the interrogator are not recorded, and the detainee's voice is expressed through the linguist or native speaker interpreter, then again through the person who is recording the interrogation. Many of these transcriptions seem to have been written a couple of days after the activity actually took place.

Furthermore, released in response to the ACLU-led FOIA lawsuit, most of the transcriptions are redacted to some degree (meaning that chunks of text are blocked out). Thus the voices of the participants are filtered and multiply refracted: through the interpreter, the individual taking the notes, the individual writing the narrative reports, and the lag between the actual interrogation and the construction of the narrative. Moreover, the collection is incomplete: there are only a half-dozen transcriptions or less per month, and many months are missing. As a result, while these transcriptions make for fascinating reading, assembling them into any kind of master narrative is challenging, like trying to put together a jigsaw puzzle that is missing many pieces.

In working with these documents, I pursued an iterative qualitative coding approach. First, I sorted the transcriptions by date, then read each transcription and made a list of themes contained in each. After sorting through this list of themes, I created a set of ninety-seven thematic codes and then grouped these into fifteen different code families (some codes belong to more than one code family). I used these code families to recode the transcripts, counting the number of transcripts in which a particular theme appeared. The most prevalent topics of the interviews included detention and capture stories in which the detainees related how they ended up at Guantánamo; discussions about Islam and Christianity; detainee views of the United States; and detainee accounts of mistreatment or abuse, usually at the hands of the United States or the Northern Alliance.

In the following pages I will draw on this thematic analysis to provide examples of the structure and content of these FBI Guantánamo narratives. I indicate redactions with blackout marks that approximate the visual appearance of the transcriptions themselves. For interested readers, I provide the document numbers (for example, 2034–45), which indicate the series number where the documents can be located on the University of Minnesota website (http://www1.umn.edu/humanrts/OathBetrayed/index.html). For ease of reading, I have left out the word "DETAINEES" on each document number, which is actually used as a document designator in all of the source transcriptions.

The Transcriptions

All transcriptions open with a header indicating who the participants were and the location and time of the interrogation. Gender is not included in the report information, but the pronouns indicate that all detainees in these transcriptions are male. Since few of the detainees speak English, most of the conversations occur through a linguist or interpreter. The opening comments of the transcriptions describe the interrogator introducing him- or herself and explaining the purpose of the "interview" (again, an FBI term).

> On 23 July 2002, ████ was interviewed at Camp Delta, US Naval Base Guantánamo Bay Cuba. Present during the interview were Special Agent ██ Air Force Office of special investigations, SA █, Federal bureau [sic] of Investigations, and ██████ Civilian Linguist ██ provided ██ translation. [3870]

> ██████ was interviewed at Camp Delta, US Naval Station Guantánamo Bay, Cuba, by SA ██ (FBI), SA ██(NCIS) and SA ████ (US Army (CID)). This interview was conducted in English. After being advised of the identities of the interviewing Agents and the nature of the interview, ██ thereafter provided the following information.... [3972]

These opening comments also include contextual information about previous interview sessions, which seems to derive from opening statements and questions from the detainee being interrogated. In these comments, we learn several things: first, that detainees go through multiple interrogation sessions. Second, the interrogation teams seem to repeat questions, which the detainees find tedious. Third, the detainees are aware that information about their lives is being amassed in one of the most important artifacts of interrogation: the file.

> ██████ again stated that he had already provided this information, but then agreed to answer the interviewers' question anyway. [4035]

> ██████ refused to answer any questions that have been previously answered by him from prior interviews and is already contained within "the file." [3912]

After the opening comments, the transcriptions move into narrative summarization of the detainees' responses to the interrogator's questions.

More than half of these transcriptions begin with detailed stories in which the detainees describe how they ended up at Guantánamo. Often the detainee seems to be telling his interrogators that his imprisonment is accidental, that he was in the wrong place at the wrong time. For example, in an interrogation that took place on September 24, 2002, the prisoner explains that he was conscripted by the Taliban:

> ████████ described his Taliban conscription in the following manner....Every year different families would be forced to send male members of their family to serve a one month tour of duty with the Taliban...[and] once ██████ was notified that he was conscripted, he went, the next day, to ██████ District, where he reported to the Taliban....He was armed with one Kalashnikov rifle and one magazine holding a total of 30 rounds [3256].

When the war started he was captured and imprisoned by the Northern Alliance, something that happened to approximately a quarter of the detainees represented in this set of transcriptions. As another detainee recounted,

> When they were placed into the makeshift prison in Bamyan, the prisoners were under the overall control of ██ a senior official of the Northern Alliance...[and] he and the other prisoners went through simple interrogations...; during this period, the prisoners were beaten with the butts of rifles and endured several more interrogations. [3902–5]

As they are recounting the chain of events that brought them to Guantánamo, many of the detainees describe being moved from prison to prison as they are transferred from Northern Alliance to US custody: from Bamyan to Baghram to Kandahar to Guantánamo. Along the way, it appears that the prisoners get to know each other; indeed, the transcriptions indicate that the conditions of imprisonment may have created a dense social network of Afghans, Arabs, Pakistanis, and people of other nationalities caught in the post-9/11 web of the Global War on Terror. For example, when asked to pick out faces he recognizes from a set of FBI photo books, one detainee points out nineteen faces, all of whom he recognizes from his time at different prisons during his detention, but claims not to have known any of them prior to the invasion of Afghanistan after 9/11.

Along those lines, in many of the detainees' accounts we learn that 9/11 was not only disruptive to the United States but to a good portion of the Islamic world. Detainees repeatedly point to 9/11 as a turning point in their lives, either because it caused them to commit to Jihad, because they were conscripted into Taliban military service, or because 9/11 started a chain of events that led to their current imprisonment in Cuba.

> ████ first heard of the terrorist attacks in the US on ███ version of Voice of American [sic] radio. He initially could not believe it was true. He had no prior knowledge of the attacks and had not heard any rumors of anything about to occur. [3842]

> ████ made the decision to join the Jihad shortly after September 11th. He had seen a CNN news report that the US bombing campaign was taking place in the mountain regions and not in the cities. He wanted to be part of the Jihad, but in a peaceful capacity. [3876]

From this point, the narratives evolve into complicated exchanges in which the interrogators and the detainee jointly offer, counter, and question each other's narratives of the events that brought them into the room. Underlying all these exchanges is the theme of trust, or rather the lack thereof, a problem that recurs over and over again in the transcriptions. Interrogation seems to involve sorting through conflicting stories, sifting through the detainee's experience to get to some kind of truth about involvement in terrorist activities, though clear proof seems elusive. Indeed, most of the detainees seem to be making an effort to take back previous confessions, which they explain were given under either fear of duress or actual torture, particularly while in the custody of Northern Alliance forces, though several complain of forcible treatment on the part of US personnel as well (see, for example, 3883, 3884, 4056, 4072). Perhaps not surprisingly, many of the detainees report suffering from mental health problems:

> ████ advised he was taking medicine twice a day with his meals. A review of his medical records at Camp Delta revealed he was diagnosed with post-traumatic stress syndrome and depression. [3870]

> ████ advised of problems with the other detainees....He said it puts great stress on him to the point that he has thoughts about suicide. ████ believed he is spying on them. At the time of this interview, he stated he has seen a doctor [3908].

The problem of trust runs both ways, however; the question is not just whether or not the interrogators trust what the detainees are telling them, but whether the detainees trust the intentions and reassurances of their captors. If they do not, one wonders how the interrogators can convince them to cooperate with their investigations. Indeed, discursive resistance is a prominent theme throughout these exchanges, as when detainees refuse to answer questions, when they pray instead of responding to the interrogators, or when they deploy sarcasm.

> ████was asked if he liked Americans and responded, "Of course" (Arabic translator advised that the response was sarcastic). ████ further elaborated,[11] "why would someone not like someone who treated him badly on the way to Guantánamo Bay and hit him?" [4023]

When another detainee is asked if he "deserves to leave Camp Delta," he responds, "No. Ask me why." When the interrogators do so, the detainee responds, "Because I'm Muslim." Still another transcription evokes George Orwell's essay "Shooting an Elephant" when the detainee tells the interrogators that

> the detainees see the guards as babies, especially the "big American guards that fill the doorway." This is because the guards are supposed to be strong, yet they walk around with a "camel" (a backpack water storage device with a drinking tube attached) on their back sucking on the tube of water all of the time. A strong man is able to go without water for long periods of time. [3913]

And finally, a detainee dryly observes that "if the prisoners did not hate the United States before 9/11, they do now" (4049).

Resistance to imprisonment and interrogation is another consistent theme. The interrogators frequently ask the detainees if anyone in their cellblock is telling them to lie or not to answer questions (the detainees' response to this question is invariably "no"). The interrogators seem to be concerned about incipient prisoner revolts. Most of the respondents deny knowledge of such plans but admit that a great deal of communication takes place among the Guantánamo detainees; that most have experienced similar tribulations in the course of their detention experiences; and that many of the prisoners are unhappy with the conditions of their detention and consider it unjust. In one transcription (3860–63) the prisoner is asked if he knows about "specific plans to cause disruption to Campo [*sic*] Delta or the assault of a guard/guards or other detainees." The prisoner responds that he knows of nothing specific, but

> ▆▆▆▆ simply stated, "If an opportunity exist [*sic*], they will take it."....▆▆▆▆ stated that he felt "oppressed" but would not by [*sic*] violence. If there were an opportunity to escape, he would take it.... ▆▆▆▆ reassured the interviewers that if he heard anything regarding plans to attack US interests, or plans to cause a disruption or assault on Camp Delta, he would tell us. [3861]

Some detainees seem inclined to mistrust anything the interrogators tell them; one detainee dismisses his interrogators contemptuously as "government pawns" (2922). When trust is gained, it can be lost. One prisoner expresses frustration that he has been interviewed "approximately six (6) times since he has been in US custody." After willingly cooperating with the investigators he states he no longer trusts his American interrogators since an interrogation at Guantánamo by representatives of his native government leads him to believe that US government personnel passed on information about his family, and the prisoner is now worried that their safety is threatened. "It's unbelievable, this is a US prison, in the US, and ▆▆▆ government is able to come here and do anything they want. It makes me wonder who's running this prison" (3924).

Everyone, it seems, is searching for a philosopher's stone, some independent arbiter of veracity. The detainees want proof that the interrogators are going to send them home, while the interrogators are seeking proof that the detainees are telling the truth, though the nature of truth—is a self-professed Jihadist really a terrorist?—is itself elusive. For example, one wonders if a detainee who admits he "made the decision to join the Jihad shortly after September 11th....He wanted to be a part of the Jihad, but in a peaceful capacity" realizes the subtle differences between Jihad and terrorism might be lost on US government officials (3876).

In any case, the detainees marshal what discursive resources they can as proof of honesty: "▆▆▆...swore that he would sign his own execution order if he had lied to the interrogators" (3861). Another detainee, after providing information about an incipient hunger strike, tells the interrogators—one male and one female—that he respects them. He "claimed he was going to write the male interviewer's name on his heart and the female interviewer's name on his right upper arm. He claimed he respected the interviewers" (3914).

In this equivocal realm both detainees and interrogators look to the polygraph as a divining rod. Interrogators offer detainees the polygraph; detainees ask to take one to prove their innocence. Even the polygraph is a point of resistance, however. One detainee who apparently failed his polygraph accuses the polygrapher in Afghanistan of "playing with the machine" and he tells the interrogators that a Red Cross worker from Saudi Arabia warned him not to trust polygraphs. The interrogators respond that the polygraph is indeed accurate and that Red Cross workers "are not investigators and should not advise him on his case" (4086). Still another detainee insists that polygraphs are against Muslim religious beliefs and accuses the interrogators of trying to "trick" him (3091).

The most interesting transcriptions, however, reveal complex exchanges in which interrogators and prisoners deploy and discuss competing narratives about the significance of 9/11, the Global War on Terror, whether Islam is synonymous with radicalism, the fundamental precepts of American democracy, and the nature of American empire. These exchanges give some sense of what this "clash of civilizations" looks like at the level of individuals in the interrogation room. These exchanges also have a psychological element, as interrogators first elicit, then challenge a prisoner's worldview in an effort to cajole information from the detainee.

One transcription in particular dramatically evokes the techniques that Marshall Sahlins relates in his conversations with Mr. X, Captain D, and Captain Y, three US interrogators working in Vietnam. They explain to Sahlins the importance of breaking down the ideological ties that bind an individual to a particular sociopolitical movement to encourage the individual to give up critical information. Similarly, in this particular case, the interrogators seem to believe that the detainee played a key role in the 9/11 attacks. The prisoner has apparently complained previously of being tortured; however, rather astoundingly, "The interview agent strongly told [the prisoner] torture is not an issue and he knows it.... When this goes before a tribunal, the torture argument will not be considered because the USG does not torture anyone in it's [sic] custody" (4032). Later, the interrogators show footage of the 9/11 attacks, then begin questioning the prisoner about his beliefs: does he believe that this is in line with what Islam teaches? Does he not see that 9/11 was an attack on all humanity, on Christians, Jews, Hindus, and Muslims alike? The interrogator tells the detainee, "No God, regardless of religion would condone the murder of so many innocent unarmed people. Those who did this in the name of God and Islam without a doubt abuse and malign the religion and will feel God's anger and wrath on judgment day." The transcription notes that the prisoner looked "visibly shaken by this realization." The agent follows these observations by telling the detainee that "the most powerful tool is the truth," and that they will give him some time to think about his decision—though the exact nature of that decision is unclear from the transcription. The end of the transcription is striking: "At the conclusion of the interview, the interview team wished [him] luck and that God may accept his prayers. After exiting the room, the interview team witnessed [the prisoner] with his head down on his hands on the table in front of him....He was crying and sobbing with tears falling on the table when he lifted his head" (4027–34).

These documents collectively provide insight into the dynamics of both interrogation and the conditions of detention at Guantánamo; indeed, it was in reading these that I began to conceptualize the interrogation room as a front line in the Global War on Terror. As Leo (2008:119) points out, *"The goal of police interrogation is not necessarily to determine the truth"* (his italics); instead, interrogation involves the active elicitation and joint shaping of a narrative of events, which may or may not be "true," but which is increasingly successful (in the eyes of the police) if the interactions lead to incrimination, prosecution, and conviction.

THE PERSISTENT COMPLEXITIES OF GWOT INTERROGATION

Legal scholar Richard Leo has argued that interrogation is legally, ethically, and socially intensely problematic, despite its popular representation as a cat-and-mouse game of verbal parrying and trickery between driven police investigators and recalcitrant detainees, fueled by TV shows like *Law and Order* and *CSI: Miami*. This obfuscates the complicated reality of interrogation as a site in which fundamental (and perhaps irreconcilable) paradoxes about the relationship between the citizen and the state in consensual democracy play out (Leo 2008:9–40). Leo tells us that interrogation is a "symbolic matter" in that it "goes to the heart of our conceptions of procedural fairness and substantive justice, and raises questions about the kind of criminal justice system and society we want to have" (2008:1).

In the context of the Global War on Terror interrogation gets to even deeper questions about the relationship between the United States and a rapidly changing world. Detention and interrogation operations are an extreme form of "cultural transfer" that pull human beings into worlds radically, even agonizingly, different than the ones they have known (Metcalf 2001). If the state is more than "a set of institutions staffed by bureaucrats who serve public interest," we might consider interrogation in the context of a larger conglomeration of "cultural and political forms, representations, discourse, practices and activities, and specific technologies and organizations of power that...help to define public interest, establish meaning, and define and naturalize available social identities" (Nagengast 1994:116). An ethnographic approach to the state means that we look for its manifestation in the lived experience of individuals, including the identities and practices of the professionals who comprise, enact, and extend its institutions. Anthropologists are particularly good at eliciting the relationships between microbehaviors and macrostructures, which gives us a unique perspective on the dynamics through which America is made, unmade, and remade in spaces like the interrogation room.

Notes

1. Monty Python performer and political activist Terry Jones (2002) commented, "What really alarms me about President Bush's 'war on terrorism' is the grammar. How do you wage war on an abstract noun? It's rather like bombing murder."

2. Revisions to US GWOT detention and interrogation legal opinions were occurring in the early years of the second Bush administration. For example, in 2005 assistant attorney general nominee Steven Bradbury opined that the federal prohibition on torture did indeed apply to individuals detained by US armed forces. Policy revisions continued until the very last hours of the Bush administration: on January 15, five days prior to the Obama inauguration, the Office of Legal Counsel (OLC) in the US Department of Justice issued a memo warning that opinions expressed in nine separate memoranda issued between 2001 and 2003 "were not consistent with the current views of the OLC, and we advise that caution should be exercised before relying in other respects on the remaining opinions identified below" (Bradbury 2009:1). The memoranda included opinions regarding rendition, military conventions, the status of enemy combatants, standards of conduct for interrogation, congressional jurisdiction over the actions of the executive branch in regard to the detention and treatment of enemy combatants and prisoners of war, and other controversial elements of the Bush administration policies regarding detention and interrogation operations under the Global War on Terror (see Bradbury 2009).

3. Specifically Executive Order 13491, "Ensuring Lawful Interrogations." Although the CIA was ordered to close all facilities that it operates, the Executive Order excludes from its provisions "facilities used only to hold people on a short-term, transitory basis." This has been interpreted as a loophole that would allow the CIA to conduct renditions—something that at least a few intelligence experts see as a probability, even under the Obama administration (e.g., Gerecht 2008; Miller 2009).

4. Salon.com maintains a website with the entire collection of Abu Ghraib photos (www.salon.com/news/abu_ghraib/2006/03/14/introduction; accessed March 23, 2009).

5. While the ACLU's electronic repository is the most comprehensive, other activist sites provide access to parts of this FOIA collection as well: the Center for Public Integrity, for example (http://www.publicintegrity.org), and the Minnesota Human Rights Library (http://www1.umn.edu/humanrts/OathBetrayed/index.html).

6. In the summer of 2002 members of the DoD's Joint Task Force Guantánamo (JTFG) began conferring with the Joint Personnel Recovery Agency (JPRA) Survival, Evasion, Resistance, Escape (SERE) program to adopt training techniques used in SERE for application in interrogation sessions. These techniques included sensory and sleep deprivation, humiliation, waterboarding, and stress positions (Levin 2008). JTFG counsel Diane Beaver (2002:1) argued that "the detainees have been able to communicate among themselves and debrief each other about their respective interrogations…[so] their interrogation resistance strategies have become more sophisticated." Navy counsel worried that if new counterresistance approaches were witnessed by external monitors, such as Red Cross observers, this would bring international scrutiny to US interrogation practices, potentially undermining the efficacy of new techniques. The navy thus recommended that any new counterresistance techniques be classified top secret (Thompson 2002). Later, with the Abu Ghraib scandal, this chain of decision making backfired devastatingly (Dunlap Jr. 2009).

7. The process of "developing confession" is quite fraught, as legal scholars and critics of criminal justice interrogation are quick to point out. Critics of criminal justice interrogation question the ethics of deceptive techniques; point out that psychological techniques can be coercive, leading individuals to make false confessions; and argue that lie detection is far less reliable or robust than its proponents indicate (see, for example, Bunn 2007:156–178; Holden 2001:967; Kassin et al. 2007:381–400; Leo 1992; Leo and Skolnick 1992; Tiantian and Burgoon 2007:152–169).

3

Counterinsurgency, Vietnam, Thailand, and the Political Uses of Militarized Anthropology

David Price

The days of naïve anthropology are over. It is no longer adequate to collect information about little known and powerless people; one needs to know also the uses to which that knowledge can be put.

—*Joseph Jorgensen and Eric Wolf, 1970*

The generation and application of anthropological knowledge is embedded within social contexts; and as with any other cultural knowledge system, the knowledge-base and application of anthropology is inevitably linked to the symbolic systems, political economy, and infrastructure in which it is produced, practiced, and consumed.[1]

While post–World War II branches of medical and social science have incorporated ethical standards derived from principles articulated in the Nuremberg Code to moderate human research protocols, there has been a general skittishness among most scientists to connect their uses of their work to the political or military uses to which their work is put (see discussion in the introduction to this volume).

The physical and social sciences share unvoiced disciplinary assumptions that avoid confronting the political context in which the produced knowledge is used, which leads to a position of imagined political neutrality. But such decisions to avoid political contexts do nothing more than empower the status quo uses of knowledge. Not to evaluate or challenge the political uses of scientific knowledge is not a neutral act; it is a decision to empower the dominant political power structures.

The lines separating distinctions between political and ethical issues raised by anthropological research are not always clear, but there are basic distinctions to frame considerations of ethical and political contexts of anthropological work. Professional ethics delineate acceptable methodological standards of practices for researchers, standards that are explicitly concerned with providing parameters protecting the well-being of research subjects.[2] Professional ethics codes delineate principles for doing things like obtaining voluntary informed consent and protecting informants, guidelines for maintaining anonymity, secrecy guidelines, and so forth. Professional ethics codes rarely venture into macropolitical realms.

Political considerations tend to focus beyond the immediate details of a particular interaction between anthropologists and the individuals they interview and instead focus on the political ends to which anthropological knowledge is applied. In the context of warfare, political considerations tend to focus on the justness of the cause that anthropological research supports, but other political considerations could address issues such as the application of anthropology to support or challenge the economic, racial, or gendered stratification of a social system.

As ethics and politics are distinct categories, it would be logically possible for anthropologists to conduct ethical research in what could be viewed as politically "bad" wars, to conduct unethical research in what could be viewed as politically "bad" wars, to conduct ethical research in what could be viewed as politically "good" wars, or to conduct unethical research in what could be viewed as politically "good" wars. Obviously, ethical research standards are open to debate as are evaluations of political considerations.

While ethical considerations focus on whether an anthropologist followed accepted ethical protocols (for issues such as protecting the identities of research subjects), political considerations focus on the sort of power relations, or political and military outcomes, that anthropology supports. Both ethical and political considerations can be concerned with issues of right and wrong, but these considerations are generally concerned with distinctly different categorical issues, with political considerations focusing primarily on "ends" and ethical considerations focusing primarily on "means." Professional ethics categorize practices into limited considerations focusing on small-scale interactions between researchers and subjects and seldom focus on systemic issues or the sort of systematic power relations embedded in outcomes in the way that political considerations do. While ethics codes focus on the "means" of good standards of fieldwork and other practices (for example, protecting informants' identities or obtaining voluntary informed consent), political considerations focus on the political "ends" to which anthropological research is put.

It is easy to understand the hesitancy of professional associations to officially address the political issues embedded in militarized uses of anthropology for counterinsurgency (though organizations like the American Anthropological Association [AAA] frequently weigh in and take sides on all sorts of political issues such as racism, antigay marriage legislation, and intercultural adoption). Instead of confronting the political issues embedded in counterinsurgency, professional associations like the AAA or the Society for Applied Anthropology (SfAA) primarily limit their institutional focus to the ethical rather than the political issues raised by their discipline's contributions to counterinsurgency. Many anthropologists frame ethical concerns in terms of "professional interests," while political concerns tend to be categorized as much more "personal" in nature. But when recurrent patterns of use and consistent outcomes become linked with the discipline itself, decisions not to engage, critique, or challenge the political contexts in which the military uses anthropology risk becoming passive endorsements of these outcomes regardless of postures of discomfort, willful dissociative ignorance, or naïveté.

This chapter, therefore, examines the context in which anthropologist Gerald Hickey's Vietnam War–era knowledge contributed to a series of RAND Corporation reports; Hickey's work is contrasted with the decision of Delmos Jones, an anthropologist contemporary with Hickey, to withhold his research from those who might use it for militarized ends. These two historical examples provide a frame through which to consider not only some of the ways that anthropological research is inevitably linked to both ethical concerns and political contexts, but to examine the approaches and outcomes of two significantly different reactions to wartime efforts to draw upon anthropological knowledge. I am interested in pursuing Jones's position that ethnographic research is inevitably linked to the larger needs of state regardless of individual anthropologists' naïve intentions, and that while anthropologists acknowledge and incorporate ethical limits in framing their research, the field of anthropology's inability to acknowledge the possibility of a larger parasitic dynamic passively commits the discipline to politically aiding the waging of neocolonial wars against those it studies (González 2007a).

GERALD HICKEY: THE NOT SO QUIET AMERICAN

Gerald Hickey (1959) earned his doctorate in anthropology at the University of Chicago in 1959 with a dissertation on the "Social Systems of Northern Vietnam." From the late 1950s throughout the years of America's involvement in the Vietnam War, no other American anthropologist had more fieldwork experience with the cultures of Vietnam than Hickey. He spent much of the war working in Vietnam, producing reports for RAND, SEDAG (Southeast Asian Development Advisory Group), and other organizations interfacing with US military and intelligence personnel. Some of Hickey's reports and recommendations broke with American military policies, and he conceptualized much of his work as devoted to saving the lives of Vietnamese groups that were misunderstood by the US military.

The reports that Hickey produced during the war, the responses by and uses of these reports by policymakers, the anthropological community's reactions to his work, and Hickey's later postwar analysis (2002) provide an opportunity to evaluate the particulars of Hickey's experiences and to consider the possibility of systemic problems associated with impacting policy changes facing anthropologists working in settings dominated by military and intelligence bureaucratic hierarchies.

Hickey conducted fieldwork in Vietnam in 1956 and 1957, which was when he met many of the individuals who would figure prominently in his future research. Hickey was in Vietnam when director Joseph Mankiewicz filmed the original 1958 Hollywood production of Graham Greene's *The Quiet American* and even appeared as an extra in a scene shot with Michael Redgrave (at about the fifty-minute mark). Hickey's cameo in *The Quiet American* provides an ironic frame for viewing his contributions to American military and intelligence Vietnam policies over the next dozen years, but it also marks his very early awareness of Graham Greene's critique of the CIA's interventions and intentions in Vietnam.

In 1962 Hickey and John Donnell (Donnell and Hickey 1962) coauthored a preliminary report based on ethnographic research for RAND entitled "The Vietnamese 'Strategic Hamlets.'" The Strategic Hamlet Program was a counterinsurgency operation that uprooted entire villages and relocated them in areas where US military and intelligence personnel could more easily monitor and control the peasants and reduce their contact with and support of the Vietcong. While the stated goal of these new "hamlets" was to isolate and move villagers from the "path" of insurgents, functionally, the new hamlets were essentially locked-down encampments that maintained illusions of open-door free movement (complete with deadly fortified barriers). They also isolated and controlled populations in new regions in ways reminiscent of the World War II–era War Relocation Authority camps that relocated Japanese-American citizens or the wartime relocation camps of other nations.

The Strategic Hamlet Program relied on forms of full-spectrum dominance to control villagers' economic, political, and physical needs as entire villages were relocated from direct contact with the Vietcong in the highlands. Strategic Hamlet targeted village members suspected to be Vietcong supporters, and it installed village informers who reported to US military and intelligence personnel on subversive activities. Donnell and Hickey (1962:2–3) described the program as designed to:

> consolidate governmental authority in pacified areas through a defense system and administrative reorganization at the hamlet level. In each hamlet, the military basis of the system comprises a Self-Defense Corps (SDC) unit that may number anywhere from five to twelve men, and auxiliary warning and/or guard force composed of members of the Republican Youth, and more or less extensive fortifications. In addition, the program involves the political and social organization of the inhabitants in a way that permits close surveillance of their political activities, of their social participation in such government-controlled mass movements as the Republican Youth, and the contribution to labor projects for community development. Once these programs are established, the system is further designed to serve as a basis for wider programs of rural economic reconstruction, including agricultural credit and extension services.

Strategic Hamlet created panoptical microcosms that were artificially engineered not only to move villagers from regions of Vietcong movement but to redesign village economic and social dynamics. As inducement to leave their village homes, families were given small pieces of land to build homes within the perimeter of the strategic hamlet compounds, with access to farmlands outside the compounds. Sometimes farmers were left outside these compounds to collect intelligence (Donnell and Hickey 1962:6–7).

Hickey understood that controlling physical space was as important as controlling cultural space and that "the reorganization of a hamlet's social and administrative organs is regarded by all officials as at least as important as the construction of physical defense facilities" (Donnell and Hickey 1962:7). Units known as "Rural Reconstruction Teams" supervised the reorganization of villages and helped install a number of social, agricultural, and economic programs that on the surface appeared to be aid programs, but that also increased the contingencies of control under which villagers further subjected themselves, thereby increasing their dependency on their new keepers (see Donnell and Hickey 1962:7; Milhauser 2008). These Rural Reconstruction Teams also tried "to learn about families with pro-Viet

Cong sentiment who should be regrouped near a military post for easier surveillance" (Donnell and Hickey 1962:7).

The scale of the Strategic Hamlet dream was massive. In 1962 the US military planned to install twelve thousand strategic hamlets in a six-month period (Donnell and Hickey 1962:3). Such increasingly large visions of total control are logical and inevitable once militaries become dependent on counterinsurgency. These contrived "hamlets" installed governing advisory units known as the "Council of Elders" that consisted of wealthy and influential community members who could be manipulated to steer public opinions and policies (Donnell and Hickey 1962:8). Rural Reconstruction Teams always began their work by conducting a census, an act that according to Donnell and Hickey (1962:7), "often prompt[ed] some pro-Communist individuals to flee the hamlet."

Hickey's support for "improving" and intensifying the Strategic Hamlet Program found him deploying anthropology in the service of social engineering. The program's dependence on censuses illustrated the importance of what James Scott (1998) refers to as "legibility" as a dominant feature and outcome of the Strategic Hamlet Program. Just as cadastral surveys beget uniformity and empower those who administrate them (see Scott 1998:37–40), Hickey's Strategic Hamlet vision was one of uniformity and social engineering designed to sever connections with preexisting cultural life, supplanting order and control in ways fitting the needs of the US military and keeping inhabitants legible to them. Though Hickey thought of his work as reducing harm for those peoples forced into relocation, the Strategic Hamlet's manipulation of these people raised many disturbing questions about the application of anthropology for counterinsurgency.

Hickey's report provided US policymakers and military and intelligence agencies with an ethnographic view of why the Strategic Hamlet Program would fail. The report outlined how the debts, disruptions, ill-will, and economic losses generated would outweigh any benefits of surveillance and disruption of village aid to the Vietcong. The report made the motives and lives of Vietnamese peasants legible to these agencies seeking to control them. It clarified that Vietnamese peasants were "more favorably disposed to the side which offers [them] the possibility of a better life," yet the inherent problems in the Strategic Hamlet Program could easily lead these farmers to turn against the American designers (Donnell and Hickey 1962:15).

Hickey explicitly supported the transformation of the Strategic Hamlet Program into a form that would better meet the needs of its villagers while maintaining the US military's control. Hickey urged that conditions be manipulated so that farmers living in strategic hamlets could derive direct benefits from the programs in which they were forced to participate. Using concrete examples to illustrate why rational peasants would despise their relocation and disruption of their normal agricultural activities (for example, the report explained that farmers had short-term views of future payoffs, and thus the immediate reductions in tobacco cash crops were viewed as a "defeat" rather than an inconvenience), Donnell and Hickey (1962:16–17) warned that if the cultural views and needs of these people were not accommodated, the villagers would be lost as allies:

> These farmers are the backbone of the village warning and auxiliary guard systems. In our opinion, they will participate in these security activities willingly and effectively only if, in the very near future, they see evidence that the strategic hamlet to which they have made such heavy contributions in time, materials, land, and reduced secondary crop yields is capable of improving their economic, social, and political welfare beyond the narrower aspect of the greater physical security it offers them.

The report made a number of recommendations. Primary among these was that the peasants be viewed as rational actors whose needs and values should be understood and respected if the Strategic Hamlet Program were to achieve its desired ends of control. The authors did not recommend the end of the forced relocation of villagers. They instead recommended that peasants be compensated for their work and cooperation—and specific recommendations for increased compensation, along with increased political involvement in decision making, were made.[3]

But Hickey's vision of an "improved" hamlet program ignored larger problems of costs and scale. In explaining the vision and scope of the program, Roger Hilsman (1998) (who was John F. Kennedy's director of the State Department's Bureau of Intelligence and Research) later commented that

> in Malaya, the British tried all sorts of things against the Communist insurgency, [a] jungle based Communist insurgency, and failed over and over again. Finally, under a man named R. K. G. Thompson, they hit upon what they called a strategic hamlet program. In a sense what they did was, they took villages and fortified them, and then controlled the flow of rice and food and ammunition and so on and so forth. And it took a long time, this so-called strategy, but it worked. Now what happened in Vietnam was that R. K. G. Thompson was the

liaison officer from the British and after his experience in
Malaya, why he was [an] absolute wonderful choice, he tried to
persuade Ngu Dinh Diem and company to adopt a strategic
hamlet program. *It would have taken twenty years, but it would have
worked.* Instead of chasing Communist troops all over the jungles,
you would have slowly enlarged the secure areas, like an oil
block with strategic hamlets moving out. [emphasis added]

Hilsman's vision was that US forces could have increasingly locked
down Vietnamese peasants in strategic hamlets until well into the early
1980s with little concern for the financial costs or the neocolonial implications of imprisoning people of a foreign country. While not considering
such logistics, Hickey shared the belief that better-designed forms of mili-
tary-enforced cultural engineering could prevail. In evaluating the historic
importance of Donnell and Hickey's RAND report, historian Eric Bergerud
(1991:52) wrote,

Hickey and Donnell knew that unless the Strategic Hamlet
Program was utterly reshaped it was going to fail. Despite sharp
and acrimonious criticism from both American and South
Vietnamese officials, they prepared a report and gave a series of
high-level briefings that vividly showed the self-defeating nature
of the centerpiece of Diem's war effort in rural Vietnam. When
Diem was overthrown, the junta in Saigon ended the Strategic
Hamlet Program immediately citing as reasons many of the
points raised by Hickey and Donnell.

I would not argue that Hickey and Donnell's analysis of the failures of
Strategic Hamlet was necessarily wrong. I am sure they were correct in
proposing that many of the features of these hamlets alienated the very villagers they were designed to "protect." Even though Hickey's critique did
not confront how difficult to implement, expensive, and lengthy such a
program would be, the fundamental problems with Hickey's RAND work
were political and ethical.

Even if Hickey had developed a magic bullet that efficiently co-opted,
pacified, and rapidly moved hundreds of highland villages effortlessly, such
a plan would have necessarily manipulated these people to conform with a
US military policy that many of these villagers saw as counter to their own
wishes and interests. It is difficult to imagine how any such plan could have
been *anthropological* regardless of how much *culture* Hickey might have
incorporated into such a "solution."

Ethical Considerations circa 1962

Accepting Hickey's observation that Strategic Hamlet would fail if it continued to be administered in the ways he observed does not clarify whether such intensive and expensive forms of counterinsurgency could ever be achieved, much less whether anthropologists' contributions to such manipulative schemes would be ethical. Considering such an ethical question presents many problems, not the least of which is lack of clear anthropological ethical standards in 1962, when Hickey undertook this work. While the AAA had no ethics code when Hickey did his initial RAND work, there were two obvious resources offering ethical guidance on these issues: the Nuremberg Code (itself the basis of all twentieth-century social science ethics codes) and the Society for Applied Anthropology's ethics code.

An anthropological evaluation of the Strategic Hamlet Program more aligned with the concerns of the Nuremberg Code might have focused first on understanding, then giving voice to Vietnamese villagers and their concerns, rather than primarily striving to understand these villagers and their concerns so that they could be manipulated and moved in ways aligned with US military policy. At a minimum it would have disclosed to the villagers being studied that their participation would assist the military's increased control over their lives in uprooted, artificial villages. Conditions of warfare often present actors with a Hobson's choice; nonetheless, it seems a contradiction even to attempt to gain voluntary informed consent in armed settings, much less to gain permission to study communities so that one may better manipulate them into collaborating with the desires of a foreign military. But this is what Hickey and Donnell would have had to do in order to comply with Nuremberg's principle of voluntary consent.

The Nuremberg Code's fundamental demand of voluntary informed consent expresses a core element of anthropology's central mission to maintain a basic alignment with studied populations. It is difficult to reconcile using anthropological research to support Strategic Hamlet's forced relocation of entire villages by external military forces with the Nuremberg Code's demand that "voluntary consent of the human subject is absolutely essential" (Nuremberg Code, point 1; see Loue 2000:32). Military planners undertake such planning every day, but they are military planners, not anthropologists. When anthropologists undertake such tasks and rely upon field research with affected individuals, they are bound by ethical standards that are rooted in Nuremberg's commitment to voluntary consent.

The SfAA's ethics code was a product of the problems encountered by anthropologists during World War II (see Price 2008b:272–279). The SfAA code was already a dozen years old, and while not directly solving the problems facing Hickey, it cautioned against elements of such disruptive forms of social engineering with admonitions like the following:

- the applied anthropologist must take responsibility for the effects of his recommendations, never maintain that he is merely a technician unconcerned with the ends toward which his applied scientific skills are directed;

- specific means adopted will inevitably determine the ends attained, hence ends can never be used to justify means;

- the applied anthropologist should recognize a special responsibility to use his skill in such a way as to prevent any occurrence which will set in motion a train of events which involves irreversible losses of health or the loss of life to individuals or groups or irreversible damage to the natural productivity of the physical environment. [SfAA 1949:20–21]

The SfAA code's weak language leaves it open to broad interpretations, but the code's concerns over the irreversible losses of health and life and warnings against anthropologists becoming technicians less concerned with the means of manipulation than desired ends provides a basis for ethical concern. Hickey's use of ethnography to openly facilitate improved means of surveillance (Donnell and Hickey 1962:7) is an unusual and problematic use of anthropology that loses sight of "means" for "ends."

Concerns about such "ends" and "means" raise political questions about the ends to which Hickey's ethnographic means were put. That his anthropological skills were harnessed for use in a war striving for neocolonial ends must be factored into political considerations of this work. But lines separating political and ethical distinctions are not always clear; the use of these anthropological skills for neocolonial ends also raises ethical issues. That his RAND report humanized and clarified cultural motivations of villagers in this neocolonial war does not mean that Hickey could "maintain that he is merely a technician unconcerned with the ends toward which his applied scientific skills are directed." To focus only on "means" (ethnography) without acknowledging the "ends" (pacification and domination of a studied population) is counter to the SfAA's 1949 commitment to avoiding irreversible damage to studied communities.

Hickey's unheeded Strategic Hamlet recommendations were not just relegated to the files of history. The rejection of his evaluation by policy analysts has been recently trumpeted by Montgomery McFate as an argument for militarizing anthropology today. But McFate did not acknowledge the logistical (that is, the likely decades of occupation), ethical, or political problems with Hickey's recommendations. She instead assured her military audience that had Hickey been listened to, the Strategic Hamlet Program would have been a glowing success, writing:

> Hickey's research indicated that the strategic hamlets might be successful if farmers saw evidence their communal labor and contribution of time, land, and building materials actually resulted in physical and economic security. Although Hickey's observations were probably correct, his views were often dismissed as too pacifistic. When Hickey debriefed Marine General Victor Krulak, the general pounded his fist on his desk and said, "We are going to make the peasants do what's necessary for strategic hamlets to succeed!" As Hickey noted, peasants have many methods of passive and active resistance, and force is often counterproductive as a motivator. Disliking the results of the study, the Pentagon pressured RAND to change the findings and, in the interest of impartial research, RAND refused. In the end, none of Hickey's findings were implemented, and the Strategic Hamlet Program was a failure. [M. McFate 2005a:34]

McFate laments that policymakers ignored Hickey's Strategic Hamlet recommendations and selectively portrays Hickey's hamlet recommendations as having supported the expanded use of hamlets and the forced relocation and occupation of tribal people in fortified villages, but she does not acknowledge that Hilsman and others admit this program would have had to continue for decades as cultural engineers struggled to expand their control over the country outward like "oil droplets."

Regardless of McFate's favorable spin on the Strategic Hamlet Program, her and Hickey's support for such manipulative forms of counterinsurgency avoid fundamental ethical problems raised by anthropological contributions to counterinsurgency. At the heart of these issues is the fact that counterinsurgency necessarily risks betraying anthropology's stated and assumed commitments to the worlds we study (commitments made far clearer in more recent versions of the AAA code of ethics). As argued in some detail elsewhere, the ethical problem is not that counterinsurgency seeks to influence or impact a world that includes warfare; it is rather that counterinsurgency uses anthropology for manipulation in contested political settings, often under conditions of military occupation. It plays people, exploiting culture and situations for political gains, often in violent settings supporting neocolonial domination (Price 2010). Such applications of anthropology neglect anthropology's critiques of power and subvert anthropology for the needs of states in ways that connect to our discipline's colonial past. But Hickey expressed no awareness or concern about these issues. Instead, he viewed such work as necessary if he were to protect these groups caught in the path of war—a view that neither confronted the roles played by those who would read his report in promulgating this war nor addressed the unvoiced ethical issues of using anthropology to defeat the Vietcong villagers he studied.

Hickey's Other RAND Reports

Hickey was not deterred when RAND ignored his 1962 recommendations, and he continued to produce military-related reports for RAND throughout the decade regardless of their lack of impact. In 1964 Hickey published a RAND report describing "the major ethnic groups of the South Vietnamese highlands." On the surface the report was a typical area-centered description of the basic features of tribal cultures of the Vietnamese southern hill areas, but the political context in which it was produced, funded, commodified, and consumed transformed this work into a tool of conquest. Hickey's failure to acknowledge this context in the report, much less in his 2002 memoir, is remarkable. Hickey presented ethnographic information on six tribal groups using a common organizational format detailing basic cultural information for each group, then described settlement patterns, sociopolitical organization, and religion. The standardized cookie-cutter organizational structure of this report was reminiscent of the Civil Affairs handbooks produced by George Murdock for the Office of Naval Intelligence and the Office of the Chief of Naval Operations during World War II. These similarities derive from the like ends to which these works were independently put: to provide basic cultural information to otherwise nondiscriminating military and intelligence personnel who would be operating in these theaters of war and occupation (Price 2008b:91–96).

Hickey stressed that villages were the basic political unit in highland culture and that political decision making was patriarchal, while matrilineal descent gave women control over property. He described the importance of village-level councils of elders and village headmen as the dominant body of political organization, and the nature of intravillage alliances. He outlined the basic principles of the "village-centered justice" system and the importance of rituals (Hickey 1964:8). Hickey (1964:9) paid specific attention to historical traditions of intervillage warfare and traditional institutions of alliance and peacemaking—providing historical lessons from efforts by French colonialists to control highland warfare and noting that "alliances can be a means of gaining allies with whom to carry on a war more effectively. And families or clans can ally themselves so as to be able to carry out vendettas." Given RAND's wartime role, Hickey's analysis of these alliances moved beyond ethnographic description to stressing the uses of such knowledge for gaining strategic combat allies.

The context and organization of Hickey's scholarly narrative had an implicit purpose: not simply to impart cultural knowledge, but to do so in a way that informed the tasks of domination and control. Hickey (1964:14) situated his presentation on cultural distinctions not only with frames of geography, but also with frames of history and domination, writing that "the history of the highlands reveals the persistent role of the area as a buffer zone in the struggles among the Khmer, Cham, Siamese, Lao, Vietnamese, and colonial powers, as well as in the recent war between the French and the Viet Minh, and in the current conflict between the Viet Cong and the government of South Vietnam." Hickey (1964:15) noted how the Sedang, Stieng, and Mong tribes successfully resisted French domination and staged revolts, explaining how these groups combated external control with religious revelations such as the 1935 reincarnation of the Thunder Spirit's son. Even Hickey's (1964:17) discussion of highland ninth- through twelfth-century history stressed the region's struggles and resistance to outside domination and its historical role as a "buffer zone, which often passed from the control of one side to that of the other." Themes of sorcery, recurrent tales of rumored ghostly spirits undermining colonial efforts, intertribal warfare, revolts, the importance of gifts to highland leaders, and failed efforts of missions to dominate the highlands marked Hickey's historical summary.

Given his military audience and the state of the war, his discussions of blood oaths, tribunals, and friendship rituals mandating alliances were much more than anthropological musing about social formations; in this context these were descriptions of social features that could be leveraged (see Price 2008a). Hickey made no direct recommendations on how such information might be used, though the Phoenix Program and the Civil Operations and Revolutionary Development Support (CORDS) program would later weaponize just such knowledge in its armed counterinsurgency campaigns (see Valentine 1990).

Hickey's (1965:iv) Advanced Research Projects Agency (ARPA)/RAND assessment of American military advisors in Vietnam was based on ten months of fieldwork during which he interviewed "several hundred" American military advisors in Vietnam.[4] Hickey analyzed factors influencing the effectiveness and hindrances of American advisors and Vietnamese counterparts, noting such things as cultural differences; time spent in battlefield settings; training levels; failures of American advisors to learn to speak Vietnamese; a lack of skilled translators; different forms of military training; and a lack of training about the specific conditions that American advisors would face in Vietnam, elements that connect Hickey's doomed Vietnam project with contemporary visions of Human Terrain Teams.

In September 1967 RAND published Hickey's (1967) most substantial ARPA report on the social and economic development of "The Highland People of South Vietnam." This was an impressive piece of anthropological work (198 pages in length) that combined data Hickey (1967:iii) had collected from villages of all twenty-one highland ethnic groups. Hickey drew on ethnographic fieldwork he had undertaken throughout the previous decade, but he also drew on work in which he stayed with special forces units. He had the assistance of the government of South Vietnam's (GVN) Special Commission for Highland Affairs, the Summer Institute of Linguistics, the ARPA field unit in Saigon, the Military Assistance Command, Vietnam Advisory Groups, and the United States Agency for International Development (USAID) (Hickey 1967:iv).

Hickey's analysis sometimes strayed from anthropological realms to advocating military strategies. Hickey actively advocated that the South Vietnam government should end its opposition to the Front Unifié de Lutte des Races Opprimees (FULRO) and proclaim support for its members' cultural autonomy. The benefits Hickey (1967:vii–viii) identified from such an alignment included

> the immediate acquisition of an estimated 3000 to 5000 armed men skilled in jungle warfare and familiar with the mountain terrain near Cambodia, [and] it would greatly help the government's intelligence network at the village level in areas where FULRO has much popular following. Also evidence of FULRO's pro-GVN stand and of the government's willingness to let the Highlanders assume a larger role within the nation would lessen not only the chance of open discontent and protest but also the demand for autonomy and, most important, the Highlanders' susceptibility to the appeal of the Viet Cong, whose presence in the highlands would thus become increasingly untenable.

Such Machiavellian calculations ran counter to Hickey's latter-day protestations that he was not actively providing strategic advice. Hickey conceived of this stance as an ethical position aligned with the highland peoples he studied and whose interests he hoped to protect, but in the context of providing these reports to influence US military strategists, any such motivations became subsumed under the needs or goals of the military.

Hickey's 1969 RAND report, "U.S. Strategy in South Vietnam: Extrication and Equilibrium," analyzed how the United States misunderstood the nature of the war it was waging—arguing in part that the United States did not understand the political nature and nuanced history that the war overlay, but also outlining suggestions for withdrawal scenarios. Hickey's last RAND Report (1971) acknowledged his reliance on the Institute for Defense Analysis, ARPA, USAID, and the CORDS program and made development recommendations for highlander economic programs. In this final RAND report he retreated into increasingly detailed historical analysis of past Vietnamese historical incidents, generating a narrative disconnected from the military realities traumatizing the Vietnam of his present; he wrote as if this past offered a historical lesson for the present. Hickey did not seem to understand that his audience of military and intelligence personnel could not be bothered with the complexities of nuanced cultural information and arguments for economic programs as this audience was overwhelmed with the daily activities of overseeing the inevitable American military defeat in Vietnam.[5]

Over the course of a decade Hickey's work for RAND traced him shifting from counterinsurgency support efforts involving the destruction of tribal villages in order to save them, to more actively providing cultural information of strategic value. Hickey's RAND reports display the path of an anthropologist who did not understand just how different his own imagined mission was from that of the missions of the larger military and intelligence institutions consuming his reports. But this disconnect and what appears to be an enduring, uneducable, naïve hope of prevailing over deep institutional forces kept him engaged with RAND and the military for years.

Hickey's Back Home Retcon
Hickey wrote to Fred Eggan in late 1970 to inquire about the possibility of teaching as a visiting professor at the University of Chicago. Eggan expressed excitement at this prospect. Money was scarce, however, and when Eggan advised that Hickey might need to secure outside funds, Hickey turned to Ford and RAND. But Eggan warned him that "there is also a

strong feeling on the part of some students and a few of the faculty about research for the government and even stronger feeling about classified research" (Hickey 2002:297). These "strong feelings" in part related to the ruckus brewing in the AAA over the Student Mobilization Committee's circulation of stolen documents indicating anthropological military consultancies. In a memo to the University of Chicago anthropology chair, Bernard Cohn, recommending Hickey for a yearlong appointment, Eggan wrote that he knew of "no evidence of any violation of ethic standards, as I have practiced them and as I have tried to teach them to graduate students" (Hickey 2002:298). But when Eggan next wrote to Hickey, he reported that there were growing concerns in the department about the "secret" research Hickey had done for RAND and the Department of Defense. Hickey replied, in part, that his work had been "classified" but not "secret"—apparently missing the larger point that writing noncirculating reports that military and intelligence agencies could access was the real problem (Hickey 2002:298). While Eggan and Hickey's exchange focused on the particulars of what Hickey's noncirculated reports might be called, the real issue had more to do with the neocolonial *political* context of Hickey's work than it did with the *ethical* propriety of secret reports. When Eggan wrote that Chicago's anthropology department voted against Hickey's one-year position, Hickey interpreted this as an "emotional" response. On November 18, 1971, the *Wall Street Journal* ran an article on "McCarthyism of the Left" that discussed Chicago's decision to not offer a position to Hickey (Hickey 2002:301).

Hickey's (2002:297–300) anger over this rejection from his alma mater was rendered clear in his memoir *Window on a War*. He complained that his advice was largely ignored by RAND and the military and that in the early 1970s he was demonized by his fellow anthropologists, writing, "if my accommodation-coalition approach earned me the reputation in some American political [military/policy] circles of being a heretic, my being in Vietnam with the RAND corporation earned me pariah status among my academic colleagues" (Hickey 2002:296).

Thus Hickey's memoir contains bitter reflections of his long record of ignored Vietnam recommendations stretching from the early 1960s into the 1970s. His experience was not one in which his influence decreased over time. In fact, from his earliest years onward, his experience was that his colleague Price Gittinger's ethnographic "report was suppressed and mine was ignored" (Hickey 2002:350). Indeed, the history of Hickey's efforts to enlighten American policy in Vietnam is a history of ignored recommendations. Hickey had not given up when his Strategic Hamlet evaluation was ignored, but neither did he seem to question the ethical issues raised by such battle fieldwork or contributions to counterinsurgency; nor did he seem to adequately consider that his declared interests in the people of Vietnam were so at odds with the US military's institutional behaviors and values that his contributions stood no chance of accomplishing what he envisioned.

There is an otherworldliness in the ethnographic representations of Hickey's later RAND reports. He wrote as if he was living between dimensions in a world where traditional Vietnamese ethnic and linguistic groups maintained an existence outside of the American carpet bombing and spraying of Agent Orange. Hickey created these tight little just-so story vignettes where hardworking capitalist entrepreneurs rose above their poverty with cash crops like coffee (just so long as the frame of their success was not expanded to incorporate capitalism's war raining down on them).

The political and historical context in which Hickey produced his reports transformed them into works with meanings and uses far beyond the sum of their parts: meanings hinge on uses, and Hickey took pieces of ethnographic work produced by himself and others and transformed disparate elements into weaponized knowledge—political knowledge that he knew would be used to manipulate the "Major Ethnic Groups of the South Vietnamese Highlands" and would be used in military contexts. Despite Hickey's latter-day complaints about military and intelligence agencies' abuses and neglect of the "proper" use of his research, his continual participation in this process documents a form of complicity that is difficult to reconcile.

DELMOS JONES AND THE COMPLICITY OF ALL

In stark ethical and political contrast to Gerald Hickey's approach to anthropological engagements with the military is Delmos Jones's reaction to US military and intelligence agency efforts to acquire and use his anthropological knowledge to assist their wars in Southeast Asia. In 1965, while a doctoral student in anthropology at Cornell University, Jones received a Foreign Area fellowship from the Ford Foundation that funded his first fieldwork in Thailand (Linda Jones, personal communication, March 3, 2008). Delmos's wife, Linda, and their children accompanied him to Thailand. Jones's family lived in Chiang Mai, and he collected data later used in his dissertation on "cultural variation among six Lahu Villages [in] Northern Thailand" (Jones 1967).

The Jones children attended school in Chiang Mai while Delmos stayed in the Lahu Villages conducting research, though he regularly traveled back to his family in Chiang Mai. A small US Air Force installation in Chiang Mai had significant radar facilities, and Jones and others in the community assumed that this base was being used to monitor Chinese communications. In short, it was obvious to Jones that some sort of intelligence operation was being run out of Chiang Mai.

According to Delmos's former wife, Linda Jones, even back in 1965, "We were aware of American activities being conducted out of Chiang Mai. 'Air America' had lots of planes flying in and out of Chiang Mai airport (an otherwise pretty sleepy place). People who ostensibly worked for various American agencies but who were known to be CIA would board helicopters and go off, sometimes never to return. Their wives could never get any information and were eventually removed from the country" (personal communication, March 3, 2008).

Most of this information was never discussed in public, and great efforts were made to maintain a pretense that Chiang Mai was not a covert-ops base. But the Jones family had a good understanding of the extent of these activities because their children played with the kids from these other families in their homes and at the area's only English-language school. What was unusual about this situation was not that it occurred—loads of anthropologists have conducted fieldwork in political settings where they encounter what appears to be clandestine military or intelligence operations. What was unusual was how much this militarized backdrop troubled Jones, and as these background activities later began to creep into the foreground of his work, the knowledge of the ends to which this work was being put became increasingly difficult for Jones to ignore.

After returning from the 1965 fieldwork Delmos Jones (1967) finished his dissertation research and successfully completed and defended his dissertation at Cornell without delving into the political backdrop of his traditional comparative village study; Cornell's anthropology department's alignment with a broad range of cold war counterinsurgency projects spread around the globe would have made this a difficult proposition for a young and vulnerable scholar.

In 1970 Jones received a Fulbright fellowship sponsoring his return to Chiang Mai, where he was to expand upon the village-based research studies that he'd undertaken five years earlier. Linda Jones (personal communication, March 3, 2008) recalls that what had initially been background knowledge that American military and intelligence operations were occurring in the Chiang Mai region now moved into the foreground:

> I remember we were quite proud of [the Fulbright fellowship],
> but discovered how naive we had been when we discovered

that in Chiang Mai we would report to USIS (United States Information Service; known to be CIA). Shortly after we settled in Chiang Mai, we went to the Chiang Mai hotel for dinner. While we were eating, an American came over to speak with us. He told Del that he was part of an ARPA (Advanced Research Projects Agency) program collecting information about the Hill Tribes. Del was uninterested in cooperating. This fellow said it didn't matter. They had computerized and indexed all of his papers and notes anyway. Eye-opening shock number 2! So it went for I think about 5 months when Del had had enough of the situation. He told the head of USIS that we wished to leave Thailand immediately. In return, he was told that our fare home would not be paid. Del threatened to publish what he knew and they backed off. Our fare was paid and we left.

It was out of this ferment that Del began to write and speak about how the work of anthropologists could be used, even if they did not explicitly cooperate with governments. We talked about how it was common for anthropologists to note in their reports the names of village leaders, population counts, and geographical locations. These facts could then be used in ways that would not be in the best interests of the tribes. At that time, the tribal villages were suspected of harboring communists. To remove this opportunity, entire villages would just be uprooted and moved against their will. The idea was to get them out of the mountains, but their knowledge of agriculture was geared to that environment, not to that of the valleys. Also, the Thais were very prejudiced against the tribal people. Once they were relocated to the valleys, they were handy targets for mistreatment.

Jones had not been looking to become involved in a contentious political issue, but it became increasingly clear to him that his research would be co-opted and used for militarized purposes that he did not approve of, and for purposes that his research participants had not agreed to support.

By the time Delmos Jones came to understand how anthropological knowledge was being harvested for counterinsurgency uses by military and intelligence agencies, such practices had been going on for so long without anthropologists raising public objections that one can understand why these ARPA operatives took such umbrage that Jones would not acquiesce to the hijacking of his research for the needs of state.

Jones returned to the United States and wrote about how troubled he was by what he had seen in Thailand. The following year he published a short piece in *Current Anthropology* on "Social Responsibility and the Belief in Basic Research: An Example from Thailand," describing the dangers facing all anthropologists and their research participants, not only when anthropologists engaged in the sort of military-linked work that Hickey and others were doing, but when they engaged in basic research that could be used to inform counterinsurgency (Jones 1971b). In this article, after describing the political and economic importance of lowland and delta regions in Vietnam, Jones (1971b:347) described the military importance of highland villages because they "can be of tremendous strategic importance for storing supplies and establishing camps for guerrilla forces." Jones (1971b:347) connected these same dynamics with the political situation in highland/lowland Thailand and then asked and answered the question: "Did the anthropologists who rushed into the area to do basic descriptive studies consider these political facts? It is safe to say that most of us did not." Even more fundamentally, Jones (1971b:348) asked if it was a coincidence that funding for research on the cultures of these highland peoples had been increasing throughout the decade and noted that only a portion of this research was funded by "questionable government sources, chief among these the Advanced Research Projects Agency (ARPA)."

Jones (1971b:348) outlined how ARPA "controlled and funded" the Thai Information Center that had amassed more than fifteen thousand documents that he argued were by Thai and foreign bodies desiring to control the highland cultures described therein. But Jones's (1971b:348) criticism was not just directed at ARPA-funded anthropologists—he included himself among those sharing culpability for this state of affairs—because "most of us who have conducted basic research in Thailand have in fact contributed to that end, we might as well have taken ARPA's money. The question of ethics and responsibility may have little to do with the source of funding and much more with the social and political context within which the data are produced."

Jones (1971b:348) described how specific publications focused on counterinsurgency and the control of highland populations, and then he argued that

> the more information there is available, the easier it is to develop new techniques of dealing with the people whom the government is trying to manipulate. The techniques may not be ones the social scientist himself conceives; the results may not be

ones he would approve. Nevertheless, those approaches that have been developed and are being developed by the United States and Thai governments to deal with hill peoples have been aided by all of us who have done research on hill culture.

Given this *political* context, Jones (1971b:349) saw the *ethical* course of action as clear: anthropologists should "consider seriously the political implications of research and publication and cease doing both where the situation warrants." Jones didn't stop there. He insisted anthropologists should embrace their political values and use their scholarly research to advance their political causes, regardless of the political cause they supported, writing, "Thus, anthropologists who wished to aid the counterinsurgency efforts of the United States in Southeast Asia should do so, and do so with conviction. Such persons can at least be respected. I would class as unethical only those who attempt to hide behind the idea of pure research while their activities aid the preservation of the status quo" (Jones 1971b:349). This was an odd but interesting point as it bestowed respect on anthropologists like Gerald Hickey while damning anthropologists who believed in the neutrality of research even while opposing the wars of Southeast Asia.

Jones (1971b:349) ended with a call for anthropologists to stop chasing funding and publishing opportunities that advanced their careers but could endanger those they studied, arguing that "there is no longer any excuse for any of us to pretend that the results of our research are not being used to help bring about the oppression of groups. This has been the traditional role of the anthropologist, it seems."

An article published by Joseph Jorgensen and Eric Wolf in late 1970 in the *New York Review of Books* brought Jones's critique into wide circulation, and he found his stance being used by war critics in ways that made him uncomfortable, even though the article portrayed Jones as a lone hero among a field of naïve or corrupt anthropologists (Jorgensen had seen a prepublication version of Jones's *Current Anthropology* article). Jorgensen and Wolf ended their piece praising an unnamed anthropologist (clearly Delmos Jones) who had heroically resisted efforts by US military and intelligence agencies to co-opt his work for their ends. Jorgensen and Wolf (1970:34) wrote that "this lone dissenter has called on anthropologists to help create radical political alternatives for the people among whom they work, people whose social integrity is already—and whose physical existence may soon be—at stake."[6]

Throughout his career Jones remained committed to working through the ethical issues presented by anthropologists working toward desired, engaged change, and he continued to address problems arising when anthropologists' work and recommendations are not only used but also ignored by sponsors and others. Later, "as the lone anthropologist who refused to cooperate with the CIA in [their Thailand] project, Jones was subsequently commended by the American Anthropological Association Committee on Ethics" (Susser 2000:582). In 1976, in an analysis of some recurring failures of applied anthropological projects, Jones (1976:227) concisely observed that "when policy makers don't listen, this could mean [applied anthropologists] are not telling them what they want to hear"— an observation with meaning to most of us who have worked in applied settings, but one with particular resonance with the failures of Gerald Hickey and many others advising entrenched military bureaucracies. And while Jones's statements and stance had a ringing impact on anthropological debates of the early 1970s, many of his fundamental concerns drifted toward the edge of the discipline. However, recent political events have brought his concerns back to the fore.

THINKING ABOUT POLITICAL ENDS AND ETHICAL MEANS

It is remarkable that Hickey worked with RAND for as long as he did. While his military and intelligence audiences recognized their lack of understanding of Vietnamese culture, their fundamental purpose of conquest were decidedly nonanthropological. And while Hickey sincerely wanted to reduce harm for those he studied in Vietnam, he does not appear to have understood how different his anthropological purposes were from those who consumed his RAND reports. Hickey wanted to steer the military toward a kinder form of conquest while arguing that he was serving the needs of those to be conquered. While the internal contradictions of this approach do not appear to have bothered Hickey or his sponsors, it reveals a significant degree of cross-purposes that served the military's needs and may have been a salve for Hickey's conscience.

It is tempting to simply declare Hickey a "slow learner" and to condemn his inability over the course of a decade to acknowledge that the larger forces unleashed when anthropologists engage with military decision makers necessarily doomed his ability to control how his ethnographic reports would be used. I do not completely dismiss such a conclusion and am tempted to temporally extend an even broader conclusion, that military and intelligence agencies have historically (from World War II through Vietnam to the present) repeatedly used anthropological knowledge and theories that already align with their understanding and desires. Given Jones's unheeded call for the development of a more aware, less exploitable anthropology, any argument that Hickey was simply a "slow learner" implicates not just Hickey, but the entire discipline of anthropology.

Hickey's and Jones's visions of the proper ways for anthropological knowledge to interface with military and intelligence agencies failed to come to fruition, but they failed in distinctly different ways. The availability of research funds impacted both Hickey's and Jones's failures. In Hickey's case, the ongoing availability of generous funds provided reinforcement for his efforts to try to align anthropological knowledge with military needs, even if the military was not using this knowledge in the ways he desired, and his continued RAND sponsorship encouraged him to continue this relationship. The failure of a movement that followed Jones's call for resistance in publishing research to materialize was the flip side of Jones's funding dynamic: such mandates are necessarily unfunded. While Hickey bemoaned the University of Chicago's decision to not offer him a one-year visiting professorship in 1971, plenty of funding sources were offering to pay for the effort to spread Hickey's vision of a more military-aligned version of anthropology at Chicago. Hickey and other anthropologists working for RAND during the war were as well funded as today's highly paid, military-aligned anthropologists. Institutional funding for scholars pursuing Jones's nonpublication approach were and are almost nonexistent, and with increased militarization of universities, compliance with military needs is increasingly the rule (Giroux 2007).

Jones's recommended strategy for resisting the militarization of anthropological knowledge cut to the heart of the problem (for example, anthropologists pursuing "pure research" are providing data for military uses), but it ignored the larger political economy governing the lives of most anthropologists. Consider the professional outcomes of following through on his recommendation that anthropologists "consider seriously the political implications of research and publication and cease doing both" (Jones 1971b:349). In academic settings where struggles for tenure and promotion guide many of the contingencies regulating research and publication decisions, such an altruistic call not to publish seems doomed to lead to an evolutionary dead-end (to abuse an evolutionary metaphor) since those following this ethical call for silence would inevitably be "selected against." Outside the academy, applied anthropologists choosing not to write reports would face even grimmer survival prospects.

Hickey and Jones offer stark choices to anthropologists with needed expertise during times of war: a choice between blind optimism that individuals can redirect institutional uses of knowledge and a stance of recalcitrant silence. Some will argue that there are viable third or fourth choices, but I have a difficult time seeing them—especially when it comes to using anthropology for counterinsurgency. Too much history blocks my view, history arguing that anthropology's commitment to those we study and who share their lives with us is often at odds with the military's desired uses of our knowledge for counterinsurgency's smoothing of conquests in wartime—regardless of individual anthropologists' intentions.

I would only add a mitigating factor that aligns with Jones's insistence that anthropologists understand that there can be no such thing as political neutrality: anthropologists can individually (or in professional organizations, perhaps collectively) decide if they support or oppose the political cause of a *particular* war and then engage or withhold knowledge accordingly.[7] Such a stance would be counter to that of many contemporary military-engaged anthropologists who insist they oppose the US wars in Iraq or Afghanistan even as they offer anthropological services to those fighting these wars.

Such a partisan anthropological position does not solve the large, systemic problem that scholars have already published ethnographic resources of use to military and intelligence agencies; this may simply be an endemic problem unless scholars disengage from (or at least limit) publishing entirely in a hermit-like response to Jones's concerns. Publishing is itself a political act, as Georges Condominas (1977:xvii, xxv) discovered to his horror when he learned that the Green Berets had secretly used an unauthorized translation and printing of his ethnography of highland Vietnamese village life to conduct deadly highland operations.

Hickey believed he could steer the military straight; Jones believed that military and intelligence agencies would steal his work for their own ends and that he had no control over these uses. While Hickey's memoir chronicles his dissatisfaction with the ways that his reports were used only in selective ways, Hickey underestimated the possibility that structural dynamics governing the military's consumption of anthropological knowledge necessarily lead to such outcomes—unless anthropologists pre-align their assumptions to meet with military culture, a process that often seems to increase the longer that anthropologists work in these environments. Hickey did not consider the possibility that these structural dynamics themselves are rooted not only in the forms of military decision making but also in the deeper contingencies bred within forms of warfare in neocolonial states seeking to suppress occupied insurgents. Hickey dismissed this possibility, but we should not.

Given his own proximity to these events and a general lack of historical research documenting the ways that anthropological knowledge was selectively used and largely ignored during World War II, it is understandable that Hickey might fail to inquire into these possibilities. But contemporary anthropologists should not be constrained by such a limited understanding of past military engagements. Strands of contemporary postmodern particularism dissuade anthropologists from trying to make such far-reaching metanarrative connections. I find so many recurrent instances of anthropologists' work being used for unintended ends that the discipline's inability to cope with these recurrences leaves it unable to cope with the serious political consequences these recurrences present to the discipline.

Anthropologists should not essentialize the past (or present). However, they also should not overlook the possibility that recurrent patterns of abuse of anthropological data could be tied to structural features of the military and intelligence agencies with whom anthropologists engage. Hickey overlooked these dangers, and there is plenty of funding available for contemporary anthropologists who can learn to overlook these possibilities in the present. Anthropologists need to consider the political uses of their work and understand that they are limited in how they can control the ends to which it is put.

Hickey seems to be a tragic figure—but *why* he's tragic changes with different readings. One can read him as naïve, martyr, willfully ignorant, tragic hero, or self-serving; but there is no reason for contemporary anthropologists to not learn from his experiences. Some will likely claim the moral of Hickey's story is that we must work harder to make the military understand what anthropology has to offer, but such interpretations ignore the importance of institutional culture and the possibility of larger contingencies governing military uses of anthropological knowledge.

Notes

1. This chapter benefited from correspondence with or the comments of the SAR seminar participants, as well as Roberto González, Linda Jones, Steve Niva, Eric Ross, Marshall Sahlins, and Ida Susser.

2. In contemporary professional parlance the term "research subject" has been replaced with the more collaborative term "research participant," but the word "participant" implies levels of voluntary informed consent that are inappropriate when discussing Vietnam War–era social research, so I intentionally use the term "research subject."

3. It is striking to compare these recommendations with those made by a variety of anthropologists working in the War Relocation Authority camps during World War II. In both settings anthropologists inclined toward cultural engineering advised that better management and control could be achieved over relocated populations by

improving living conditions and adding more elements of normalcy to their daily existence (see Price 2008b:142–170).

4. In order to consider the ethical issues raised by Hickey's work, it is important to note that as Hickey shifted his focus of analysis from the ethnic groups of Vietnam (as was the case in his 1962 and 1964 RAND reports), different ethical issues were raised. Specifically, when Hickey studied American military advisors and their Vietnamese counterparts, his ethical commitment shifted from representing (and protecting) Vietnamese ethnic groups to doing so for the military advisors he was studying.

5. Hickey's final work in Vietnam was for the Herbicide Study Group. He documented the horrors that Agent Orange had brought to highland villages in a report that was highly critical of US action and was submitted to the US Senate in February 1974 (Hickey 2002:341–346).

6. Though Jorgensen and Wolf had made Delmos Jones the hero of their piece, Jones (1971a) wrote a terse response, published in the *New York Review of Books*, correcting errors found in the original piece (see also Wakin 1992).

7. Regardless of the particular war, anthropologists must not abandon the standards of proper ethical practice as specified under anthropological codes of ethics. These ethical decisions must transcend individual or collective political choices—and if the current AAA code of ethics had been present during Hickey's work supporting the Strategic Hamlet Program, such work would have certainly been ethically problematic given the impossibility of achieving voluntary informed consent due to the way this program operated.

4

Should Anthropologists Provide Their Knowledge to the Military?

An Ethical Discourse Taking Germany as an Example

Maren Tomforde

In 2007 members of the German Association of Anthropology (GAA) were asked to consider a motion that would require that members working "for a domestic or foreign secret service" be suspended from the association (Motion A 02, resubmission from the annual meeting in 2005).[1] In discussions with colleagues I learned that the motion was proposed for two reasons: firstly, it was seen as a response to US programs such as the Pat Roberts Intelligence Scholars Program (PRISP)[2] and the Pentagon's Human Terrain System (HTS),[3] both of which explicitly call for cultural knowledge to be better incorporated into US intelligence and military activities. Secondly, some GAA members had heard that the German Federal Ministry of Defense and the German Armed Forces (the Bundeswehr) had created staff positions for civilian social scientists. This generated concern that some GAA members might be working in some covert capacity for the German government.

As an anthropologist who has worked for the German Federal Ministry of Defense since 2003, I am acutely aware of such concerns. After the fall of the Berlin Wall and the reunification of Germany, the Bundeswehr was transformed in the 1990s from a purely defensive force into an operational military that participates predominantly in international peacekeeping and stability operations. Recognizing that this new mission required soldiers to develop "soft skills" such as social or cross-cultural competence, some German military leaders sought to incorporate social scientists into training and operational programs. The actual creation of social science posts was slow, mainly because enthusiasm for hiring sociologists and cultural scientists[4] was not uniform across the Federal Ministry of Defense and because of fiscal constraints on hiring and investment in new programs. However, the Bundeswehr has hired a handful of anthropologists since 2000.

I am one of those anthropologists, and to my knowledge the German government has not invested the kind of resources and effort into recruiting anthropologically trained scholars that the United States has. Nevertheless, there is a great deal of concern among members of the GAA that anthropologists like me, working for the Bundeswehr, might be violating the ethical tenets of the profession. This is a question that deserves consideration and investigation. Unfortunately, the motion presented in 2007 was poorly informed; it failed, for example, to differentiate among the German intelligence services, the Bundeswehr, or the Federal Ministry of Defense; nor did its proponents attempt to discuss their concerns with anthropologists working in such institutions. The motion was finally withdrawn after my colleagues and I had clarifying talks with those who had submitted it. However, in September 2009 the same motion was yet again set on the agenda by an anthropologist from Tübingen University for the next GAA conference in October 2009.

The ethics of social science in this context are indeed worth considering, particularly in the context of German history. Contemporary anthropology in Germany is deeply liberal; scholars are aware of the legitimizing role that academic knowledge has in the political sphere, and they do not want their work abused for a state's hegemonic interests. In Germany such reservations have deep historical roots. Anthropological knowledge in particular played an important role in supporting Germany's colonial expansion and, later, in legitimizing National Socialism and the rise of the Nazi state in the 1930s and '40s. Indeed, under the Third Reich a considerable number of anthropologists supported the National Socialists, and their symbolic capital helped to legitimize the genocidal state (Seidler 2005). Thus it is perhaps not surprising that German academics today, particularly in the social sciences and humanities, tend to be quite critical of the security state and deeply suspicious of any involvement in military affairs (Leonhard and Werkner 2005:13).

Exploring the historical relationship between German anthropologists and the nation-state raises still-salient questions about the social, political, and moral responsibilities of social scientists as citizens. In this chapter I will describe the history of German anthropology and use that as a frame through which to explore the ethical, moral, and practical issues that pertain to German anthropology in the context of the Bundeswehr, with which I have several years of professional and research experience. My employment forces me to consider my own role in supporting policies and activities of the Bundeswehr's peacekeeping and stability operations. It is worth noting that even the Bundeswehr's peacekeeping mission is a matter of controversy among many German activists and academics, particularly those in the German peace studies community, who tend to argue that military intervention necessarily perpetuates violence. They express concern that Western models of freedom and democracy are being imposed in a neoimperial manner in places like Afghanistan, without regard to local political, historical, or social structures (see Münkler 2009; Rubinstein 2008). At the same time, peacekeeping is an activity legitimized by a popularly elected German parliament, which implies that all German citizens are in some sense responsible for the Bundeswehr's new role.

Given this political, historical, and national context, should anthropologists actively support the Bundeswehr, for example, in preparing soldiers for stability operations abroad? If we do so, how can we prevent our knowledge from being used to harm others? I do not think these questions are easy to answer, nor do I believe that anthropologists in Germany have discussed them enough, particularly in the context of post-9/11 international security challenges. We are not ready to address the new challenges and responsibilities that Germany's engagement in the world might present us as scholars and as citizens.

So I will engage these questions in both a historical and professional context. I will address the role of anthropology under National Socialism and examine how the discipline dealt with this history in the postwar era. Then I will describe post–cold war security policy and the missions of the Bundeswehr abroad to provide greater context for understanding how the Bundeswehr draws on anthropology in its current work. I will attempt to summarize some of the arguments with which I am familiar, both for and against the involvement of German anthropologists in the Bundeswehr and in security work. Lastly, I will offer my own opinions about how anthropologists can do ethical work in a military context and describe how the field of military anthropology might evolve in Germany.

THE MILITARY AND ANTHROPOLOGY UNDER NATIONAL SOCIALISM

"*Ethnologie*" is the present-day German equivalent of social or cultural anthropology as practiced in the other parts of the world. *Ethnologie* is a relatively new term, however. In the past the discipline of anthropology was generally known in German-speaking countries (Germany, Austria, Switzerland) as *Völkerkunde*, or ethnology/study of the world's peoples, a term coined around 1770 in Germany and following from the term *Erdkunde*, or study of the earth. The purpose of Völkerkunde was to study "peoples without a written language" and foreign cultures on an international and comparative basis (Gingrich 2005:70–87; Hauschild 1995a:22; Fischer 1988:4). Later, at the end of the eighteenth century, *Volkskunde* (ethnic studies) also came into existence, referring to archaeological and linguistic studies of one's own (German) people.[5] In a period characterized by Eurocentrism and paternalism toward colonized peoples, Germans saw themselves at a "naturally higher level of development" (Byer 1995:64) in relation to "civilizationally inferior ones" (for example, Africans) (see also Renner 2000:116–117).

Under the Third Reich such racialized discourses were reified into a unified anthropology strongly oriented toward racial biology (Hauschild 1995b:9). The emergence of an overtly racial anthropology can be traced to the Treaty of Versailles, signed June 28, 1919, under which the German empire accepted exclusive responsibility for the war. Most Germans saw the Treaty of Versailles and the French occupation of the Rhineland as humiliating and unjust. The Treaty of Versailles had a multitude of economic, social, political, and psychological consequences for Germany,[6] where a dire economic situation, a barely functioning parliamentary democracy, the loss of its colonies, reservations about its neighbors, and a sense of wounded national pride set the stage for the rise of German nationalism and the racialized ideology of National Socialism (see also Renner 2000:115; Hauschild 1995a:19). With the seizure of power by the National Socialists in 1933, racial thinking became manifest in nearly all fields of social, political, and scientific life, as terms like *Volksseele* (national soul of the people), *Herrenrasse* (master race), *Blut und Boden* (blood and soil), and also *Auslese* (selection) and *Untermensch* (under-man) became part of the everyday German lexicon (Braun 1995:17). "Völkerkundler" Wilhelm E. Mühlmann (1940:212) captured the nation's mood when he wrote, "The German upheaval of 1933 was a revolutionary self-liberation, as Germany had been in a state almost of colonial exploitation and mental infiltration by the victors in the previous years."

Under the Third Reich scientists of all disciplines engaged in "self-mobilization" (Weisbrod 2002:18), so that science became a supporting pillar for the survival of the fascist regime: "The fascist state assigned a task to fascist science; it was solved with fascist energy" (Conte 1988:246). Academics cooperated and actively worked for the cause of Nazis for a range of reasons:

economic self-interest, political ambition, social pressure, and last but not least, inner convictions (Hauschild 1995a:31; see also Byer 1995:70–71).

German anthropologists quickly embraced National Socialism, and not only because doing so enabled them to keep their jobs and pursue research (Hauschild 1995a:21). For most Völkerkundler, the overt racism of the National Socialists was not a great discursive distance from their own Eurocentric, racist colonial paradigms. Secondly, many ethnologists welcomed the National Socialist government's goal of regaining Germany's colonies so that they could pursue new research projects. Moreover, the government also promised a "revaluation of the discipline as a practical science" (Braun 1995:66). Gretchen Schafft (2004:1; see also 48–54) writes that research was pursued "without respect for standards of scientific thought and process," while Jürgen Braun (1995:53) and André Gingrich (2005) describe how physical[7] and sociocultural anthropology were united in support of German "racial hygiene" in Germany. Indeed, the work of biological anthropologists like Josef Mengele, Eugen Fischer, and Otmar von Verschuer and sociocultural anthropologists including Richard Thurnwald, his student Wilhelm E. Mühlmann, and Ludwig Kohl-Larsen are best understood as part of the same general school of work.[8]

German anthropologists provided "scientific" expertise to the government on both colonial and domestic populations throughout the 1930s and '40s. Sociocultural anthropologists advised government administrators that it was the white man's task to research "negroes" and bring African people proper culture, civilization, and freedom (Conte 1988:246–249; see also Hauschild 1994). With regard to Germany's colonies, anthropologist and National Socialist Ludwig Kohl-Larsen (1943:36–37) wrote:

> It is important to not regard blacks a priori as wogs, but rather as human beings of a different race, who have certain functions in common with all human beings....The indigenous always has to feel the great racial difference and the resulting superiority of the white race, he must be kept at a distance.

Renowned anthropologist Hermann Baumann made the "colonial task" of anthropology as well as the "colonial question" the main themes of his teaching activity and provided research results to the National Socialists to be used for their purposes (Braun 1995:72; see also 31). Thus Thomas Hauschild (1995b:7) speaks of a "coexistence of understanding and annihilating the other," a discourse typical of fascist anthropology.

For the Third Reich, anthropological research was particularly important for the state, as racialized social science lent scientific legitimacy to concepts of racial hygiene, helped to legitimize state expansion on the basis of a superior European self-concept (Byer 1995:69–70; see also Schafft 2004:37; Hauschild 1995a:31; Said 1978), and confirmed the "racial superiority of the Nordic race" (Mosen 1991:15; see also Grüttner 1997:141–143). Indeed, significant university positions in anthropology were soon filled with supporters of National Socialism's racial policies (Schafft 2004:70, 77). Anthropology under National Socialism embraced eugenics: "The goal of the anthropologists who were active under the Nazi regime was to create a state in which the German gene pool became homogeneous and the racial and genetic qualities of the citizens matched their national identity as Germans" (Schafft 2004:152). Prominent sociocultural anthropologists included Thurnwald, Mühlmann, and Kohl-Larsen, as well as Leo Frobenius, Walter Krickeberg, and Hermann Baumann. Anti-Semitic thinking permeated much of their work between 1933 and 1945 (Spöttel 1996). Thurnwald, for example, embraced racial hygiene quite early in his career (Dostal 1994:254), and he and Baumann opposed the democratic orientation of the Weimar Republic and openly aspired to create a Germanic *Volksgemeinschaft* (people's community), exclusive of any non-Germanic influence (Braun 1995:32). Mühlmann (1940:214–215) wrote about "racial political self-help" and the importance of cleansing Germany of "harmful elements":

> This…applies to racial policy measures against domestic groups, which are intolerable from an ethnic, cultural or economic point of view and racially unmeltable. In this context, it is first and foremost and almost exclusively the Jews who come into question for the modern great peoples.

Mühlmann (1936:442) supported strict racial segregation, describing its importance as an objective matter of fact. He also furthered his career by making positive statements about Adolf Hitler as an "omnipotent savior" in politically opportune publications (Mühlmann 1970:133, 138–139).

Anthropologists not only failed to challenge anti-Semitism and concepts of racial purity but legitimized and extended such concepts in their work (Schafft 2004:222): "There is sufficient evidence to place anthropologists in the German Third Reich squarely within the category of perpetrators. In every way, they prepared the German population for the Holocaust and helped it almost to succeed" (Schafft 2004:250).[9] Scientific articles in academic journals legitimated National Socialist ideology and racial goals, even though these did not have a wide public readership. We see "generative ethics" at work (Byer 1995:75), in which anthropologists promulgated the concept of a healthy German people needing defense from the existential threat of a racially impure "other." As racist and fascist values permeated the "social unconscious" (Fromm 1962:89), the epistemically powerful work of social scientists underwrote National Socialists' genocidal policies with disastrous consequences.

The Postwar Era: Professional Denial, Responsibility, and Guilt

After the war ended Germany went through a process of de-Nazification in which National Socialists were systematically removed from positions of influence. The focus was on state and judicial institutions, not science or academia, and as a result, most German anthropologists managed to escape censure.[10] The same can be said of many German academic disciplines (see also Weisbrod 2002), although as I have argued, German anthropology played a particularly important role in legitimizing Nazi ideology.

Indeed, German anthropologists not only failed to critically assess their involvement in the Third Reich but turned completely away from it—as if German anthropology did not have a past at all (Hauschild 1995a:37–39). At its first postwar professional meeting in 1946 the Deutsche Gesellschaft für Völkerkunde (GAA) hailed a "renewed spirit" in the discipline (Seidler 2003:1; see also Fischer 1990:218–220). Some semantic self-purification ensued: for example, anthropologists dropped the term "race," speaking instead of "*biotypus*." Yet the depth of this disciplinary conversion is debatable: "occasionally one reads between the lines and finds the content is still there" (Schafft 2004:243; see also Seidler 2003:95, 100–101; Hauschild 1995b:9). Although anthropologists like Mühlmann, Baumann, Thurnwald, and Kohl-Larsen later claimed they were never true believers in National Socialism, their publications indicate otherwise (see also Seidler 2003:99; Renner 2000:121; Michel 1995:142; Hauschild 1995a:50; Braun 1995:58; Fischer 1990:218). However, most, even overt supporters of the Third Reich, managed to reestablish themselves in postwar academia, continuing to teach and do fieldwork and write (Schafft 2004:188–192; Braun 1995:87; see also Renner 2000:121–122). For example, Baumann, an avowed National Socialist associated with reactionary, extreme right-wing associations such as the Kampfbund,[11] remained fundamentally convinced of "the unity of culture and race" throughout his career, even after 1945. Until his death in 1972 he remained a respected don of anthropology: he kept his academic position, continued teaching and doing research, was elected chair of the GAA in 1963, and received numerous awards (Braun 1995:42–44, 119). Indeed, Baumann's *Völkerkunde von Afrika* (*Ethnology of Africa*) is still regarded as a standard in African cultural history (see Haberland 1974:1).

His colleagues either underestimated or ignored Baumann's former political leanings, many of them also "disregarding their own actions and activities and their own responsibility" for the regime (Seidler 2003:99). Anthropologist Ludwig Kohl-Larsen was among the few who were not able to maintain their careers. He was senior leader in the Sturmabteilung (the so-called Stormtroopers, or the Brownshirts, were a paramilitary organization that helped Adolf Hitler to gain power in 1933) and banned from his profession in 1946 for "being handicapped by his political past" (Renner 2000:124).

During the 1980s social scientists and historians began to conduct research on individual participation in the Third Reich. The ideas, ideologies, and convictions of individual actors, including scientists, became legitimate topics for investigation (see, for instance, Schafft 2004; Diewald-Kerkmann 1995). Within this framework the activities of anthropologists have come under scrutiny so that we now know more about their activities during the Nazi regime and how anthropologists helped to legitimize racial hygienic measures such as deportations and mass murder.

Yet German anthropologists have still not conducted a critical reassessment of their discipline's history (Fischer 1990:209–210). Certainly, this avoidance of the past was and still is part of a larger societal struggle to come to terms with the Holocaust—it doesn't just concern anthropology, but all of German society. Regarding academia, Gretchen Schafft (2004:227) writes, "Professional denial is created by a silent consensus, and its only authority is the willingness to avoid discussing discrediting events and conform to a version of the past that is threatening to the profession and the individuals within it." There are manifold reasons for such avoidance: professional pride, a desire to protect German anthropology from criticism, and the difficulty of confronting the trauma of genocide, among others. Moreover, with greater distance from the war, it became increasingly difficult to confront Nazi perpetrators who held respected positions in academia, particularly when their de-Nazification records were not easily accessible (Schafft 2004:240; see also Hauschild 1995a:36).

Debates about the "amount of responsibility and guilt" of former anthropologists do erupt (Streck 2000). For example, in summer 2006 the forum "Anthropology during the National Socialist Period" was founded at the Institute of Anthropology at the University of Hamburg in order to collect information about the anthropological work during the Third Reich and discuss previously disregarded aspects of the topic via the Internet (see http://www.ethno-im-ns.uni-hamburg.de/index.htm). Officially, the debate started in the early 1990s when anthropologist Hans Fischer

(1991:591; 1990:227–232)[12] wrote that no German anthropologists had ever been active National Socialists, even if they might have been national-ist, militaristic, or anti-Semitic. In doing so, he appealed to his colleagues not to self-righteously blame their predecessors, arguing that many Germans were both perpetrators and victims of the regime. Fischer was heavily cri-ticized as an apologist, although some have applauded his attempt to open a taboo subject (Streck 2000:7–8). Others have detailed the roles of Völkerkunde researchers under the Third Reich. For example, André Gingrich (2005:134–135) argued that Wilhelm E. Mühlmann might "well be considered anthropology's Holocaust ideologist"—despite Fischer's assessment otherwise.

Under fascism, racism was not understood as a moral category but rather as a scientific one with logical political implications embedded in the discursive practices and *dispositifs*[13] of that time (see Ahmed 1973: 263–264). So, were Mühlmann, Baumann, Thurnwald, Kohl-Larsen, and others victims of their time, blinded by discourses of scientific eugenics, or were they conscious participants? We can certainly identify a dialectic, mir-roring, mutually reinforcing relationship: as the ideology of racial hygiene influenced ethnological discourses, National Socialist anthropology helped to refine and promote politically charged concepts of racial purity. If there is one lesson in the history of German anthropology, it is that academics must remain aware of how popular discourse can influence scientific think-ing, which brings us to the present, and the question of how anthropolo-gists, academics, and citizens should approach current security policy. Thomas Hauschild (1995a:10) speaks of retaining one's ability to think flexibly and independently in "the sway of everyday practice." That this is a challenge will become clearer in the following sections in which I describe the post–cold war transformation of the Bundeswehr and German security policy. I will also describe the current role of anthropologists in the German Armed Forces and discuss the pros and cons of anthropological research in, for, and on the military.

THE NEW SECURITY ENVIRONMENT AND THE BUNDESWEHR

Since 1989 two major events have shifted German security policy: firstly, the peaceful revolution in Eastern Europe, which led to the fall of the Berlin Wall. After 1989 many Germans looked forward to enduring peace and great efforts were made with regard to disarmament (see Münkler 2002). However, these hopes were dashed when violent conflict broke out in the former Yugoslavia in the 1990s. The second major event was the 9/11 attacks against the United States, after which Germany sent

FIGURE 4.1.

Logo of the German Bundeswehr (Bundeswehr, Bucurescu).

troops to Afghanistan in support of American efforts to overthrow the Taliban. In response to these events, the Bundeswehr has undergone a process of drastic transformation from a purely defensive army to an active operational army that contributes to international crisis management and conflict prevention within the frameworks of the United Nations, the North Atlantic Treaty Organization (NATO), and the European Union. The Bundeswehr sees itself engaged in "operations for peace" (*Im Einsatz für den Frieden*), an ethos captured in its official logo, in which emphasis is put on protection, help, and mediation, not fighting (figure 4.1).

A more active Bundeswehr emerged in the early 1990s when German soldiers became part of UN peacekeeping operations in Somalia. What most Germans did not expect was to engage in military activity in Europe itself: in the wake of World War II, the Federal Republic of Germany maintained only a defensive force, and Germans were generally reluctant to deploy soldiers to areas that were occupied during the Third Reich (Geis 2007:39). However, when conflict broke out in the former Yugoslavia, the Bundeswehr became part of the NATO Stabilization Force (SFOR; later called the European Force, or EUFOR) mission in Bosnia and Herzegovina. Since 1999 it has been part of the NATO Kosovo Force (KFOR) mission in Kosovo as well, and it joined the US-led International Security Assistance Force (ISAF) in Afghanistan in 2001. These three remain the Bundeswehr's most prominent missions.

Many German citizens support the Bundeswehr's efforts to provide assistance within the framework of peacekeeping missions, as long as fighting and killing are minimized (Bulmahn and Fiebig 2007:6–9; see also Kühne 2007:74). Indeed, the Bundeswehr is a parliamentary army, meaning that a democratically elected German parliament must approve all deployments as stipulated in the German constitution of 1994. Every twelve months the German parliament reviews all Bundeswehr mission mandates. Many politicians see peacekeeping as Germany's contribution to international stability. For now, conflict management is relatively easy to justify to a German populace that accepts peacekeeping (Kümmel and Biehl 2000:12).

Still, not all Germans are sanguine about Germany's military activities. Memories of fascist militarism run deep, and there are limits to German willingness to accept combat missions (Bulmahn and Fiebig 2007:9; Kühne 2007:66). Some groups are openly critical of the post–cold war Bundeswehr, including members of the German peace movement and, surprisingly, many German security experts. While peace activists worry about the "beginning revival of militarist German Wehrmacht ambitions" (Kühne 2007:70), conservative security experts and military leaders—many of whom "came of age" during the cold war—tend to see peacekeeping as an unwieldy task, a paradoxical blend of diplomacy, reconstruction aid, and military force.

In his speech on the occasion of the fiftieth anniversary of the Bundeswehr in October 2005, Federal President Horst Köhler lamented the "friendly indifference" of Germany's citizens toward their armed forces (see Geis 2007:39). A recent survey conducted by the Bundeswehr Institute of Social Sciences revealed that less than 10 percent of Germans know basic facts about the Bundeswehr's current missions, including the reasons for deployment of German soldiers in Afghanistan. Missions that seem more humanitarian get greater support than riskier military operations, such as ISAF (see Bulmahn and Fiebig 2007:6–7; Bulmahn 2006:44). While humanitarian operations theoretically pose minimal risk to soldiers, the reality of peacekeeping can be quite different: for example, rising attacks in northern Afghanistan drew German forces into fighting operations, causing much debate about whether or not Germany should remain involved in ISAF. The NATO air attack on two gasoline trucks near Kundus, authorized by the German Provincial Reconstruction Team commander, at the beginning of September 2009 triggered heated discussions about Germany's role in Afghanistan as more than fifty civilians were killed during the attack—a caesura for Germany's out-of-area engagement (Kornelius 2009:4). Once again critics demanded that the German government finally admit its troops are involved in war-fighting activities in Afghanistan and no longer distribute lies about robust peacekeeping. In addition, debates about the combat mission in Afghanistan get conflated with domestic political dynamics, clouding the public's understanding of and commitment to ISAF (see Tutakhel and Gardizi 2008:2; Schoch 2007: 6–7). We can speak of a certain ambivalence in German security policy: for example, a recent article by Michael Rühle (2008:8), head of the Policy Planning and Speech Writing Section at NATO in Brussels, pointed out the futility of believing that "German security interests could be advocated almost without any risks in the future by participating in collective post-conflict management" in the twenty-first century.

The German state is thus confronted with a dilemma: on the one hand, it would prefer not to deploy its forces, much less to engage in combat,[14] but on the other, it does not want to refrain completely from engagement, as does, for instance, Switzerland (see Rühle 2008:8). This is not just because of international treaty obligations (for example, NATO), but also because Germany wants to be recognized as a sovereign and equal partner in global politics. As Europe's economic powerhouse, located in a geostrategically important position, Germany seeks permanent membership in the UN Security Council (see Geis 2007:46–47).

German academics, including anthropologists, are similarly ambivalent about the Bundeswehr's activities. Recently, Christoph Antweiler (2005:19) publicly challenged his colleagues to consider the question, "Terror in New York—War in Iraq: Can and should the field of anthropology publicly react to such incidents, and is it willing to do so?" Antweiler received little response, I think partly because German anthropologists share their fellow citizens' "friendly indifference" toward involvement in peace operations, and partly because German anthropology tends to be somewhat ponderous in responding to contemporary issues. Yet the GAA conference in October 2009 started with a discussion forum on the topic of "Anthropologists in conflict areas and war zones: Ethical aspects of a new field for our profession." Among the discussants were university professors on the one hand and anthropologists working for the Bundeswehr and NGOs in conflict areas on the other. To sum up the panel discussion, the professors generally argued against research for the military even though they were not up-to-date on the wide spectrum of new job and research fields. The practitioners pointed out that they could not afford to categorically reject job or research offers in the security sector and would thus decide from case to case whether or not these offers met their ethical standards.

Perhaps the most important reason for our reluctance to engage in discussion of military issues and security policy is German anthropology's history. This is despite the fact that anthropologists in other countries are increasingly concerned with problems of culture in the context of war and the military (see, for example, Guttman and Lutz 2010; Lucas 2009; Tomforde 2009c; Rubinstein 2008; Gusterson 2007) to the point of generating a paradigm shift in anthropological research on violence, warfare, and conflict, which was until recently focused on "the tribal zone" (Ferguson and Whitehead 1992). In contrast, more anthropologists are now looking at peace and conflict in industrialized nations, including studies of Western militaries, with an interest in sustainable conflict management, conflict prevention, and postconflict management (Snyder 2002:7; see also Rubinstein 2008; Simons 1999:85ff; Ben-Ari 1998, 1989; Nordstrom and Robben 1995). However, German anthropologists have yet to conduct additional similar studies among German military personnel.

At the same time, the relationship between anthropology and the Bundeswehr may be changing, if only because the German Armed Forces are interested in engaging anthropological research. Accordingly, in the following sections I will address the role of anthropologists within the Bundeswehr, discuss previous ethnographic research, and concentrate on my own research work with the German Armed Forces, also critically examining my activities from an ethical perspective.

ANTHROPOLOGISTS IN THE BUNDESWEHR

Currently there are three anthropologists working with the Bundeswehr: one at the Psychological Operations Center (PSYOP Center),[15] one at the Bundeswehr Geographic Information Office, and one at the Führungsakademie der Bundeswehr, the German Command and Staff College. In addition, a few anthropologists work with the Bundeswehr on a freelance basis.

I began to work with the Bundeswehr in 2003 as a research assistant at the Bundeswehr Institute of Social Sciences (SOWI), where I conducted ethnographic research on the Bundeswehr's missions abroad for four years. I spent several weeks mostly at the Bundeswehr's camps in the Balkans and in Afghanistan and conducted most of my research on German troops, looking at the sociocultural dimensions of deployment, soldiers' motivation, family and deployment, aspects of multinational cooperation, and relations between German troops and host country cultures. I was not allowed to conduct research on host country populations because of the precarious security situation in the theaters of operation. I submitted my research results in the form of expert reports to the Federal Ministry of Defense, which officially sponsors all studies carried out by the SOWI. My reports contained not only my research results but also recommendations on improving soldiers' preparation for intercultural activities in host countries and optimizing multinational cooperation. In addition, the majority of my studies were published in journals or edited volumes (see, for example, Tomforde 2005, 2006b, 2008, 2009b, 2009c).

In March 2007 I resigned from my temporary employment at the SOWI and accepted permanent employment as a senior lecturer for anthropology at the social sciences department of the Führungsakademie der Bundeswehr in Hamburg. The Führungsakademie is the Bundeswehr's highest educational institution. Professionally experienced officers, most with academic degrees, are given further training and education through courses and seminars. This helps them qualify for new assignments and promotions. For example, officers with various years of professional and mission-related experience study several weeks in college and, upon passing a final exam, are qualified for assignments as staff officers. Another course at the Führungsakademie lasts two years and qualifies officers for general or admiral staff assignments. The Führungsakademie trains and educates officers from Germany as well as from NATO/EU and non-NATO/EU countries, which contributes considerably to the multinationality of the college. For example, the International General/Admiral Staff Officer Course trains students from more than fifty countries.

The Department of Social Sciences, where I teach, consists of predominantly civilian lecturers (political scientists, sociologists, educationalists, economists, lawyers, and theologians) who teach students about the relations between the armed forces, state, and society. The position that I hold was created in March 2007 in response to concerns that soldiers in the theater of operation needed intercultural competence in addition to military training. I was given full leeway in choosing my lecture topics, which have included violence and war from a comparative cultural perspective, anthropological conflict and peace research, and the sociocultural dimensions of the Bundeswehr's missions abroad. Moreover, I developed a curriculum in which different seminars and courses collectively address the issue of cultural awareness for military operations. For this purpose, I regularly exchange ideas with the other three anthropologists working with the Bundeswehr who remain involved in practical problems of improving cross-cultural competence in military contexts. My colleague at the PSYOP Center prepares mission-relevant information on African countries and lectures in the field of cross-cultural competence. A third colleague working at the Bundeswehr Geographic Information Office develops materials examining the regions of deployment, providing troops with information about the history and culture of local ethnic groups from an anthropological perspective to help the troops better prepare for missions abroad.

It is possible to study the Bundeswehr from an external perspective. For example, at least one anthropologist is with the Hessische Stiftung für Friedens- und Konfliktforschung (Peace Research Institute, Frankfurt). She conducts research on the identity and self-image of soldiers. Because she works outside the Federal Ministry of Defense, she has limited access to information on the Bundeswehr and its theaters of operation. However, she is also perceived among her anthropology colleagues as less biased in favor of the German Armed Forces, while my two colleagues and I are often criticized for our closeness to the security sector. On the other hand, our positions in the Bundeswehr mean that we can contribute to better democratic control of the armed forces by informing the public of structures and sociocultural practices that we ascertain through research conducted directly amidst the troops.

An Evaluation of German Military Anthropology

Despite the small number of anthropologists studying the German military, German anthropologists are debating such engagements. These debates are somewhat marginal; for example, they do not take place in respected German journals such as the *Zeitschrift für Ethnologie* (*Journal of Anthropology*) but in meetings and symposia, as evidenced by the GAA motion and by the discussion forum I described earlier. Although such debates occur partially in response to events in the United States (such as the establishment of the Human Terrain System), German anthropologists also have historical reasons for their ethical and moral concerns about a renewed utilization of anthropological knowledge for Germany's security interests: fears of an "anthropologization of the military" (Rötzer 2008). Like their counterparts in the United States, German anthropologists are discussing whether or not anthropologists should be allowed to work with or conduct research on the military, if only because the military naturally represents the use of force—something that is incompatible with anthropology's dedication to nonviolence. One might argue, on the other hand, that anthropologists are morally obligated to support the military in the context of a "just war": see, for example, the work of Margaret Mead, Ruth

91

Benedict, Geoffrey Gorer, or Erik E. Erikson during World War II (Price
2002a:14; see also Bräunlein 1995:27, 40).

The Pros and Cons

Some of my colleagues are very critical when they learn of my work as
a lecturer at the Führungsakademie der Bundeswehr. Although very few
know of the Führungsakademie, the association with the Bundeswehr is
enough to generate criticism. The reasons for this criticism include the aforementioned history of anthropology's contribution to National Socialism, as
well as a general leftward orientation in German anthropology that is characterized by opposition to anything military.

However, my colleagues do raise important ethical considerations that
I shall examine below. For instance, is our work necessarily influenced by
the fact that the Federal Ministry of Defense both employs us and sponsors
our research—is it even possible to be critical and independent of the
sponsor? According to Stephan Feuchtwang (1973), the idea of independent science on a material level is naïve and romantic. It is already the
financial aspect of anthropological field research that unhinges the illusion
of "scientific freedom." This holds true for anthropologists working for
armed forces as well as for scientists financed by other institutions. Working
for an organization, be it the Bundeswehr or any other organization, one
always needs to keep a critical distance to one's employer and its activities.
This critical distance and moral veracity is normally taken for granted
among academics, yet instantly questioned regarding people working for
armed forces—regardless of their type of work and convictions. Scholars are
even concerned that cooperation with anthropologists working on the military is "polluting" and harmful to their careers (see Brown 2009).

My colleagues and I at the Führungsakademie try to conduct research
on the Bundeswehr as critically as possible.[16] For this reason, the Department
of Social Sciences (founded thirty years ago) has had a reputation for lean-
ing to the political left, something that makes it unpopular with more conservative elements in the military. Yet we play an important educational and
research role as we are the only civilian department that critically examines
the military, and we attempt to give the soldiers studying with us a differentiated understanding of societal issues.

Others question whether or not I am able to maintain my objectivity as
a member of the Bundeswehr. For example, in the four years that I was
working with SOWI, I mainly conducted research on the armed forces. As
part of this I completed a one-month military training for civilian personnel, familiarized myself with the fundamentals of being a professional

soldier, and, while working in Afghanistan, I wore a uniform. For many fellow ethnologists, this was a step too far. They had no objections to my research on the military, but to do so for the Bundeswehr while wearing a uniform was too much.

I saw this differently. Most anthropologists undergo some form of socialization when they enter their field site, and my experience with the Bundeswehr was no different. For example, during two years of ethnographical research on cultural concepts of spatiality in northern Thailand (1999–2000, 2001–2002), I learned the local languages and, later on, wore the local costume—as expected of me by the villagers. However, wearing the local costume did not mean that I "went native." Instead, I integrated as well as I could into the communities I was studying but never lost sight of my ethical perspective or of my status as a researcher. To conduct my ethnographical research on the Bundeswehr I went through an analogous socialization process—I had to learn the language of the military and familiarize myself with its basic cultural patterns, including wearing the "local costume" during predeployment training and while in military camps such as in Kundus (Afghanistan). However, I never became a soldier or identified myself with the institution to the extent of forgetting my ethical perspective or status as a researcher; and up to today, I remain a civilian critical of the Bundeswehr's engagement abroad. In other words, working for and researching the military does not necessarily mean that one violates the ethical principles of informed consent, of doing no harm, of making research results open to the public, or of not providing information to the secret service or other people or institutions potentially harmful to the people researched (see Ferguson on the HTS in this volume). On the contrary, all of my research results have been published in journals or edited books. Neither the Bundeswehr nor the Ministry of Defense restrained me from doing so, as these institutions are only barely interested in ethnographical data on the German Armed Forces and as they almost "fear" articles in Bundeswehr internal publications read by soldiers and officials within the Ministry of Defense as opposed to external publications read by an anonymous civilian public. As I did not conduct any research on the local populations in the mission areas, I did not run the risk of providing the military with intelligence to use against Afghanis, for example. Rather, I showed that Bundeswehr culture changes considerably through engagement in peacekeeping missions and, as a result, that the organization is confronted with a serious generational conflict (Tomforde 2009d). Without proper ethnographic research among soldiers deployed abroad, I could not have validated these results.

Many anthropologists worry about clandestine research, in which the identity and motivations of the anthropologist are kept secret from the peoples one is studying. According to the American Anthropological Association's Code of Ethics (1998),[17] the primary ethical responsibility of the anthropologist is to do no harm to the people one is studying and to ensure that they are fully aware of the motivations and goals of one's research so that they can choose whether or not to participate. Anthropologists working clandestinely can tarnish the reputation of the entire discipline since all anthropologists might be perceived as spies. However, at this point my colleagues and I focus exclusively on studying the Bundeswehr and its interactions with host nations; we are open about our work and do not conduct clandestine research on host populations.

At times discussions of my work can become highly polarized. For example, during the first meeting of the recently founded Peace and Conflict Studies in Anthropology group in Halle, Germany, a colleague told me that my work was inherently unethical because I am sponsored by the Bundeswehr, which kills innocent Afghanis. Although this individual also studied conflict, she saw her fieldwork in Papua New Guinea as ethical because she relied on public research grants—interestingly, claiming that research grants provided by the German government are morally "pure," while research money from the German Ministry of Defense is "polluted." I believe that such perspectives stem at least partially from the discipline's activities under National Socialism. Many German humanists remain convinced that it is naïve and unethical to provide knowledge to the military, as one does not know how the research results are used. Yet, looking at my work within the Bundeswehr, I—as a critic of German peacekeeping missions—know fairly well in what ways my research results will be used (or rather not used, due to lack of interest in ethnographical data on the military), at least as much as National Socialist anthropologists—as convinced racial ideologists—knew exactly how their work was being used. I believe that anthropologists working with the military are rather aware of how their data are being applied and are therefore in a good position to address this issue responsibly. For example, it is possible that the German Armed Forces might use social science research to optimize their own striking power, and my current work as a lecturer might provide my students with such cross-cultural competence as to improve their fighting capabilities. However, any anthropological study on Afghanistan might provide the military with more inside knowledge than my readings on culture theories, the anthropology of religion, or the anthropology of war.

I work constantly to critically evaluate the impact of my research on the

Bundeswehr by discussing my work with colleagues inside and outside the military. I give lectures at universities and I publish in anthropological journals and books (Tomforde 2006b, 2009d) on the topic of "ethics and the military" to guarantee a continuous discourse on this important theme with a wide range of people. As a researcher I have a responsibility not to allow myself to be absorbed unconsciously into particular ways of thinking —for example, believing unreflexively that peacekeeping work in NATO, the EU, or the United Nations is critically important for Germany's future. As a result, I take an increasingly critical stance toward the Bundeswehr's missions abroad (see also Münkler 2009), and I ask my students to question whether or not presence of weapons and the enforcement of the Western model of democracy and the nation-state can help to establish sustainable peace in conflict regions. I point out that in the past fifty years the field of development cooperation has painfully illustrated that top-down models do not work and that only participatory procedures can be successful in terms of sustainability (Tomforde 2009b). This is true as well for peace-keeping missions (see Rubinstein 2008).

I continue my work with the Bundeswehr because I am convinced that different and differentiated thoughts are important to introduce to the armed forces. Within the Bundeswehr there are critical thinkers seeking new ways to resolve conflict who are looking at the conflicts of our time and want scientifically based perspectives on conflict and cooperation. Emerging concepts, such as networked security, local ownership of resources, and interagency cooperation, indicate that the Bundeswehr is open to new ideas. Anthropological teaching can indeed help to change military perceptions of the Bundeswehr's work and mission in positive ways.

Moreover, I think that my work as a lecturer of anthropology and cross-cultural competence can improve soldiers' awareness of different ways of life and perspectives. This is not about making soldiers more efficient at launching strikes against local populations but rather about teaching them, for example, more about culture theories, their own cultural background, and their self-image in order to make them more sensitized to the "other."

OUTLOOK

A careful discussion about the role of the military has been absent in German society, largely for historical reasons. Nor have anthropologists in Germany engaged the military as a field of study, and the armed forces have been held in low esteem among academics. Not surprisingly, in Germany the field of military anthropology is perceived as a suspect form of practice. As a matter of principle, scientists who conduct research on or for the military are presumed insufficiently self-critical, unable to make ethical and moral judgments about the import of their work.

I have attempted to show that anthropologists working in the Bundeswehr can thoughtfully raise critical questions about doing research in and with the military. I argue that doing so is particularly important in Germany, where anthropologists in the past dedicated themselves to the service of an inhumane political regime. Anthropologists such as Mühlmann, Baumann, and Kohl-Larsen consciously defined "knowledge as a mental weapon" and willingly provided it to the fascists. Rather than condemning these individuals as immoral and walking away from further consideration, we might learn something about our present by studying the context of their actions—as Pierre Bourdieu (1993) has advised. This means going beyond mere condemnation and trying instead to develop a profound understanding of what was going on at that time, to understand how human rights could be so easily disregarded by extremely intelligent scientists with apparently little reflection or guilt. I have attempted to draw on some of this history since I believe that doing so can help us understand as scientists and as politically mature citizens how our current societal discourse is part of a larger historical context.

Because of this history, and because of the acute human consequences of military action, research in, with, and for the military must be critically questioned and constantly examined. We have a particular ethical responsibility to critically reflect on our work and to question what we are doing, lest we become instruments of the political system. As Doris Byer (1995:70) has observed, "It seems to be very difficult to detect hidden values and judgments, even more so, the more current they are and the more directly we are affected by them." This is not just true for anthropologists who work with the military but for all academics who engage in any form with the military. We are all wise to remember that "the printed word always implies a participation in the public life—no matter whether the author is willing to do so or not or whether the author is knowing it or not" (Galeano 1995:5).

In this regard, I believe that anthropology in Germany can provide a differentiated, holistic, comparative perspective in the current discourse on security. However, to do so the discipline needs to further open itself to the (immediate) study of security-related issues in order to be able to better contribute specifically anthropological competences to the public discussion (see, for example, Antweiler 2005:19). Against the background of a rapidly changing world, anthropologists need to conduct research on the military because it will provide valuable insight into sociocultural processes of violence, conflicts, war, militarism, interculturality, identity formation, subcultures, and organizations. Moreover, anthropologists working in and around crisis areas, whether as part of the military or as independent researchers, should disseminate their work quickly and in a generally understandable manner to the public, including soldiers. This could help all of us engage in an informed discussion about the dynamics of conflict management, which today involves a wide and confusing array of actors: governmental and nongovernmental organizations, armed forces, local representatives, physicians, development workers, and others. Doing so might help to minimize intercultural misunderstandings, counter emerging prejudice, generate support for the de-escalation of conflict, and even save lives.

Both engagement and resistance can be unethical and can lead to outcomes that are morally questionable. Moreover, a security situation never is static or stable—it is always subject to evolution and change, which can affect our positioning. Making an effort to maintain critical distance always is appropriate. However, a critical distance does not mean that anthropology should exclude a social phenomenon like the military from its research, nor refrain from participating in the current discourse on security policy. Instead, we should follow Michel Foucault's advice: "It is not my point of departure that everything is evil, but that everything is dangerous, which is not the same as evil. When everything is dangerous, we will always have something to do" (Dreyfus and Rabinow 1987:268).

Notes

1. I thank Laura McNamara and Robert Rubinstein for their comments on an earlier version of this paper and for their manifold support.

2. The PRISP, signed into law in December 2003, is intended to help fifteen US intelligence agencies recruit new analysts possessing "critical" linguistic or scientific skills by awarding scholarships to undergraduate and graduate students who in return acquiesce to working for the intelligence community for a set period of time (see Jaschik 2006; http://www.aaanet.org/press/an/infocus/prisp/nuti-faqs.htm, accessed July 12, 2011).

3. See Gusterson 2008. Hugh Gusterson is one of the founders of the Network of Concerned Anthropologists (NCA). The network examines the Pentagon's new policy of hiring social scientists for new types of military assistance like the HTS, which embeds social scientists in combat teams in places like Iraq and Afghanistan. NCA asked anthropologists to sign a pledge not to do covert work or work in occupied territories (see http://www.concerned.anthropologists.googlepages.com/home, accessed July 3, 2008).

4. The distrust between humanities scholars and the military is neither unknown nor new but has been part of the history of anthropology since World War I (see Gusterson 2007:156–157). The relationship is characterized by colliding professional concepts, and forms of communication and self-concepts, and by differences in dealing with research results. Moreover, it is generally difficult to overcome these contrasts. While the working methods of humanities scientists are geared toward transparency and coherence, the military rather works behind closed doors in its barracks.

5. Despite great efforts to unify Volkskunde and Völkerkunde/Ethnologie, it is still common practice to differentiate between Ethnologie and ethnic studies/ European ethnology (see Haller 2005:5; Kaschuba 2006).

6. Scientific books on race and on the prominent place of the "Aryan race" in a racial hierarchy were popular among the German population of that time, as such publications helped to compensate for the notion of defeat and "revitalise the spirit of the German people" (Schafft 2004:62).

7. The German term *Anthropologie* represents the field of biological anthropology and is, due to its connection to the genocide in the Third Reich, still seldom used as a synonym for Völkerkunde/Ethnologie (see Fischer 1988:24).

8. For a list of anthropologists' activities in the Third Reich, see Schafft 2004:Appendix 1.

9. Franz Boas and Bronislaw Malinowski were among the very few anthropologists brave enough to openly campaign against fascism and Nazism (see Carstens 2007:70–75; Hauschild 1995b:8–9; Fischer 1990:209). Not only very few international academics but also very few international scientific institutions challenged the scientific assertions of Nazi racial ideology (Schafft 2004:208; Barkan 1992:285).

10. After 1945 Nazi anthropologists protected each other "from disgrace or, even worse, prison. Due to the political realities of the time, they avoided court trials, but also the German public aided them to sidestep sanctions by their unwillingness to have one more defeat: the loss of respect for their intelligentsia" (Schafft 2004:225).

11. The "Kampfbund for German Culture" was a political organization founded in 1928 by one of the most influential Nazi ideologists, Alfred Rosenberg. The aim of the organization was to inform cultural life in Germany along anti-Semitic lines.

12. Professor Emeritus Hans Fischer is one of the most renowned postwar anthropologists and worked at the Institute of Ethnology at the University of Hamburg until 1999.

13. The term "dispositif" was developed by Michel Foucault (1978:119–120) and refers to the network of discourses, regulatory decisions, laws, doctrines, scientific statements, and so forth, of a particular time.

14. However, this does not keep German enterprises from engaging in the highly profitable arms business. In 2006 Germany was among the top three arms exporters after the United States and Russia. The worldwide arms business has seen record figures for years and the one-trillion-dollar mark has long been surpassed. Hans Blix, head of the UN Monitoring, Verification and Inspection Commission, recently stated that global military expenditures had risen by 30 percent between 2001 and 2006: "We are experiencing a revival of the Cold War policy, but without war, a sort of Cold Peace" (quoted in Leyendecker 2008:1).

15. There are more posts for anthropologists at the PSYOP Center, but currently these are held by social or regional scientists.

16. See, for example, our critical reflections on German peacekeeping missions (Jaberg et al. 2009).

17. The Deutsche Gesellschaft für Völkerkunde (German Anthropological Association, or GAA) has not yet agreed upon one ethical guideline. There is still an ongoing debate within the association whether such an internationally compatible guideline is needed or not (Vorstand und Beirat der Deutschen Gesellschaft für Völkerkunde 2008:18–19).

5

Plowing the Human Terrain

Toward Global Ethnographic Surveillance

R. Brian Ferguson

This chapter is one of a pair in which I am trying to think through some of the foreseeable implications of the Pentagon's new quest for culture. The planned companion piece (Ferguson forthcoming), will go wide, engaging with engagement in its broadest senses. The present work is narrow, focused on the Human Terrain System (HTS), which in time may be seen as a comparatively simple topic. In years to come anthropologists will deal with ethical, moral, and political issues in innumerable professional contexts. Most will come in hues of gray. To cope with those challenges, it is important to have a sense where the slippery slope goes off a cliff, where professional ethics can be transgressed. That point, I will argue, is reached with the HTS.[1]

I accept that those who advocate or sign up for the HTS have good intentions. They hope to use ethnographic understanding to save lives and lessen the destruction of war. I will argue that the information they gather in the field also can be used to help identify enemies for "kinetic" targeting, the application of military force. That is why participation in Human Terrain Teams crosses the ethical line. Anthropologists must not help militaries figure out whom to kill. More than that, the HTS folds into a projected worldwide monitoring of indigenous peoples for security threats by the Department of Defense (DoD). Anthropologists should not do that either.

Some of my colleagues expect the HTS will go away because of its many problems: three team members killed in the line of duty, one convicted of manslaughter, one under investigation for espionage, loud whistle-blowing about incompetence in multiple areas, inadequate training, unacceptable scholarly and anthropological standards, unclear and unworkable chains of command, intractable personality collisions from top to bottom, sudden changes in management and training locations, inability to recruit competent social scientists, appointment of unqualified personnel and cronies, an investigative finding of sexual harassment and creating an intolerable work atmosphere, abrupt pay cuts midstream followed by resignation of many civilian employees, and so on (see Bill and Bob's Excellent Afghan Adventure 2009; Forte 2009a, 2009b; Glenn 2007; Isenberg 2009; Nature 2008; Pelton 2008; Piatetsky 2009:3; Price 2009; Weinberger 2008a; see also ongoing postings on Matt Tompkins's blog, *Iraq's Human Terrain*, e.g., Helbig 2008; on *Wired's* "Danger Room" by Nathan Hodge, Noah Schactman, and Sharon Weinberger, e.g., Schactman 2008, 2009; and on *Zero Anthropology* by John Stanton, e.g., Stanton 2008a, 2008b, 2009). On top of those problems, the HTS, and the larger emphasis on counterinsurgency and global "stability operations," face stinging critiques from within the military (Bacevich 2008; Connable 2009; Dunlap 2008; Katel 2008; Ricks 2009).

If this were anything but a Pentagon program, it would be dead by now. Yet the HTS seems locked in as a cornerstone of current DoD doctrine (see Albro 2009), promulgated by David Petraeus and his brain trust and backed by name by Defense Secretary Robert Gates (Connable 2009:63; Gates 2008:3; Jaschik 2008:2). Some $200 million is sunk into it (Redden 2009:1). The Obama/Gates plan for Afghanistan expands HTS:

> [M]ilitary officials say that they have worked hard in recent years to come up with creative programs that can win the population's trust, crucial to any effective counterinsurgency strategy. The human terrain program has become a cornerstone of that effort. A Pentagon study completed this month recommended that the Joint Chiefs of Staff increase the number of such advisors across the military "by factors of three to five," along with a large expansion of cultural training for members of the military. [Stockman and Bender 2009:2]

THE HUMAN TERRAIN SYSTEM

The HTS consists of Human Terrain Teams (HTTs) attached to field combat brigades and Reachback Research Cells (Kipp et al. 2006). The first HTT was deployed to Afghanistan in February 2007, and five teams were in Iraq by early September 2007. The plan was to embed one HTS team in all twenty-six of the US combat brigades in Afghanistan and Iraq (Rohde 2007:1). In March 2009 the number of teams was on target, with twenty-one in Iraq and six in Afghanistan (Landers 2009b). It is not clear, however, how many of these teams were fully operational or how many anthropologists were involved (Rob Albro, personal communication, February 13, 2009)—and that count was before the pay reduction and turmoil that led to many resignations.

The stated mission of the HTS is "to provide commanders in the field with relevant socio-cultural understanding necessary to meet their operational requirements" (Human Terrain System 2008a:3). To quote one of many similar passages in the *Human Terrain Team Handbook*:

> The HTT will research, interpret, archive, and provide cultural data, information, and knowledge to optimize operational effectiveness by harmonizing courses of action within the cultural context of the environment, and provide the commander with operationally relevant, socio-cultural data, information, knowledge and understanding, and the embedded expertise to integrate that understanding into the commander's planning and decision-making processes. [Finney 2008:35]

Throughout the *Handbook* the HTT is conceptualized as a fully integrated part of the command vision, showing "how the culture influences the battle space" (Finney 2008:16).

Appendix B of the *Counterinsurgency* manual (United States Department of Defense 2006a) gives a general idea of the product expected. One map overlay (B-3) displays the location of ethnicities. Another (B-2) is of "population support," which marks and labels local population clusters and numbers as "supports host nation," "supports insurgents," and "neutrals." The *Handbook* also details information to be collected for other kinds of mapping, including social networks, association matrixes, and event coordination registers (Finney 2008:36–37).

In public statements, defenders of the HTS claim that their goal is to find ways to reduce killing and destruction. For example:

> My job in Iraq was to represent the population to promote non-lethal planning and operations. When a mission is conceptualized, when course of action recommendations have to be made, when decisive points are identified for the commander, my job is

to present what the population wants and expects, how it will react, and at all times promote nonlethal options. [A. Silverman 2009:1]

This vision of "war without blood" (West 2009:6) appeals to humanitarian sentiments. That goal is conspicuously absent in articles written for military audiences. In those writings the point is that anthropology can help our side fight smarter and *prevail*. For example, an architect of HTS wrote, before the system was formulated,

> Successful counterinsurgency depends on attaining a holistic, total understanding of local culture....To defeat the insurgency in Iraq, U.S. and coalition forces must recognize and exploit the underlying tribal structure of the country; the power wielded by traditional authority figures; the use of Islam as a political ideology; the competing interests of the Shia, the Sunni, and the Kurds; the psychological effects of totalitarianisms; and the divide between urban and rural, among other things. [M. McFate 2005a:37]

HTS has two faces—one for the military and one for the public. The public relations campaign has been remarkably successful, but available facts do not support this claim of harm reduction

Organization

The original plan for HTTs was for four members commanded by a military team leader:

- Cultural Analyst: Specs: Civilian, MA/PhD, Cultural Anthropologist/ Sociologist. Duties: Advise HTT and unit staff, conduct/manage ethnographic/social science research and analysis.
- Regional Studies Analyst: Specs: Civilian, MA/PhD, Area Studies. Fluency in area language. Duties: Provide local area interpretation of compiled human terrain information and run focus groups with locals.
- Human Terrain Research Manager: Specs: Military, W-2 to 0-34, MI. Duties: Integrate human terrain research plan with unit intelligence collection plan. Serve as first CI [Combat Intelligence] screen for HT data. Secondary human terrain data advisor.
- Human Terrain Analyst: Specs: Military, E-6 to 0-3/4. Any MOS.

Trained debriefer. Duties: Primary human terrain data researcher. [Kipp et al. 2006:13]

As the program developed, changes were made, as reflected in the new *Handbook* (Finney 2008:11–27). The standard size has increased to up to nine members. The title of "regional studies analyst" is gone, and the local cultural and language knowledge they were to bring is folded into the description of "human terrain analyst" (HTA). "Cultural analysts" are now called "social scientists," and there are to be two per team, along with two "research managers."

The HTAs, up to four of them, are the main field agents. Their extensive job description paints each as a veritable Lawrence of Arabia: operating with substantial autonomy, moving from place to place, gathering a volume and quality of information that would be impressive for a trained researcher with years in the field, building alliances, cutting across channels, and generally getting things done. Just half of the HTA's "essential task list" reads:

- Identify specified and implied cultural data requirements.
- Analyze the operated area against cultural data.
- Analyze available sources of local cultural information.
- Assess other characteristics of the battlefield (leaders, population, demographics, social, ethnic, and religion, etc.)
- Develop Human Terrain Information Requirements.
- Determine indicators and specific information requirements for supporting Commander's Critical Information Requirements, Decision Points, and Names Areas [*sic*] of Interest. [Finney 2008:23–24]

The social scientists themselves seem primarily tasked to attend meetings, frame research strategies to meet command needs, interpret data at higher social science levels, and serve as trusted counselors to the commander.

The duties and products of each HTT are so all-encompassing as to be impossible, a fantasy of what ethnographic attention can provide. This fieldwork miracle is to be accomplished by people who may have little to no social science training, little to no prior experience in the area, and very little time in one location to gather information and make friends. As an HTT research manager at Bagram told a reporter in March 2009, "Time spent on the ground in days, not minutes, is vital to building friendships" (Zumer 2009).

The civilians in HTTs receive training, serve in uniform, and are issued weapons (MTC Technologies 2008). The practice of carrying weapons varies (Ephron and Spring 2008:1; Middle East Online 2008; Mulrine 2007:36). A sympathetic reporter describes the fieldwork of Audrey Roberts, an anthropologist in Afghanistan, in this way:

> When the Salerno Human Terrain Team arrives in a village for interviews, the commotion and the presence of heavily armed soldiers make it highly unlikely that Roberts will be invited for tea. Still, she has an ingratiating smile. Even though they are often nervous about being seen talking to an "American soldier," Afghans quickly open up to Roberts with complaints about the lack of security in their villages....She works the streets of Afghan villages wearing combat boots, a helmet, Army fatigues, and armored vest and ammo clips for the M-16 rifle she carries, though usually her work tools are a notebook and a pen. [Landers 2009b:2]

Another reporter comments about Roberts's team: "At a recent meeting with elders of the Mangal tribe...HTT personnel mingled and chatted to guests through Pashtun interpreters while stressing that they are not conventional military intelligence gatherers. Whether the tribesmen really get the distinction is unclear, but partners in the local government seem receptive" (DPA 2008). The uniforms and guns were among the circumstances noted by the AAA Commission on Anthropology's Engagement with the Security and Intelligence Communities in concluding that HTT members could not guarantee voluntary informed consent by studied populations (American Anthropological Association 2007:31).

Informed consent is the ethical cornerstone of anthropological field research, but "social scientists on HTTs do not submit their research to an institutional review board, as would normally be required for human research" (Weinberger 2008b:584). The HTT *Handbook* declares that an "accompanying document is written outlining how the research will comply with the protection of human research subjects according to 45 CFT 46 to ensure the research falls within accepted ethical guidelines" (Finney 2008:55). It goes on to state, "Our research is performed in the same manner in which academic social scientists conduct their research and is similarly rooted and theory and complete with ethical review boards" (56). To my knowledge, no substantiation has been made public of these claims of ethical guidelines and independent review boards. For that matter, attempts to find the meaning of "45 CFT 46" came up with nothing.

WHAT DO HTS FIELD TEAMS DO?

HTS advocates claim that the system benefits local populations and reduces the violence of war. Does it? They vigorously deny that they provide information that can be used to target people for violent action. Is that so? At present there is very little public information about the actual practice and impact of Human Terrain Teams. The first six HTTs were billed by Montgomery McFate as "proof of concept" that would produce a publicly available report of HTT activities. Responding to a critic's request for evidence that HTTs reduced casualties, in February 2008 she replied:

> Professor González laments the lack of independent data to support the claim that HTS assisted in reducing lethal operations.... The qualitative and quantitative data from both Iraq and Afghanistan substantiating this claim will be included in the HTS Assessment Report. Given that HTS is a new project, it is not possible to have mature outcome evaluation data at this stage. Professor González will have to wait until next summer for the completed assessment, just like the DoD. [M. McFate and Fondacaro 2008:27]

That summer, and the next, came and went—no report for Professor González, or for anyone outside the DoD loop.

Advocates of the HTS, and of generally increasing engagement between academia and the military (Jaschik 2008), have pledged openness to outside scrutiny. HTS fails this test: no ethical review information, no research products, no evaluative reports or statistics, no metrics about the operations of HTTs—none of that has been made available. Even the HTT *Handbook* went public through a leak (Price 2008c). Our main source is news reports. Of course, news media access requires the approval of military and HTS administrators or officers. On that biased basis, here is "the news," first for Iraq, then for Afghanistan.

Iraq

Dave Matsuda of the Eighty-second Airborne's Second Brigade Combat Team is described in a Fort Hood newsletter as studying and explaining local tribal organization and hierarchy and counseling on necessary rituals, local scripts, and appropriate symbols. For a wanted poster he suggested an illustration of two open hands, derived from the Koran, instead of a Western scales of justice. Matsuda's executive officer comments, "It's great having them. They add a critical dimension to the fight, one that has been missing up to now" (Pryor 2007).

Marcus Griffin, the anthropologist with the 1-76 Cavalry's Charlie Company, developed indicators of local well-being, such as how the local market is stocked, and interviewed locals about schools and electricity, for example. Prior to joining the HTS his work had been on "Freegans," environmentalists who scour dumpsters, and in Baghdad he rummaged through trash for ideas (Ephron and Spring 2008:2). Griffin's (2007) blog describes other insights from a helicopter overflight: accumulated rubble and flooding by stagnant ponds and sewage probably led to increased stress in the population, and those problems should be addressed.

Another Iraq team with the First Infantry Division's Fourth Infantry Brigade Combat Team was led by Matt Tompkins, fiancé of whistle-blower Zenia Helbig, who was dismissed from HTT training when she joked about jumping sides (Helbig 2008). When an American officer suggested buying two hundred goats for a local sheik, his team recommended finding out first if the sheik wanted goats, or maybe something like work on the power grid (Mulrine 2007:35). When his unit needed to get a local police commander to crack down on subordinates suspected of aiding insurgents, the team suggested appealing to his pride. They pointed out that the subordinates were mocking him, which made him visibly angry (Ephron and Spring 2008:2).

Tensions about the role of this team are evident. When commanding officer Ricky Gibbs returned from a two-week visit home to first meet cultural anthropologist Lisa Verdon and area specialist Fouad Lghzaoui, he wondered how they would operate within the chain of command.

> After the team ticks off a few planned projects, for example, Gibbs has a question: "Who told you to study those things?" What he most wants to know, he says, is the following: "How do I make [Iraqis] realize that I'm thinking what they're thinking?" The questions keep coming. "How do I approach them in a way that helps? How do I get into the clique? How can I win the information campaign using the way they think?" Gibbs ends the exchange with a final query: "Are you all going to help?" "We will try," answers Lghzaoui. "Inshallah [God willing]." Verdon winces. Gibbs looks at his team. "There is no trying," he says. "We're going to do an American inshallah on this one." That means, he says, "We're going to do it." Later Verdon digests the encounter, noting the teams have to be sensitive to the can-do American military culture too. [Mulrine 2007:36]

Gibbs also told the reporter that over time, HTT input was invaluable. For instance, the team informed him that an image of a snake on some wall posters was a positive rather than a negative symbol, helping him better understand local attitudes. But problems with this team did not go away.

Another reporter noted that the "social scientist on [Tompkins's] team had no relevant field-research experience,...and their de facto translator was a Moroccan who barely spoke English" (Weinberger 2008b:584). Their cultural adviser "was pulled from Iraq only after five months of her military team leader reporting not only her inability to contribute, but her open refusal to acknowledge his authority, support information requests from the supported unit or coordinate with anyone on the team" (Helbig 2008:3). Following Helbig's criticism of the HTS, Tompkins was returned from Iraq and released from the program (Helbig 2008:6).

In a later news article, Tompkins was critical of HTS impact.

> Tompkins...said he thought his team provided helpful input to its brigade, but the contribution was more superficial than planners of the program had conceived. "Without the ability to truly immerse yourself in the population, existing knowledge of the culture...is critical....Lacking that, we were basically an open-source research cell." [Ephron and Spring 2008:2]

(The mention of "knowledge of the culture" refers to the fact that social scientists recruited to HTS often have had no research experience with Middle Eastern cultures.)

> Tompkins...says that for every success in Iraq, he has suffered multiple frustrations and failures. And he doesn't believe his team members were uniquely qualified to provide the input they did. Tompkins says many of the officers and grunts he worked with had more-relevant knowledge and experience than the anthropologists, having served in Iraq twice or three times before. "These are dedicated individuals who are often intimately familiar with many of the nuances of the society and culture they are trying to engage with." [Ephron and Spring 2008:2]

This last observation is widely confirmed by others. For instance, Connable (2009:62), a foreign area officer, comments on reports of HTS successes:

> These examples demonstrate common sense in a COIN [counterinsurgency] environment, not breakthroughs. Hundreds of Army and Marine staffs that accepted culture as a significant

element of terrain have been doing these things on a daily basis across Afghanistan and Iraq for years without HTS support. [See also Sepp 2007:218]

The best described Iraqi HTT is IZ6. Adam Silverman (2009), a non-anthropologist HTT social scientist, says his job was to represent and empower the local population and promote nonlethal options by the Second Brigade Combat Team/First Armored Division. His team, he says, was "able to directly or indirectly conceptualize and influence virtually all of our brigade's problem sets and provide nonlethal options to resolve them" (A. Silverman 2009)—quite a claim. The only example he gives is this: "I provided information that presented a set of nonlethal options for resolving a problem regarding a local mosque." His team did a lot of research, producing reports that "provide very important insight and findings regarding Iraqi tribal behavior, Iraqi politics, religion, rule of law, as well as the stabilization and reconstruction that is being undertaken" (A. Silverman 2009). Their findings were shared across the military spectrum and with the embassy and State Department (A. Silverman 2009).

A master's thesis at the Naval Postgraduate School (Schaner 2008: 49–67) uses Silverman's HTT as a case study based on interviews with the "IZ6 lead Social Scientist" (Silverman is not identified by name). This unit operated in a rural area south and east of Baghdad that was "comparatively stable" and an "ideal area for agricultural development and revitalization" (Schaner 2008:49–50). Two of the three IZ6 activities described have the character of postconflict stability operations. In one case brigade planning had prioritized the revival of local fish farming, and the HTT, working with military Civil Affairs teams, developed information about water infrastructure, local ideas of what worked in the past and could work in the future, and which laborers to hire to improve local ties. In the other case, in response to land disputes involving displaced persons in the area, the HTT created a plan for an arbitration system attuned to local values and law. Both sound like worthwhile projects, but the world is awash with failed plans for promoting prosperity and justice. No information is provided about implementation or results of these plans. Results are what matter, as the third HTT case demonstrates.

The most illuminating illustration of how an HTT can work in a conflict situation came about accidentally. The team leader was attending a "municipality development conference," and in one session where other US military personnel were not present (my emphasis throughout), a senior Shia tribal Sheikh started shouting and was subsequently escorted out by a senior Sunni tribal Sheikh. A translator explained to the IZ6 Team Leader that the tribal Sheikh was shouting about how *things are never done right, never completed, and how things are never improved.* However, the tribal Sheikh's comments in front of his peers *directly contradicted what the Social Scientist heard the tribal Sheikh say to his American associates in a different forum.* An Iraqi conference participant revealed that the tribal Sheik's apparently contradictory behavior had root in a great amount of confusion that exists among Iraqis over what America is trying to accomplish in Iraq. The Iraqi conference participant elaborated on this reasoning by further explaining that most Iraqis do not understand how a nation like the United States could invade a country like Iraq, and then turn around and rebuild it. In the eyes of Iraqis and *in Iraqi culture, these are two contradictory and confusing endeavors that generate mistrust and confusion,* and sit at the root of the tribal Sheikh's contradictory behavior. [Schaner 2008: 59]...[*This*] *unique instance in which the HTT Team Leader observed a candid outburst of a prominent Shia tribal leader in a setting with no American military leaders present...was somewhat startling and indicated that perhaps Iraqi-American relationships still needed improvement with respect to this segment of society.* [59, 60]...IZ6 enables the BCT [Brigade Combat Team] to better bridge into the population by first identifying the true perceptions of local citizens and leaders. Having this kind of knowledge allows for an improved quality of interaction between the BCT and the civilian population. This in turn *helps the BCT refine all functions it performs with respect to the population (e.g., security, counterinsurgency, and reconstruction).* [62]

A straightforward interpretation of these events is that local Iraqis see US development efforts as incompetent failures, that they still see the army as occupiers, and that they tell the conquerors what they want to hear. The HTT analysis, instead, portrays this as an expression of "Iraqi culture," which renders locals "confused" and prone to "contradictory behavior." This accidental revelation was "startling" to the HTT social scientist—who identifies himself as the representative of the local population to the US military. Good thing he was privy to this meeting, or else the brigade might not have learned that its relationship with local peoples still needed some tweaking. As it was, a report of the "Sheikh outburst" was submitted, and the BCT staff used it to draft new "assessment and updating population engagement practices" (Schaner 2008:60). "[B]etter practices can be implemented that address the principal concerns and confusions claimed to be endemic within Iraqi citizens" (61). What practices, exactly, are not clear. They are to be discovered by trial and error. Other more targeted implications are obvious.

Sheikh X is identified by the HTT as very angry at the Americans and duplicitous. "IZ6 greatly contributed to enhancing awareness and insight into the truth about what a senior local Shia tribal Sheikh actually believed versus what he conveyed to his American associates. Given that this particular tribal Sheikh is a senior leader in his community, such beliefs most likely reflect the sentiments of his constituents" (Schaner 2008:59). If there were a new wave of IED killings in the area, would not this identification of Sheikh X as duplicitous and angry at the United States put him and his followers under increased suspicion? At the Society for Applied Anthropology meetings that preceded this volume, Adam Silverman adamantly asserted that his work provided no information that could be used to identify potential enemies, but "the truth" about Sheikh X is precisely that kind of information.

Montgomery McFate, lead spokesperson for the HTS, gave a reporter one example of how an Iraq HTT reduced local violence. The case involved a young man detained by the military because they found what they thought was

> jihadist literature and an illegal weapon. These detentions...can easily escalate into major conflicts with the local community. But in one recent case, researchers helped defuse a potential conflict. Analysts working for a "human-terrain team" informed a US commander that the "jihadist" literature...was ordinary religious teaching material, and the weapon—a riflescope—was for a pellet gun that beekeepers in the area use for shooting birds. The suspect was promptly released, and his family ended up helping US forces by revealing the location of a large improvised explosive device. [Weinberger 2008a:583]

Told to another reporter, this story got better—much better.

> [A]fter an HTT officer identified the prisoner as harmless and the commanding captain was ready to release him, the HTT officer explained that the local Iraqis would consider the release insulting unless it was done in accordance with their culture.

McFate said that after the captain released the prisoner in what the townspeople considered a respectful manner, the local sheikh was so impressed that he volunteered to drive out Al Qaeda himself, and also informed the American military of the location of several weapon caches and improvised explosives. [Swire 2008]

Sharon Weinberger (2008a) checked McFate's tale with the commander of that HTT. He confirmed that the team helped defuse the situation— without any mention of any subsequent benefits—but clarified that no anthropologist was involved. The recommendation to release came from himself and "an Iraqi-American analyst. There wasn't even a social scientist on the team at the time" (Weinberger 2008a:584). This example illustrates why many anthropologists are skeptical of unsubstantiated claims by HTS advocates. And as Weinberger (2008a:483) herself asks about McFate's story, what if the HTT had determined that the young man really did have jihadist literature?

Afghanistan

The first HTS team in Afghanistan, with the Eighty-second Airborne's Fourth Brigade, received a great deal of publicity centering on Tracy St. Benoit, a non-PhD anthropologist and a former combat aviator (Featherstone 2008:62–63; Gulfnews.com 2009; Rohde 2007). Not knowing what to do with these strange ducks (members of the HTT), brigade commander Col. Martin Schweitzer installed them as part of intelligence analysis. The team improvised. They built rapport with Afghan workers on the base and speeded up repair of the base mosque. They advised on medium and content for a broadcast message against people becoming suicide bombers. They opened up communication with women; they counseled soldiers on body language. They explained to the commander the Pashtun code of ethics. "'That's when we started understanding Pashtunwali,' [Schweitzer] said. 'The minute (the HTT) plugged in their computers.' The team held meetings in dozens of villages to better understand Taliban influence, and found it was not based on ideology, but on lack of income and security" (Featherstone 2008: 62–63). St. Benoit identified a long-standing dispute over timber rights that divided the large Zadran tribe and interpreted Taliban actions as efforts to play off this division. She suggested actions to help bring the Zadrans together, such as building a school to be used by different factions and convoking *shuras* (local assemblies) to discuss problems (Rohde 2007). A reporter (Featherstone 2008:66) accompanied a non-HTS Provincial

Reconstruction Team (PRT) mission to a village St. Benoit had not visited because it was thought to be "stable." The local doctor complained to the soldiers of Pakistani Taliban infiltrating the area and said that they needed killing, not reconciliation. On the mission's return, St. Benoit provided her perspective to Featherstone (emphasis added):

> "But that sounds like a thoroughly entrenched Taliban pres-
> ence," Tracy said. "It had all the metrics.... It was too bad," she
> said. The PRT had missed an opportunity to gather critical infor-
> mation. Had she been there, *she would have interviewed the doctor at
> length about the evolution of the Taliban threat.... It was quite possible that
> the doctor was allowing the Taliban to use his clinic....* Otherwise they
> would have killed him a long time ago. She asked me if I'd
> noticed anything on the ground outside the clinic. "Rocks, that's
> about it." "Any needles?" I...recalled that a soldier had told me
> to stay away from some discarded syringes. "That's significant,"
> Tracy said. *It was a clear sign that the Taliban had been there.... Soldiers
> were too preoccupied with providing security to notice such patterns, she
> added, which is why they needed an HTT to guide them.* [Featherstone
> 2008:66]

Consider this report against the denials that HTTs gather tactical information about enemies.

One of St. Benoit's contributions was reported first in the *New York Times* (Rohde 2007), but the anecdote is often repeated—up to the Secretary of Defense (Jaschik 2008). In one incursion into a valley in Paktia Province, "'Tracy identified an unusually high concentration of widows in one village,' Colonel Woods said. Their lack of income created financial pressure on sons to provide for their families, she determined, a burden that could drive the young men to join well-paid insurgents. Citing Tracy's advice, American officers developed a job training program for the wid-ows" (Rohde 2007:3). That makes good press, though the notion that a job training program for widows by a temporary occupying military force will change their living circumstances seems highly unrealistic. What is not noted in the anecdote's repetition is that St. Benoit has thus identified wid-ows' sons as potential insurgents, a point that could become part of stan-dard profiling techniques in insurgent areas. Will that help their mothers?

In another illustration of the utility of a "woman's perspective," St. Benoit's questionnaires revealed that mullahs in "the more conservative tribes" preached against contraception. "'And so one of the things that came out of this was an evolving metric for Taliban influence,' Tracy said. 'Female contraception. Who would've thought?'" (Featherstone 2008:63). Does this not help identify locations where Taliban are strong?

A "preliminary assessment" of this HTT was completed in August 2007. It was not made public, but glowing highlights are posted on the HTS website, including three particular accomplishments. In one case, a village had been firing rockets at a local base. On HTT advice village elders were brought into a discussion. They claimed it was not them but the Taliban firing and pledged to stop them if the coalition would pay occasional friendly visits to the village and give them a volleyball net. Both were done, and the rockets stopped. In another area, an HTT advised the military to reach out to local mullahs rather than village elders who were supporting the Taliban. That led to an immediate cessation of attacks. In a third, the HTT convinced a company commander that a local village supported the Taliban only because they were being coerced. They convened a shura, after which villagers agreed to the construction of a road and employment of local youth as auxiliary police to keep the Taliban out (Human Terrain System 2008a; see also Schweitzer 2008). These examples sound way too good to be true, or at least, enduring.

The *New York Times* story (Rohde 2007) first reported Colonel Schweitzer's seemingly compelling point, also often repeated, that this first HTT led to a 60 to 70 percent reduction in kinetic actions by the military. However, as Noah Schactman (2007) reported, "Even some HTT members have a hard time believing that figure. And [HTS administrator] Fondacaro cautions that the 4th Brigade's area of operations was relatively calm, and therefore well suited to social-science research. But the local commander insists that 53 of 83 districts now support the local government...up from just 19." David Price, failing to find evidence for this claim, contacted Colonel Schweitzer directly. The colonel replied that this claimed reduction was his own "loose estimate" (Price 2009:5; Weinberger 2008a:584). Advocates of the HTS say it reduces kinetic actions against local peoples. These dubious two-year-old claims about the first Afghanistan HTT are the only *specific* examples of kinetics reduction made public to date.

St. Benoit was the first HTT anthropologist in Afghanistan. More recently, Audrey Roberts, a non-PhD anthropologist, worked with one of the six HTTs in Afghanistan by early 2009. Her team learned that local tribal groups were trying to settle a dispute among themselves, documented Taliban attacks on local officials, reported widespread disgust about governmental corruption, relayed objections about nighttime raids that violated norms of dignity by exposing women to American soldiers,

explained that economic travails enabled recruitment by well-paying insurgents, and found that local fighters are from several distinct groups—
opium traffickers, kidnapping gangs, Al-Qaeda, and both Afghani and
Pakistani Taliban. This sounds like worthwhile information for the commander, but the glowing report in the *Dallas Morning News* (Landers
2009b) makes no reference to reducing kinetic operations. Military planners interviewed by the reporter say the information HTTs gather helps
them "identify ways to turn the insurgents against each other and to identify groups that might be willing to negotiate" (Landers 2009b). Another
reporter quotes Roberts, "We identify the environment that the bad guys
operate in, build a foundation for units so they can understand their area"
(DPA 2008).

Description of Roberts's work originally appeared in the *Dallas
Morning News* on March 8, 2009. It was picked up by the *Boston Herald* on
March 13, and from there went all over the web. There is only one substantive change in the second article, but it is a plainly misleading alter-
ation. The *Herald* ended thus:

> The work of the Human Terrain Teams is controversial. The
> American Anthropology [*sic*] Association has condemned the
> work as a corruption of social science because it provides the mil-
> itary with intelligence to use against the insurgency. Roberts said
> her work was not classified, and was available for any and all mil-
> itary and civilian groups working to support the Afghan govern-
> ment. [Landers 2009b:3]

The original story ended this way:

> The work of the Human Terrain Teams is controversial. The
> American Anthropology Association has condemned the work
> as a corruption of social science because it provides the military
> with intelligence to use against the insurgency. Roberts does not
> worry about what the military does with her information, even if
> it is fed into the intelligence used by U.S. Special Forces for
> killing or capturing insurgent leaders. "If it's going to inform
> how targeting is done...whether that targeting is bad guys, devel-
> opment or governance...how our information is used is how it's
> going to be used," she said. "All I'm concerned about is pushing
> our information to as many soldiers as possible. The reality is
> there are people out there who are looking for bad guys to kill,"

Roberts said. "I'd rather they did not operate in a vacuum."
[Landers 2009a:4]

(The *Boston Herald* posting has been withdrawn from the Internet, so all links to it are down. As of this writing, the only access to the altered story is through a Marine veterans' site, Leatherneck.com.)

MILITARY INTELLIGENCE AND TARGETING

Montgomery McFate is adamant that the teams do not collect military intelligence or participate in targeting attacks. She "vehemently denied that the anthropologists collected intelligence for the military" (Rohde 2007:3). Furthermore, as is posted on the HTS website,

> HTTs do not proactively elicit actionable intelligence [note the hedge] from the local civilian population. Team members are legally prohibited from performing active intelligence collection. Only Military Intelligence (MI) Human Intelligence (HUMINT) Collectors can answer specific questions from the brigade's intelligence unit. Furthermore, brigades do not need HTTs to collect intelligence or assist with targeting, since they already have a large intelligence staff that performs this function for them. The role of the HTTs is to help the troops better understand who is NOT their enemy. [Human Terrain System 2008b]

But how can one better understand who is *not* the enemy without better understanding who *is* the enemy?

How important is the legal prohibition when the team terrain analyst will "have a military intelligence background, " and the terrain research manager is also specified as having "a military background in tactical intelligence," with his primary duty being to "integrate human terrain research plan with unit intelligence collection plan" (Kipp et al. 2006:13)? According to the HTT *Handbook*,

> while HTT is not an intelligence asset, HTT feedback is incorporated into the S2's Intelligence Preparation of the Environment to ensure the commander is apprised of all relevant aspects of the operational environment.... [For example, HTT] Link Charts presenting any significant persons of influence who may be affected by the mission should be presented. These link charts should illustrate the relationship of the entity to the

mission and his/her position within society (including ties to key political figures, threat organizations, etc.). [Finney 2008:36–37]

So the mapper of human terrains is directly charged with identifying "significant persons of influence" in a mission area and their connections to "threat organizations."

The *Handbook* includes interview questions that obviously could elicit identification of adversaries of US forces:

> Security: Research the security situation. Ask everyone you talk to about the security situation and how it is compared to last year. Find out why it is better or worse than last year. Ask for examples. [Finney 2008:70]

And,

> Issues/friction points: Discover if there are prior or existing issues with the Coalition Forces, Local Army, Local Police, other tribes, within in [*sic*] the tribes, other villages, etc. Discover if there are past incidents with the Coalition for which the residents harbor any malcontent. [Finney 2008:71]

The *Handbook* does say, clearly, that HTT members are not to be involved in the process of deadly targeting:

> No Lethal Effects Targeting. The commander has an intelligence section for lethal targeting, what they require is a section that can explain and delineate the non-lethal environment (e.g. tribal relationships and local power structures), as well as the second and third order effects of planned lethal and non-lethal operations. [Finney 2008:82]

Is it conceivable that the commander's MI and staff will *not* make use of the mapping, network analysis, and other data gathered by HTTs in their efforts to identify targets? An experienced foreign area and intelligence officer (and vocal critic of HTS) calls the supposed separation of HTT data from intelligence "broadly inaccurate....Cultural information is inextricably linked to the intelligence process" (Connable 2009:59). "Reality is that combat intelligence staffs in both Afghanistan and Iraq have received some updated training and are aggressively collecting and analyzing cultural data" (Connable 2009:63). On this point, Lt. Col. Gian Gentile wrote to a supporter of the HTS:

Don't fool yourself. These Human Terrain Teams whether they want to acknowledge it or not...do at some point contribute to the collective knowledge of a commander which allows him to target and kill the enemy in the Civil War in Iraq. I commanded an Armored Reconnaissance Squadron in West Baghdad in 2006. Although I did not have one of these HTTs assigned to me (and I certainly would have liked to), I did have a Civil Affairs Team that was led by a major....I often used his knowledge to help me sort through who was the enemy and who was not and from that understanding that he contributed to I was able to target and sometimes kill the enemy. So stop sugarcoating what these teams do. [González 2009b:36]

Supporters of the HTS often note Colonel Schweitzer's estimate that in his second tour of duty HTTs helped reduce kinetic operations by 60 percent. Not noted is what Schweitzer says he would have done with an HTT on his *first* tour of duty, when he had not yet seen the light of culture: "I would've used it to have a better understanding of the population so I could eliminate them. You can do that with the HTT, but that doesn't win the fight" (Featherstone 2008:64). There it is in black and white—whether HTTs are used for lethal targeting depends on the intentions of the commander. The HTT *Handbook* backs up that conclusion. Teams are encouraged to develop their own plans for research, so they "are not waiting around for someone in the unit to ask us to do something that may be of an intelligence nature that compromises our ethical integrity and claim to being different from what already exists" (Finney 2008:56).

HTS advocates write as if sociocultural advising and data gathering are isolatable from violent military engagement. "HTTs work primarily with units whose function is explicitly non-lethal, such as medical personnel, Provincial Reconstruction Teams, Civil Affairs, etc. When they do work with maneuver units, HTTs improve the units' abilities to carry out non-lethal aspects of their roles" (Human Terrain System 2008b). This is an illusion. The HTT *Handbook* repeatedly emphasizes that the HTTs' work is to be fully integrated into a spectrum of command options. In its final appendix, "Commander Feedback," Col. Todd McCaffrey states: "In summary, the team has become an indispensable asset in helping me understand the complexities of tribal and political relationships and assess the potential results of a variety of lethal and non-lethal actions" (Finney 2008:119). Lethal and nonlethal, both.

Looking at the demand side, military writers are crystal clear that they want "ethnographic intelligence" and cooperative options as part of a unified approach that includes ready application of deadly force. For example, as pre-HTS commander in Iraq Morgan Mann (2007:106) writes:

> Understanding tribal organization and leadership is critical to success in rural Iraq....We must make every effort to understand an area's tribal alignment and disposition in order to focus the appropriate combat, economic, and political power needed to defeat the tribe or change its position regarding the coalition.... Just as we develop a combined obstacle overlay when analyzing terrain and enemy mechanized movement, we must develop an overlay to understand tribal influence in the AO [Area of Operations]. Overlays should display tribe names, boundaries, and dispositions, and indicate which tribes dominate in the AO. Once we understand the tribal relationships in our area, we can leverage our power in the tribal environment. We must collect names, tribal affiliations, photos, and home grid coordinates of all males in the area and meticulously record the information in appropriate computer databases.

Major Mann (2007:105) is clear that knowledge of the human terrain is key for *simultaneously* reducing violent clashes, building alliances, *and* effectively targeting the enemy:

> Because we demonstrated that we would use targeted violence whenever necessary, tribal attacks on Marines decreased and intelligence about the enemy increased. Soon we were able to broker truces with the formerly hostile tribes. Of course, the use of lethal force is not the only means of demonstrating power. There were benefits to cooperating with us or even just remaining neutral....The Caragoul tribal leadership recognized that coalition forces could and would take decisive action along a power continuum ranging from the use of deadly violence to economic and social incentives.

HTS anthropologists would not be directly involved in targeting attacks, but information they elicit, analyze, and present would be. The Human Intelligence teams that go out to identify targets will be aware of the HTT findings, even if they are prohibited from accessing individual identifications. Say a young man somehow comes to their attention.

Standard HTT research findings could tell them if he lives in X location, he must be a Y; as a member of Y, he will follow the directive of Sheikh Z; Sheikh Z has a blood debt against coalition forces because they killed his brother two years ago; Sheikh Z is a major political adversary of tribes allied with the coalition and has known connections to mullahs suspected of ties to insurrectionists; the individual in question would have few economic options and may need money as provided by insurgents to support his family. Would not all that cultural intelligence help to identify the young man as a likely enemy?

The ethical issues only get more complex. What if "the people we study" were expanded to include the military units within which anthropologists are embedded and with whose personnel they will expectably form close ties? Ethically, could an anthropologist *not* help identify adversaries who want to kill them? What if during a visit to a village a person whispers, "Those two, against the wall…they are just waiting for you to leave. They will kill anyone who works with you"? Does the anthropologist keep that to herself? The situation is impossible. Anthropologists face ethical dilemmas in many field situations, including whether or not to intervene in a situation to save a life. With HTTs this sort of quandary is built into the very nature of the job, and saving one life may imply taking another. Problems do not stop in the field.

Who Else Will Get Human Terrain Data?

Information gathered by HTTs is forwarded to Reachback Research Cells in the United States. A stated goal of the Reachback system is to enable the "sharing" of information gathered by HTTs.

> In addition to the capabilities the HTS offers to brigade commanders and other decision makers in given areas of operation, the data it compiles will be available for the training, modeling, and simulation communities to better support deploying forces in their mission rehearsal exercise scenario development. Other U.S. Government agencies will also have access to the central database. And finally, to facilitate economic development and security, the compiled databases will eventually be turned over to the new governments of Iraq and Afghanistan. [Kipp et al. 2006:14]

The "other U.S. Government agencies" that are intended to have access to HTS data are not specified, but surely include intelligence agencies. The

Defense Science Board Task Force, in its vision for a thoroughly culturized DoD, emphasizes centralization and availability of all sources of cultural information, including from the HTS (Defense Science Board 2009: xvii–xix).

Then what? One answer to "Human Terrain Data—What Should We Do With It?"—in an article of that name—is to use it to develop ever more sophisticated computer models (González 2008b:25; B. Silverman 2007). Commitment to this is on a scale similar to the HTS itself. DoD projections allocate $124 million dollars to "Human Social Culture Behavior Modeling" and other "social science modeling over the next six years" (Bhattacharjee 2007). This effort is to be integrated with high-tech gadgets for getting at the truth, such as "automated sentiment, intention, deception detection" and "geo-spatial dynamic network analysis and the combination of neuro-cognitive models and dynamic network analysis in the area of influence, attitudes, and beliefs" (Defense Science Board 2009:xvi).

In this military/intelligence fantasy, knowing eyes on the ground will track the smallest details, analyze, compare, try out practical applications, and pass results up to higher levels. There hypotheses will be tested, algorithms refined, and then sent back down for implementation by forces in the field. Doctrine will become an organic being, evolving to maximize US domination in areas of security interest by whatever approach works best. And what good is a fantasy of domination, unless it is *global* domination?

FUTURE EXTENSIONS

This DoD security vision looks beyond current conflict situations to mapping key information about local peoples in *potential* "trouble spots" all over the world. Plans to send HTTs to "the Pacific" and Africa are in process (MTC Technologies 2008). A reporter asked HTS program manager Steve Fondacaro if it was not already too late to send HTTs to Iraq and Afghanistan:

> [H]e was optimistic that his program would not only survive the outcome of these wars but thrive. There was no shortage of conflict in the world. Wars were brewing in Somalia, Nigeria, Indonesia, South America, the Philippines. "All these areas are getting ready to blow up, just like this, just like Iraq," Fondacaro said. In this world afire, Human Terrain Teams would be on the ground far ahead of military forces. Every hot spot would have a tailor-made HTT cell at its center, feeding a constant stream of analysis to policymakers and generals. "Here we have the military in the lead, in Afghanistan," Fondacaro said. "In

Mindanao, the social scientists would be in the lead."
[Featherstone 2008:68]

AFRICOM, the new unified military command for the continent, is the first non–war zone target for HTS advocates. A recent job posting from Archimedes Global Inc. looks to staff a "Socio-Cultural Cell" and a "Social Science Research Center" for AFRICOM, with more to follow. Gen. William Ward, head of AFRICOM, emphasized the importance of cultural anthropologists and recruited them himself at the UK Royal United Services Institute. They are not, however, advertising for "human terrain analysts," making a reporter wonder, "Is there some re-branding at work here? Or might the two projects work side-by-side" (Hodge 2009)?

The HTS will be only one part of the effort to "map human terrains" globally, and anthropology is only one of many disciplines that will be involved. "Social scientist" slots in HTTs can be filled by people from comparative religion, political science, sociology, psychology, regional studies, and so on. The current controversy over the American Geographical Society's Bowman Expedition, funded by DoD to map land use in the potential "trouble spot" of Oaxaca, suggests that the discipline of geography may face a greater quandary than anthropology (Herlihy et al. 2008; Mychalejko and Ryan 2009; Sedillo 2009). In the giant computational system of Pentagon fantasy, all social/behavioral data and theory will feed into one total, actionable understanding.

For a chilling look at Pentagon thinking along global lines, consider "Networks: Terra Incognita and the Case for Ethnographic Intelligence" (Renzi 2006a; see also Renzi 2006b). This is not proposed as an extension of the HTS—Renzi is notably vague about the means. The ends, however, are to maximize the Pentagon's panopticon of global indigenous surveillance.

> The proliferation of empowered networks makes "ethnographic intelligence" (EI) more important to the United States than ever before....I propose that we [look at] amassing EI, the type of intelligence that is key to setting policy for *terra incognita*....With the United States no longer facing a relatively simple, monolithic enemy, our national interests are found in a confusing cauldron of different locales and societies....Today, we have little insight into which cultures or networks may soon become threats to our national interests. For this reason, America must seek to understand and develop EI on a global scale, *before* it is surprised by another unknown or dimly understood society or network....

[A] low-key, constant interest in overt ethnographic matters would show that the United States cares and is indeed watching. Perhaps this constant attention would serve to subtly constrict the amount of safe-haven space available for dark networks. The overt information gathered by military ethnographers could complement the covert work done by the CIA (and vice versa)....Ethnographic intelligence can empower the daily fight against dark networks, and it can help formulate contingency plans that are based on a truly accurate portrayal of the most essential terrain—the human mind. United States policymakers must not commit us ever again to terra incognita. The Nation must invest in specialized people who can pay "constant attention" to "indigenous forms of association and mobilization," so that we can see and map the human terrain. [Renzi 2006a:16–22]

Will this global ethnographic surveillance enhance global targeting ability? John Wilcox, the assistant deputy undersecretary of defense, presented a PowerPoint slide at a meeting of the Precision Strike Winter Roundtable. This organization focuses on high-tech weapons systems to eliminate targets around the world at very short notice. The slide began with "Need to 'Map the Human Terrain Across the Kill Chain'—*Enables* the Entire Kill Chain for GWOT" (Wilcox 2007). GWOT, of course, is the Global War on Terror. The Kill Chain is a linked sequence of operations: Plan, Find, Fix, Track, Target, Engage, Assess. Montgomery McFate responded that Undersecretary Wilcox "is in no way connected with HTS" (González 2008b:22, 25; S. McFate 2008:27). That is the point. What HTS produces will be used by other people outside and above it.

Everything discussed in this chapter is about just one aspect of our coming security engagement. Anthropology will be a theoretically large, if numerically small, node in several dimensions of strategic planning and operations. The sort of ethnographic intelligence needed for counterinsurgency will be just as essential for stability operations (Center for Technology and National Security Policy 2008), civilian surges (Binnendijk and Cronin 2008; DeYoung 2009; Jelinek 2009), or a new foreign combat advisor corps (Nagl 2007), just as anthropology will be key for the multidisciplinary strategic research community to be created by the Minerva program of social science funding. "Culture" is pivotal in the Pentagon's grand strategy for the future (United States Joint Forces Command 2008: 46–50). This broader engagement will be the subject of a subsequent paper (Ferguson forthcoming).

HTS AND THE FUTURE OF SECURITY ENGAGEMENT

As anthropological engagement with security organizations and agencies broadens and deepens, the ethical, political, and personal challenges to anthropologists will become more and more complex. The question of participation in the Human Terrain System is valuable because now, early on in the process of engagement, we can consider basic issues in a fairly discrete and defined way. This chapter has compiled the available evidence to address the polarized claims from both sides of the controversy. Do Human Terrain Teams provide guidance that leads to a reduction of kinetic activities by US forces in Iraq and Afghanistan, and so save lives? Do Human Terrain Teams provide information that can by used by US forces to target adversaries for kinetic actions?

Two years after the publicized claim that the first Afghanistan HTT reduced kinetics by 60 percent, that claim has not been substantiated or replicated. Nor has any other credible evidence appeared showing how social science input helped to avoid violence. On the other hand, evidence that HTT information can be used for kinetic targeting is abundant and consistent. Data collected by HTTs will be fully integrated into tactical planning at all levels. It may be used to develop cooperative strategies to win hearts and minds, but it can also be used in deciding who needs to be taken out. To repeat the HTS mission statement, its goal is "to provide commanders in the field with relevant socio-cultural understanding necessary to meet their operational requirements." This is a package deal. I sympathize with HTS advocates who want to improve respect and communication between sides, to make US forces more responsive to local needs and perceptions, and to develop cooperation and alliance in place of combat. But whatever their intentions, HTS members will not decide how their findings will be utilized. If anthropologists provide information to employers who may use the information to kill, that crosses our ethical line in the sand.

Beyond ethics, there are the larger political issues that start with HTS field operations but go far beyond that. As planned, the information gathered will go freely to other US government agencies, and at some time in the future, to local governments, to use however they deem fit. In the future—starting now—the Pentagon vision is for ethnographic intelligence to be processed globally against potential unconventional "threats to U.S. security." Advocates of the HTS claim that all over the world, anthropology can help the US military exert control over local populations with less killing and destruction. The appeal of that vision is in less killing. The danger is that it comes with more effective control by the US military.

An anthropologized Department of Defense might well mean less blundering around, less shooting and bombing. A well-run imperium always finds ways to reduce the bloodshed. Increased power means decreased use of force. If HTS works as its proponents say it does, it could be an important tool in strengthening US hegemony. However chimerical the vision of global ethnographic surveillance may be, the capacity the HTS is helping to build cannot be seen as being in the interests of the indigenous peoples of the world—the people to whom anthropology is most responsible—unless their interests coincide with incorporation into a neoliberal US empire.

Note

1. After completing this chapter, I read two new books focused on HTS and related topics, *American Counterinsurgency* (Gonzalez 2009a) and *The Counter-Counterinsurgeny Manual* (Network of Concerned Anthropologists 2009). Points that I make here overlap considerably with those writings, and interested readers should consult both for additional information and ideas.

6

Military Ethnography and Embedded Journalism

Parallels and Intersections

Anne Irwin

The setting is a harvested wheat field in the Panjwaii District of Kandahar Province, Afghanistan, in July 2006. The field is filled with armored vehicles and soldiers because it has been transformed into a company echelon, a support area for an infantry company engaged in a battle about 400 meters away. The occasional piece of shrapnel skips along the dusty ground and we can hear small arms fire close by. The radio operator and I sit on the ramp of a Light Armored Vehicle (LAV). Each of us is wearing a radio headset, and we are listening anxiously to the radio traffic. The radio operator is monitoring and logging several different conversations at once, and I am listening for the voices of the members of Eight Platoon, the platoon I have been studying, and trying to catch up on my field notes.

Although the voices are distorted by the radio and by the panting brought on by exertion and heat in the mid-60s °C, we hear of two gunmen on a roof. They have good firing positions and are holding up the entire platoon. Someone who does not identify himself broadcasts "Boneca's down," a clear breach of radio protocol: casualties are not supposed to be identified by name, but by "zap number," the unique identification number assigned to each soldier, and every transmission should be preceded by the call sign of the transmitter. Those of us listening to the radio know that these protocols are deeply ingrained in every radio operator and infantry soldier; to have contravened them testifies to the exhaustion and stress through which the soldiers are operating.

Minutes later, a casualty report comes through. This time it is preceded by the appropriate call sign, and the casualty is labeled priority one, meaning life threatening and urgent. At this point we are not sure if this priority one casualty is Tony Boneca, whom we both know, or another soldier. We listen tensely as the battle with the gunmen continues and the helicopter medical evacuation is arranged. Another breach of protocol occurs when someone broadcasts that the casualty has been downgraded to priority four with VSA, or vital signs absent. Still not certain whether the casualty is Corporal Boneca or, indeed, whether the casualty is dead or alive, we continue to wait anxiously.

Eventually an armored ambulance pulls in and stops at the edge of the field. When the ramp is lowered, one of the medics pulls out a folding metal chair and sets it up on a bank in the shade of some fig trees. A civilian woman, whom I recognize as journalist Christie Blatchford, climbs out and sits in the chair. She appears to be in shock, although there are no obvious physical wounds. The medics then help three members of Eight Platoon dismount; they are all suffering from what the military calls heat wounds, and one of them is limping badly. It turns out that he has a broken leg, which he sustained while throwing a hand grenade. The three soldiers sit on the bank, and the medic inserts IVs to replenish their fluids.

Two of these soldiers are men whom I know very well, having spent much of the previous month in their LAV, so I run over to see them. One of the soldiers, John,[1] who had been Tony Boneca's best friend, looks at me and says, "I hope he's satisfied now." I take the "he" to be a reference to the unit's commanding officer about whom the soldiers have been complaining for weeks. They had constantly expressed the belief that he was taking unnecessary risks with their lives in order to further his own career. John confirms that the casualty is indeed Tony Boneca, and that he is dead. I had still been entertaining hopes that somehow it was all a terrible mistake, that he was still alive and that the "VSA" report had been transmitted in error. I sit with John for what seems like hours. He does not speak another word but stares off into space. I want to offer comfort but do not know how or what to say, so we sit in silence.

Finally, the other soldier, Frank, begins to speak. With a tear trickling down his cheek he tells me that they had been unable to kill one of the men on the roof, that he seemed to be a well-trained soldier who knew how to take up a perfect firing position. He says, "We just couldn't kill him." He begins to feel dizzy and nauseated, so the medic and I help him back into the ambulance, where the medic places an oxygen mask over his face. Frank asks me to take a picture of him in the back of the ambulance with the oxygen mask on for his wife who has been compiling a photo album of the tour.

After about an hour the ambulance crew announce that they are taking the three casualties back to Kandahar Airfield (KAF) for medical treatment in the hospital, and they ask Christie Blatchford, who has been sitting quietly in shade, if she wants to go with them. She replies, "Yes, I've got my story and have to write and file it." (When I met up with her later in the month, she told me that as soon as she had arrived at KAF she had written and filed the story that appeared the next morning [Blatchford 2006]. The story of Tony's death is one of the "fifteen days" covered in the book of the same name that was published a year later [Blatchford 2007].)

Those of us remaining in the leaguer[2] spent the rest of that day and night and the next day monitoring the battle over the radio. The gunman on the roof was finally wounded and captured, and the soldiers who escorted him, blindfolded and hands bound, back to the leaguer told me the story of how Tony had died. There was no time to mourn for him, however, because as soon as the battle for Panjwaii was over, the unit was sent on another series of operations. It was weeks before the members of Eight Platoon and I had a break in a forward operating base (FOB) with Internet access and had an opportunity to read the newspaper account of Tony's death (Blatchford 2006). The members of his platoon were dismayed by the graphic tone of the story: "He was ashen with the plug of an airway tube showing in his mouth....Past the clusters of small green grapes and the sunflowers...on the same worn paths Cpl Boneca had walked as a strong 21-year-old, his blood now dripped" (Blatchford 2006:1). They were concerned that his parents would needlessly read the details of how he had died, and they felt that the journalist had exploited his death to make a good story for the newspaper.

The intersection of my path with Christie Blatchford's and the reaction of the soldiers to her story caused a great deal of soul-searching on my part. During the course of my research in Afghanistan and for several years after my return, I sympathized with the soldiers' perspective and felt that much of the media coverage of the Canadian military's role in Afghanistan was exploitative and even sensationalistic. During the research and afterward I struggled to understand how my work differed from that of the journalists covering the war. Yet in deciding to begin this chapter with an account of Tony Boneca's death, I fear that I am guilty myself of exploiting his death in the interest of a good story.

The struggle I have been engaged in to understand the parallels and intersections between an ethnography of a military unit engaged in war and the practice of embedded journalism has been the inspiration for this chapter. While this is not a systemic analysis of military-media relations nor a critique of embedded journalism, I do explore the similarities and the differences in our attempts to represent the lived experience of soldiers in war. I begin my exploration by examining in detail the path by which I ended up in a wheat field in Panjwaii, sitting with a wounded and grieving soldier.

ACCESS AND EARLY RESEARCH

I was still an undergraduate student when I first considered the possibility of doing anthropological research with a Canadian military unit. I was interested in studying the military because before attending university I had served as an officer in the Canadian Forces (CF) reserve for fifteen years. During that period I had served in a number of different capacities, including administration, training, and commanding a military police platoon, but I had never been deployed overseas. As I took different undergraduate courses in anthropology I was frequently struck by how applicable many of the concepts I was learning were to the military and by the lack of interest in the military as an important social institution. When I proposed to do a master's degree focusing on the anthropology of an infantry unit, most of my professors suggested that while an ethnography of the Canadian military might be interesting, it would likely be impossible to gain access.

In fact, access was surprisingly easy to obtain with the assistance and intercession of a senior officer for whom I had once worked. I ended up conducting two periods of ethnographic fieldwork with the same unit, the first battalion of the Princess Patricia's Canadian Light Infantry (PPCLI), leading to a master's degree, a PhD in anthropology, and a tenure-track appointment (Irwin 1993, 2002). Both periods of research were conducted entirely in Canada. At that time, the mid-1990s, the Canadian Forces had not been deployed in a combat role since the Korean War and were primarily employed on UN-sponsored peacekeeping missions.

RESEARCH IN AFGHANISTAN

I first began to consider the possibility of doing anthropological fieldwork with deployed troops in November 2005 when then-Brigadier General Grant gave a briefing to the Centre for Military and Strategic Studies at the University of Calgary. After the presentation, during which he talked about the PPCLI's upcoming mission from February to August 2006 in

Afghanistan, he told the audience of academics that he was inviting "stake-holders" to volunteer for short visits to the theater of operations to get a firsthand look at the way the mission was operating. I approached him and suggested that I would like to go, not for a short visit but for a longer period of participant observation, beginning as soon as the university term was over in April and ending when the troops returned to Canada at the end of their tour in August. To my surprise, he was cautiously optimistic about the feasibility of my research and asked me to send him a formal pro-posal. After I had done that he forwarded my proposal to his superiors, all of whom responded positively, due in part, I believe, to two factors: my pre-vious research with the same battalion and my former military service. My MA and PhD theses had been well received by the military, and it is possi-ble that because of my prior military service I was perceived as a "friendly" researcher.

After receiving approval from the senior leadership of the Canadian Forces at the vice chief of the defense staff level, I submitted my proposal to both the CF/Department of National Defence Research Review Board for a technical and ethical review and to the University of Calgary Conjoint Faculties Ethics Review Board for an ethical review. After some negotiation and amendments my research was approved by both bodies and I pro-ceeded with other administrative details, including applying for and being granted a University of Calgary research grant. I was also required to sub-mit to a risk assessment by the university's risk management staff. On the advice of risk management I made arrangements for the appropriate vac-cinations, and all that remained was the logistical challenge of getting to Afghanistan.

In discussions with Brigadier General Grant and his staff I had deter-mined that a short pilot project would be both useful and appropriate, so I arranged for an absence from campus for two weeks in March and was flown, at the expense of the Canadian Forces, to Afghanistan by civilian commercial airline as far as the CF support base in the United Arab Emirates. There I was issued field equipment, including personal protec-tive equipment and a uniform without any badges of rank, before flying into Kandahar Airfield on a CF transport plane.

During this pilot project I encountered a number of soldiers whom I had known in 1992 and in 1995–1996 during my previous fieldwork with the battalion. They welcomed me warmly, and I spent about a week with them outside the wire, that is, outside of the protective confines of KAF. Without exception they expressed enthusiasm for my research and suggested that I was uniquely situated to be able to do the work. They identified my earlier research as the relevant factor, not my military service, which had not included war service. This positive response to my presence in the field and to my research convinced me of the feasibility and importance of conducting a longer term of research, so in May I returned.

This time I asked to travel to the theater by military aircraft with a resupply flight, and this request was approved. Consequently, I flew, again at military expense, by civilian air to Trenton, Ontario, where I boarded a military aircraft along with a number of military personnel. Some of these military personnel were returning to Afghanistan after their leave, and some were technical staff flying in for short terms of duty.

Once again, upon arrival at the Canadian support base, I was issued with the necessary equipment and boarded a military flight for KAF. Throughout my travel my expenses were paid for by the Canadian Forces, and I had a VIP tag attached to my luggage. My travel documents were signed personally by the vice chief of the defense staff, and the clerk who had made all the arrangements for me had told me that if any members of the military were less than helpful, all I had to do was show them my travel documents and they would do the utmost to assist me because of the high level at which my trip had been approved.

At no point was I required to sign any agreement or release about restrictions to what I might write. I was not asked to rejoin the reserves, nor was I asked to release the Canadian Forces from responsibility for my safety. Because of my knowledge of the National Defence Act, I knew myself to be subject to the Code of Service Discipline under the provisions governing civilians "accompanying the Forces," but no one at any time pointed this out to me. All this lack of concern over the legalities and risks involved in my research now strikes me as extraordinarily naïve and trusting on the part of both the military staff and myself. We made no arrangements for any action to be taken if I was injured, taken ill, kidnapped, or killed, other than having me complete a next of kin notification form, just as soldiers do.

There are a number of explanations for this lack of concern over what I might write and about liability and my safety. My military experience would have suggested to them that I would be aware of the provisions of the Official Secrets Act and the Code of Service Discipline, both of which I would be subject to during my research. With respect to liability and my safety, the negotiations were under way before there had been significant numbers of Canadian casualties, and no one was yet calling the operation a war. I suspect, however, that the primary reason for the lack of concern was a much more bureaucratic one: the staff officers I was dealing with were very busy, with far more important things to worry about, and to inquire carefully into issues of liability and risk would have increased their workload significantly. It was easier simply to hope for the best.

So that was what was entailed in getting to the field site, or at least to the coalition base at KAF. Once there, I still had to arrange access to the unit that was of interest to me, Task Force Orion, the battle group largely composed of members of PPCLI. The commanding officer of the task force, Lieutenant Colonel Hope, was expecting me because of the my pilot study in March. However, the unit was outside the wire when I arrived in KAF, so I spent several days waiting at the base until I heard that the unit had returned for two days of rest, refit, and replenishment.

The adjutant of the unit assigned me to Charlie Company, and I met the company commander, who suggested that I should spend the entire tour with Eight Platoon and told me to pack and be ready to leave the next morning. At the designated time I dragged my gear over to the vehicle compound, where I met the acting platoon commander whose regular platoon commander was on leave. I introduced myself to the members of the platoon after the company commander had issued his convoy movement orders, and then I climbed into the Eight Platoon headquarters LAV along with the platoon signaler and the other members of the vehicle crew.

Except for the period described in the opening of this chapter, I spent the remaining period of the tour, all of June and July, and most of August, with Eight Platoon. The great majority of this time was spent outside the wire in FOBs and on the move. Occasionally, we would come back to KAF for a few days of rest and refit, but we routinely spent weeks without returning to camp.

CANADIAN MILITARY-MEDIA RELATIONS AND JOURNALISTIC ACCESS

Journalists wishing to cover CF operations in Afghanistan also must go through a lengthy procedure, but it is quite different from and administered under a separate set of rules than those applying to academic research. And any understanding of journalistic access to the Canadian military must be informed by the particular context of civil-military and military-media relations in Canada. To begin with, the military in Canada is not the hegemonic force it is in the United States. Numbering only 64,000 regular force members and 36,700 reserve force members, the military in Canada represents only 0.39 percent of the Canadian population. The total defense budget is only Canadian $17.8 billion (MacNamara and Adams 2008).

Until Canada's deployment to Afghanistan the Canadian news media largely ignored the Canadian Forces unless they were reporting on some scandal or controversy. The torture and murder of a young Somali man by Canadian soldiers deployed on a peacekeeping mission during the 1990s was given a high profile by the media, as was the subsequent government inquiry (Bercuson 1996). For the most part, however, the news media in Canada, and the Canadian public in general, were largely ignorant of the inner workings of the Canadian Forces (Hobson 2007). In many ways, during the cold war and even after the fall of the Berlin Wall, the Canadian Forces was thought of by the Canadian public as largely irrelevant, despite the role the forces played in UN peacekeeping missions all over the world. This was also true in the academic world, except for the very small minority of scholars engaged in military history and strategic studies.

During the 1980s and especially after the Somalia tragedy, military-media relations can be described as marked by mutual distrust. Military officers perceived the media as the enemy and did not welcome what little attention was paid to the military. In turn, the media seemed to assume that senior officers were constantly involved in covering up scandals. Very few media personnel specialized in covering the military, and even fewer had any kind of military experience; consequently, there was very little expert knowledge of the military within the ranks of the media.

The Canadian government's decision to deploy a task force of the Canadian Forces to Afghanistan as part of the NATO mission Operation Enduring Freedom raised tremendous controversy, and it also raised the profile of the Canadian Forces. The news media developed a newfound interest in military matters and in soldiers and soldiering. The fact that Canadian soldiers were routinely taking on combat roles for the first time since the Korean War captured the popular imagination, as have the deaths of more than 130 Canadian soldiers (to date). The media's new interest in things military required a change in approach by the military, and thus the policy of embedding journalists was instituted. The process of gaining access for journalists is in some ways more difficult than for academics and in others easier, in part because there is a systematic process, rather than having all parties rely on an ad hoc procedure. Embedding journalists in the military during operations is now a well-established institution with dedicated staff, Public Affairs Officers (PAFFOs), managing the relationship. The policy regulating journalists and reporters accompanying the forces in an operational theater is subject to instructions issued by the commander of the Canadian Expeditionary Force Command (Canadian Expeditionary Force Commander 2007).

Journalists wishing to embed themselves with a military unit must be, first of all, accredited journalists, preferably with a recognized media outlet, although there is some provision for embedding freelancers. At any one time no more than sixteen journalists are embedded with the Canadian Forces in Afghanistan, and priority is given to Canadian national media, such as the Canadian Press and national newspapers and television stations. Before being accepted as embedded journalists, members of the media are required to sign an "embed agreement" specifying the parameters of their relationship with the military. The agreement covers all aspects of the relationship, including what resources will be supplied by the partners to the agreement, what restrictions will be placed on the activities of embedded journalists, and what action will be taken in the event that journalists are injured or killed while going about their duties. The agreement clearly specifies that journalists accompanying the Canadian Forces are subject to the Code of Service Discipline.

According to the embed agreement, the media outlets employing embedded journalists are responsible for their travel arrangements to KAF. Most journalists fly into Kabul by civilian air and travel to KAF with the aid of local Afghan "fixers." Once they arrive at KAF, their accommodation and rations are supplied by the Canadian Forces. KAF has a media compound set aside for them, including air-conditioned tents and satellite links back to Canada. Members of the media wear civilian clothing and must display their accreditation and identification at all times. During one of my sojourns at KAF I went over to the media compound and attempted to arrange to interview members of the media. None of those present would consent to participate in the form of giving me an interview: they wanted to interview me instead.

Members of the media who stay at KAF have regular access to media briefings and press conferences by commanders and military spokespersons. They do not have regular access to off-duty soldiers and are warned in their instructions not to invade soldiers' privacy during their personal time. Because of complaints from soldiers about invasion of privacy, members of them are not permitted in the tent lines where soldiers are accommodated, nor are they welcome to set up cameras or other recording devices in Canada House, the canteen where soldiers relax.

For those members of the media who wish to venture outside the wire and embed themselves with an operational unit, the competition is intense. The process of embedding journalists for sorties outside of KAF begins with the operational commander deciding that there is room in a vehicle or vehicles for one or more embedded journalists. The fact that there is space available is passed on by the PAFFO to those members of the media who have expressed an interest in participating. It is also the PAFFO who is responsible for choosing who among them will be permitted to accompany the unit. It appears that the decision as to who will be chosen is made on an ad hoc basis and depends to a large degree on the relationship between individual members of the media and the PAFFO.

Members of the media who accompany operational units outside the wire are responsible for providing their own protective gear (body armor, helmet, and so forth), sleeping bag, and other equipment, including communications equipment. They are required to stay with the unit to which they have been assigned, and they may not venture into the countryside on their own or else they lose the benefit of the protection afforded by the military. According to the embed agreement, the only restrictions placed on what they may report are those based on operational requirements; they are not permitted to report on upcoming operations or, in the event of fatal casualties, the fact that there has been a death until the next of kin of the dead soldier have been notified.

CROSSING PATHS WITH THE MEDIA

During my research in Afghanistan I crossed paths with a number of media personnel—in the cafeteria line at the mess tent at KAF, at media briefings after engagements, and in FOBs. I even met several reporters and television journalists in the media tent when I went by to try to interview a few of them. As noted above, they all refused formal interviews, but one of them ended up interviewing me instead (Cotter 2006). Journalists were not the focus of my ethnographic research, and so I was not too disappointed not to be able to interview these potential subjects. Moreover, my ethics clearance from the University of Calgary's ethics committee only applied to members of the military, not journalists. Consequently, what my field notes cover is not the practice of embedded journalism so much as soldiers' responses to the presence of journalists.

Soldiers' reactions to the presence of journalists or reporters were generally negative and unwelcoming. They constantly recounted tales (most of them probably exaggerated or entirely fictitious) about the tricks that members of the media resorted to in order to obtain a good story. One of these tales was an account of how a television film crew that had been embedded with the unit before my arrival in the country had pulled away to a distance to film a long shot of the section of soldiers. One of the soldiers supposedly discovered that the reporter had left a digital voice recorder hidden and running on the ramp. In response the soldiers filled their discourse with expletives so that the recording would be unusable in any news broadcast.

When soldiers whom I knew well introduced me to visiting or incoming soldiers, they would precede their introduction with a comment to the effect that I was "OK" because I was "not media." Yet despite the negativity toward media personnel in general, some reporters and journalists, particularly those who spent longer periods with the same unit, came to be accepted. Some soldiers developed personal friendships with these journalists, but they were always considered exceptional, and the positive attitude toward individual journalists was never extended to the media in general.

THE PROJECTS OF EMBEDDED JOURNALISM AND MILITARY ETHNOGRAPHY

I first realized that an embedded journalist had been assigned to Charlie Company on the evening of July 7 in the vehicle compound of Task Force Orion at KAF as the company vehicles were being marshaled for a road move to Panjwaii District. It was dark and there was a lot of purposeful activity going on, but I heard a woman's voice say, "I'm supposed to be going with Major Fletcher." I learned later from one of the company headquarters soldiers that she was Christie Blatchford, a well-known Canadian columnist with the daily national broadsheet newspaper the *Globe and Mail*. Because we were busy loading vehicles and getting ready to leave, and I had been assigned to one of the platoon vehicles, I was not able to meet her at that moment. The next time I saw her was after Tony Boneca's death, as I recounted in the introduction to this chapter.

By July 7 I had been with the company for more than a month and had spent most of my time with either the headquarters of Eight Platoon or with one of the sections of the platoon, depending on which LAV had room for me. There had been a number of personnel and vehicle casualties, so the platoon warrant officer had been constantly reassigning troops to correct the balance of troops to vehicles. I had become one more body to move around. On July 2 the platoon had been sent to a FOB near Spin Boldak on the Pakistan border with the task of taking up a static location in the base and sending out regular security patrols. The troops had been anticipating with pleasure what would have been a break in combat activity after weeks of mobile patrols, ambushes, and firefights. But to everyone's dismay, on July 4 there was a change of plans and Eight Platoon, along with the company headquarters, was sent back to KAF to prepare for a major combat operation in Panjwaii District, an area where they had sustained several casualties in previous operations. The terrain in Panjwaii was difficult, full of grape fields and grape-drying huts where the enemy was known to shelter and from which they routinely sprang ambushes.

The morning of July 5, before leaving Spin Boldak for KAF, the platoon warrant officer took me aside and told me that I would not be going with the platoon. He said that the official reason given by the company commander was that there was not enough room for me with the platoon, since they had received a replacement soldier for someone who had been wounded, but that they were also concerned about risk and liability. I was not clear, nor was he, whether the company commander was referring to the possibility that my presence during the operation would represent a liability in the sense of adding to the risk for soldiers, or whether he was concerned about the military's liability for my safety. He told me I would stay in Spin Boldak with Seven Platoon, which was staying behind to secure the FOB. Later in the evening, however, he came and told me that if I still wanted to go on the operation, I would be permitted, but that I would have to travel with one of the company headquarters vehicles, which would be employed in a support role rather than being engaged in any fighting. I agreed to the conditions of my participation and traveled back to KAF in the LAV captain's vehicle.[3]

July 5 was spent loading ammunition and other supplies and going over plans. A number of the soldiers confided that they were so frightened of going back to Panjwaii that they were unable to eat, and several of them told me that they had been vomiting due to anxiety. A few soldiers gave me messages to pass on to their wives or parents in the event of their deaths. A sergeant confided in me about a prophetic dream of his own death in combat that he had had since childhood. He was convinced that his death would occur in Panjwaii in the turret of a LAV.[4]

Before leaving Canada each soldier had had his or her picture taken in a classic combat pose by a CF photographer to be used in news releases. Soldiers referred to these photos as their "death pictures." One soldier who had been sick on the day the photos were taken joked that the lack of a death picture guaranteed survival of the tour. Another soldier asked me to ensure that if he was killed during the upcoming operation, the PAFFOs would not use his official "combat photo" in the death notice, but one of the photos I had taken of him smiling with his section. Although I knew that I would have limited, if any, influence, I told him I would do my best to see that his wishes were met.

As pointed out by Mark Peterson (2003:8), the goal of ethnography is to capture the richness of the complexity of everyday life. The ethnographic endeavor is also explicitly situated in a particular theoretical tradition and seeks to contribute in some way to theoretical issues of interest to anthropologists. In my case I was interested in how soldiers constitute their

identities qua soldiers through their everyday practices and in their negotiations with the military institution of which they are a part. For this reason, all these interactions made their way into my field journal, as they were
germane to my research agenda. The goal of my research was to understand the social dynamics of the unit. Since I had studied the same unit in
the context of a peacetime army training for war, I now wanted to examine
how those dynamics and relationships changed in the context of combat.
My desire to immerse myself as fully as possible in the life of the unit was
predicated on the need to observe as much as possible the full range of
activities in which the study group was engaged. The goal of ethnography,
then, is not simply description, but description with a theoretical question
in mind, grounded in the tradition of scholarship. Good ethnography is
based on accurate and detailed reporting of events and circumstances,
but it is more than that. Ethnography, as I understand it as the primary
research method of social anthropology, must search for underlying patterns of behavior.

News writers, in contrast, according to Allan Bell (1991:162–163), are
engaged in a process of systematic and progressive simplification.
Embedded journalists are there to report on events as they occur; their
understanding of social relations within the military unit is incidental to
their primary goal. Understanding how social relations work in the unit
certainly adds context to their reporting of events; at the very least, understanding the society in which they are embedded makes it easier for them
to do their job. If they understand social relations and social norms, they
can better manage their relations with soldiers and add nuance to their
reporting. So, whereas my deep immersion with the unit was predicated on
the theoretical questions I was attempting to answer, journalists were
embedded at least in part to be closer to the action, to be available to
report on events as they unfolded.

Janet Cramer and Michael McDevitt (2004:132), in arguing for journalists to adopt ethnographic methods, suggest that "ethnographic reporting challenges journalists' understanding of objectivity, neutrality, and
balance." They go on to argue that journalistic objectivity is not a singular
notion but is more complex than the way it is understood in the popular
imagination. They suggest that an emphasis on neutrality, balance, accuracy, and fairness is more appropriate than a slavish adherence to objectivity (Cramer and McDevitt 2004:132). They also argue that ethnographic
reporting has an advantage in portraying "in a responsible manner the lives
and cultures of groups that are typically marginalized through mainstream journalism practices" (2004:132). Embedded journalism at its best

approaches the agenda of a social anthropology of the military. I am thinking of, for example, the work of Sebastian Junger (2010). His book *War* both
captures accurately and illuminates clearly the social relationships among
soldiers engaged in warfare and the lived experience of those soldiers.
Indeed, Dominic Boyer and Ulf Hannerz (2006:10) have argued for a willingness on the part of anthropologists and sociologists to recognize the parallels and similarities between investigative journalism and ethnography.

While the projects of journalism and ethnography may have many similarities and parallels, particularly in terms of the practices of research, the
strategies through which journalists and anthropologists establish their
respective authority are quite different.

JOURNALISTIC AND ETHNOGRAPHIC AUTHORITY

Hannerz (1996:113) points out that both journalists and anthropologists deal with the "other" and must establish their accounts as authoritative. In the case of embedded journalists and ethnographers of the military,
the "others" we are representing are soldiers, and we both use our sustained presence with them as a means to establish our authority to speak
and write knowledgably about them (Hannerz 1998:559). For the embedded journalist, her presence is key to "getting the story," because, as Bell
(1991:147) argues, for the journalist, the story is everything. What constitutes a story is extremely limited, but the journalistic authority to tell the
story comes from proximity in space and time. Proximity in space confers
the authority to tell the story, whereas proximity in time confers the authority to tell a *news* story. For the journalist, then, who is competing with other
journalists for the scoop, time is of the essence, and the story must be told
in a timely fashion (Bell 1991).

The anthropologist must also establish her authority, which also comes
from proximity, but what is of concern is not necessarily the events that constitute the story, but the reactions of persons to events, and authority comes
from the length of the stay and from having come home again, from the
reflection that is possible and the analysis that is enabled by distance from
the field. The orientation to time, then, is quite different. Although the pressure to publish is strong in the academic world, there is less of a sense that
research must be timely or newsworthy. It is quite common for anthropologists to take years to publish (a time delay that is exacerbated by the
peer review process). Moreover, many anthropologists mine their field notes
over and over, drawing different insights and theoretical understandings
from the same material. In that sense, the anthropological endeavor is
never fully complete. Had there been no battle or death to record on July

9, my research would not have been impoverished. I would have had as much material to analyze and the data would have shed just as much light on military social relationships and identity formation had there been no firefight or death of a comrade.

This, of course, begs the question of what constitutes "an event." An event is not an a priori category; it does not exist in the real world, separate from our interpretations of it. An event must be constituted by participants and observers as an event. For the journalist, according to Blatchford (personal communication, August 5, 2007), exciting incidents such as deaths and casualties are the events that make up a good story. This is not to suggest that some journalists are not interested in the quotidian and the mundane (Hannerz 1998:571). There is indeed a genre of journalism that seeks to represent the lived experience of certain persons, and this genre of journalism does approach ethnography. However, writing this genre of journalism is an accountable matter and must be somehow explained, excused, and formulated as something of interest beyond the reporting of events. This style of journalism can be framed as "human interest" or as a "feature article" (Hannerz 1998:571). While some embedded journalists did indeed write about the lived experience of combat soldiers, there was much pressure on them to produce an exciting story, an account of an event (Blatchford, personal communication April 20, 2008).

ETHICS

Both military anthropologists and journalists must consider the ethical dimensions of their work, but again there are significant differences in their approaches to ethical concerns. After our return to Canada I interviewed Christie Blatchford and asked her if she had ever had any ethical concerns about her work, prefacing my question with the comment that I struggled daily with ethical issues. Her response was that she had never had a single ethical problem, although other journalists had questioned her ethical stance. It became clear very quickly that we had different assumptions about what constituted ethical work for our professions. In the ensuing discussion Christie made it clear that for her and other journalists, the paramount ethical principle was not to be biased but to report the facts of the story as accurately as possible. She had assumed that I was referring to the accusations that some have made that embedded journalists have been co-opted by the military establishment and that their objectivity is therefore compromised (Cottle 2006:94), as there have certainly been numerous criticisms of the ethics of embedded journalism, both in Canada and the United States (see, for example, Bergen 2009; Tuosto 2008).

ANNE IRWIN

I asked Christie about her reporting of Boneca's death, and she expressed the opinion that her story was important because it communicated to the Canadian public the realities of what their soldiers were experiencing in Afghanistan. She did not feel she had exploited his death in any way, and, regrettably, I did not describe to her the soldiers' responses to her story. And, indeed, that immediate response has been tempered in the years since his death. In fact, her book *Fifteen Days* (2007) was received quite positively by most members of the unit.

The ethical dilemmas that troubled me, however, were not related to objectivity, but to whether my presence as a researcher was in any way adding to the risk to the soldiers who were sharing their lives with me. There were a number of occasions when the possibility of having to protect me would have added significant hardship, and I worried about this. Another ethical concern I had was a result of the media presence in Afghanistan. I had promised to strive for anonymity for my informants, but since many of them had been identified by rank and name in news stories, it is much more difficult than it would otherwise be to achieve an adequate level of protection of their privacy. Although journalists can and do protect their informants, some going as far as being incarcerated to do so, protection of privacy is not one of their primary ethical principles. Authoritative journalistic accounts for the most part must include reference to individuals and to their stories. Cramer and McDevitt (2004) address this problem and suggest that confidentiality is even more of a challenge for the ethnographic journalist because of the greater readership of journalism than of academic research. For the anthropologist, the personal identity of participants in the research is less important than the patterns of observed behavior, and there is a long tradition in anthropology of disguising and otherwise hiding individual identities.

OTHER PLAYERS

Anthropologists and journalists are not the only civilians accompanying military forces in the theater of war: support workers on base, including the civilian employees of the CF Personnel Support Agency, run the canteen, administer fitness and recreation programs, and organize leave travel; civilian physicians and nurses on temporary contract augment the overstretched ranks of military medical personnel. These civilians are there, for the most part, in support of the mission, not as witnesses, although a civilian Canadian physician did publish a graphic account of the dying moments of a soldier who had been shot (Patterson 2007). And others, besides anthropologists and journalists, *are* there as witnesses. I

142

encountered one historian during my period of research and another spent several weeks conducting research with the rotation the year following my research.

The Canadian Forces also has a thriving War Artists' Program that enables graphic artists to accompany combat forces and produce graphic documentation of the experience of war. Recently the program has been expanded, and the first poet has been chosen as a war artist. Suzanne Steele briefly accompanied the unit I studied on their next tour with a view to producing poetry as witness to the experience of war (www.warpoet.ca).

Soldiers themselves are documenting the war through blogs, memoirs, and letters included in compilations (Brown and Lutz 2007; Keren 2005; Patterson and Warren 2007; Pengelly and Irwin 2010; Sanders 2006).

I began writing this chapter while I was struggling with defining my role in opposition to the role of the embedded journalist, and I initially emphasized the differences in the projects of ethnography and of journalism. I was inclined in my first draft to represent journalists as competitors and as adversaries (Boyer and Hannerz 2006:9–10). Indeed, there are differences in our goals, in our orientation to time and space, and in our primary ethical obligations. But these differences are more a question of emphasis. Whereas anthropologists are more interested in the patterning of social behavior and in the cultural factors in which the experience of war emerges, journalists are more interested in newsworthy events. Anthropologists are more interested in developing social theory than in mere description of events and circumstances. Having said that, I have always leaned more toward accurate ethnographic description in my practice than toward abstract theorizing. Certainly, the orientation to time and space is different for anthropologists and for journalists. The anthropologist has the luxury of taking the time for reflection and analysis and has the advantage and the responsibility to revisit material in response to theoretical developments. There is much less emphasis in ethnography on objectivity, and, in fact, some would argue that since the goal of ethnography is to "grasp the native's point of view," objectivity is not only impossible but undesirable.

There are definitely differences in the social contexts of the production of our work and in the institutional pressures and disciplinary traditions that influence our writing. There are also many parallels between embedded journalism and ethnography: the immersion in what is popularly seen as a closed society; the necessity of establishing the authority of one's accounts; the pressure to publish; the responsibility to "get it right." Perhaps most importantly, in the context of witnessing war, both journalists and anthropologists are involved in mediating the experience of war for a wider audience. As such, both groups form an important nexus of civil-military relations. As I rewrote this chapter I came to realize that in the end, we journalists, soldiers, poets, and anthropologists are all engaged in a struggle to transform our subjective experience and understanding of war into a coherent narrative that can be shared with others. We are each in our own way trying to tell our story and the story of others.

Notes

1. All the soldiers' names except Corporal Boneca's are pseudonyms.

2. Leaguer, drawn from the Afrikaans *laager*, refers to a temporarily protected location in which the armored fighting vehicles encircle the more vulnerable support vehicles.

3. The LAV captain is responsible for vehicle coordination and is typically deployed in close proximity to, but is not normally engaged in, the fighting.

4. In fact, he survived the tour, although one of his best friends, also a sergeant, was killed during a later operation in Panjwaii, and he believed for a number of reasons that his friend had somehow taken on his fate.

7

Ethics, Engagement, and Experience

Anthropological Excursions in Culture
and the National Security State

Robert A. Rubinstein

In this chapter I reflect on the disciplinary and personal challenges that result from security organizations' recently increased interests in anthropology and anthropologists.[1] Much of that interest is traceable to the assertion that a lack of cultural knowledge is responsible for what went wrong in the wars in Afghanistan and Iraq. As a result of this framing, branches of the US military, and other security agencies and organizations, are expending considerable efforts and resources to figure out how to fill this knowledge gap and how to bring anthropologists and other social scientists to work with them.[2]

In response to the challenges for the discipline arising from such engagement, the American Anthropological Association (AAA) established the AAA Commission on the Engagement of Anthropology with the US Security and Intelligence Communities (American Anthropological Association 2007). The response is explicitly complicated by the imperial nature of US actions in Iraq and Afghanistan, and a variety of other meetings and discussions have taken place within anthropology. Our SAR seminar occurred in this context, of which there are three important elements.

The first is the master narrative of the history of anthropology in which our conversations take place.[3] It is an anthropological truism that all knowledge is situated in the particular contexts and histories and experiences from which it derives. It is thus natural that discussions of the benefits and risks of anthropological engagement with "the military" or with "the security sector" take place in the context of particular understandings of the history and purpose of the discipline. For instance, the framing document for the SAR seminar (Whitehead and McNamara 2008) to which this chapter was a contribution situated our discussions in a narrative about the history of anthropology that asserts:

> Anthropologists have historically worked at the margins of state power, not within the apparatus of power. As Malinowski expressed it, this was to "come down from the veranda" of colonialism, and thus to become participant observers among those at the margins, or at the base, of the colonial system.

This framing of anthropology is consistent with many narratives that circulate in conversation and print about our discipline's history. Yet it is not complete. Of its two claims, the first overgeneralizes the case, is thus empirically wrong, and certainly requires more careful explication. The second claim also requires more careful explication, confusing in its present form a methodological advance for a political program.[4] I return to this issue below, since it is linked to one of the objections about engaging the security sector: that doing so might lead to anthropologists breaching their obligations to the people among whom they work and study.

Second, current discussions about anthropological engagements with military and security organizations are also placed in the context of the need to balance our responsibilities as anthropologists and as citizens. It is worth noting that this is not the first time that anthropologists have engaged this issue. Indeed, it is a theme that recurs throughout the twentieth century and often in times of war (Rubinstein 2006).[5]

The third context for our discussions is the effort to rule as outside of acceptable anthropological practice a large number of particular kinds of engagements between anthropology, the military, and other institutions of the national security state. This is reflected in efforts to reinstate in the AAA's code of ethics the prohibition against anthropologists working with secret or proprietary research. As well, such a tendency is reflected in the statements of the Network of Concerned Anthropologists.

Here, I address some of the issues raised by the current context of anthropological engagement with the military and with security organizations. Acknowledging the situated nature of my comments, I begin autobiographically. I write from the perspective of a professional anthropologist who for nearly three decades has worked at the intersection of anthropology and the security sector. During this time, using anthropological understandings as a basis for critique, I have written against US security policies, conducted ethnographic research with military units, and participated in professional military education programs.

ANTHROPOLOGICAL BEGINNINGS

In many ways my own experiences in this area reflect the tensions, ambivalences, and some of the possibilities that attend to the relationship between anthropology and the military and security communities, to which I will refer collectively throughout this chapter as "The Military." (Since one of my concerns here is that it is mistaken to treat military and security institutions as homogenous, I rely on this locution reluctantly.)

I began my anthropological career in 1976 when I completed my PhD, which focused on cross-cultural language acquisition and education. In the early 1980s I added to this area of interest a professional concern for culture and international security (Rubinstein 1983, 1986, 1988, 1992; Rubinstein and Tax 1985). I have been working among and with The Military since the mid-1980s (Rubinstein 2008). Despite these decades of work, in contexts like the SAR seminar or in visiting military installations I still feel as though I am a "marginal person," to update Everett Stonequist's (1937) phrase, or a "professional stranger," as Michael Agar (1980) describes the anthropologist in the field.[6] I don't mean by this observation something undesirable; indeed, as will become clear later, I think that this kind of liminal status is essential if anthropology is to relate responsibly to the construction of legitimate and useful cultural knowledge for the military and other elements of national power (including our intelligence and diplomatic communities).

I reach this conclusion by examining briefly a number of dimensions of the relationship between anthropology and the intelligence and military communities, including their mutual ethnocentrisms; mutual relevance of strategic, operational, and tactical levels of action; a citizen's duties and responsibilities; and the risks of cooperation. I link these concerns to traditional anthropological values of reciprocity and responsibility for those whose lives we study, and thus for the safety and development of human society in general (issues raised, for example, by Joan Ablon [1977]). In the course of exploring these concerns I call for the creation of a field of military anthropology in which the range of ways of studying or working with institutions of the national security state would be represented in a manner analogous to the variety of approaches embraced by the subfield of medical anthropology.

I came of age during the Vietnam War. The day I turned eighteen I registered for the draft, as I was required to do by law, and I filed a claim of conscientious objection. I entered college in 1969 and spent much of the ensuing three years running a draft counseling center and participating in direct action against the war, often in conjunction with the local chapter of the War Resisters League. After majoring in anthropology as an undergraduate, I entered graduate school in 1972. During this period American anthropology was still discussing heatedly how anthropological work had been misused in counterinsurgency programs in Vietnam and Thailand so that the peoples with whom anthropologists had worked were harmed, and how Project Camelot in Latin America harmed collectively the discipline of anthropology (see, for instance, Jorgensen and Wolf 1970; but see for contrast Horowitz 1967; Lucas 2009). Emerging from this intense activity was a socially conscious anthropology that sought to "speak truth to power," to break ties with colonial and imperial projects (Hymes 1972), and to turn anthropology's focus toward examining institutions of power through "studying up," using Laura Nader's (1972) memorable phrase (see introduction, note 2).

It is perhaps unusual for someone with my personal and professional backgrounds and political commitments to be involved in studying and working with The Military. How I come to be in this position is important for understanding my views, which I think of as flowing from my ethnographic and ethnological experiences.

AN ANTHROPOLOGICAL OPPORTUNITY

Concerned about the increasing militarization of our society and the dire threat of nuclear disaster, in the early 1980s I joined with my University of California–Berkeley colleague and friend Mary LeCron Foster to mobilize anthropologists who could bring anthropological perspectives to the security community. This resulted in four days of coordinated symposia, held at the 11th World Congress of Anthropology and Ethnology, subsequently published as *Peace and War: Cross-Cultural Perspectives* (Foster and Rubinstein 1986). Although the symposia included not only anthropologists but also some people from the security community, the tone and content of the discussions and of the subsequent book were largely critical of military actions and organizations and of the strategic structures of the United States and others. Assembling those symposia led me to work on the importance of considering culture in international security, even during the cold war and for conventional and nuclear strategy (Rubinstein 1983, 1988). Together with many others we formed a Commission on Peace (later the Commission on Peace and Human Rights) under the auspices of the International Union of Anthropological and Ethnological Sciences. I then spent the next few years promoting the development of the anthropology of peace.

I was interested in starting another major empirical project, and I was introduced to peacekeeping as a possible site for such work. I knew little about this instrument of international action when I started, but the idea that it brought together people from many countries to support "peace" under the auspices of the United Nations was very appealing to me. That much of the work was done by the military was something of which I took note, but it was not a major preoccupation.

By 1986 I had begun to work with the International Peace Academy (now the International Peace Institute [IPA]), then the sole institution concerned with the promotion and development of peacekeeping. I began interviewing diplomats and military officers who had been involved in peacekeeping. I talked a great deal with Gen. Indar Jit Rikhye, who was then the IPA president and who had been the military advisor to the UN secretary-general and the force commander for the UN Emergency Force (UNEF).

Through the IPA I got permission from the UN secretariat to conduct a long-term ethnographic study of the UN Truce Supervision Organization (UNTSO) in the Middle East. Thinking of this work as a great example of "studying up" and also of transnational ethnography, I began work in Egypt in 1988. It was then that my preconceptions were challenged and my views moderated.

FIELDWORK AND RECIPROCITY

One of the results of following Bronislaw Malinowski's methodological advice was that during their field research, anthropologists developed social relationships with the people among whom they worked in a manner they previously had not. This was true whether the people studied were at the peripheries of power or at its center. Anthropologists have long honored the view that they should have a concern for the people studied and that there should be some kind of reciprocity between the researcher and the people with whom she works. In a brief but perceptive article, Ablon (1977) set out some of the challenges that faced those working in their own society and those who are "studying up." She noted that in such circumstances "the anthropologist must be alert and open to different opportunities for reciprocity in the field situation" (Ablon 1977:71).

As with any fieldwork, mine with UNTSO was a mutually affecting process with lots of opportunities for reciprocities to develop. My wife and I developed deeply personal friendships with some of our "informants,"

many of whom were serving military officers. I have written about this elsewhere (Rubinstein 1998, 2008). Here, I note that in developing these relationships I began to see that The Military was, in fact, like any human
group or institution, actually a complex social system that embraced a lot
of variation. My first report of my UNTSO research, given at an AAA meeting, concluded with an acknowledgment of how my biases had been challenged and largely shattered.

True, some of the peacekeepers in UNTSO had a very narrow and deri-
sive view of peacekeeping and longed to be "doing manly things in a manly
way," as one of my informants said, and others' main aspiration was to be
shot at so that they would know themselves better. Still others were interested in what they could contribute to the international system and were
interested in furthering their understandings as foreign area officers or
their equivalents.

My research about cultural aspects of peacekeeping led me to a dual
focus on the culture of UNTSO and the importance for UNTSO of understanding the cultures of the people with whom they worked—including the
local population and the nongovernmental organizations (NGOs) with
which they cooperated.

I had no intentions of engaging in training, or institutional reform efforts,
when I began my fieldwork. That changed when the responsibilities of fieldwork reciprocity pushed me to do so. Simply, in the mid-1990s some of my
"informants"—from the military, from the UN Department of Peacekeeping
Operations (UNDPKO), and from NGOs—asked me to help them think
about culture and peace operations in a way that would further the training
and actions of senior mission personnel (Rubinstein 2008:67–69).

Almost any request from the community in which an anthropologist is
working suggests intervention and raises ethical and moral issues. The
requests I was receiving also raised such issues. Some seemed relatively
straightforward to decide. For instance, presenting my anthropological
findings about culture and peacekeeping to military audiences struck me
as unproblematic—I would say nothing to them that I would not present
and publish in standard, public anthropological meetings and journals.
Others seemed more problematic, as I describe later.

MUTUAL ETHNOCENTRISMS

Many anthropologists and many in the military have a mutual distrust
for one another. Social scientists, including anthropologists, have documented the distorting and destructive effects of US military activities both
at home and abroad (for example, Falk and Kim 1980; Lutz 2001; Melman

1986; Stade 1998). For these reasons, and because the military is an instrument often used in the pursuit of strategic ends that are politically repugnant to many anthropologists, a number of stereotypes of the military have been elaborated within anthropology, resulting in a kind of ethnocentrism where the military is concerned.[7] Reflecting on this, I realized that while anthropologists would never speak of other societies or institutions with a global and homogenizing phrase like, for example, "The Arabs," we all too quickly spoke of the "The Military" (Rubinstein 2003).

For their part, many in the military view anthropology as an arcane and exotic subject given to not particularly useful ideological rants. They can point to many anthropological studies and anthropologists whom they find quaint and amusing, and they deride anthropology as jargon-laden. Often, such claims are made by critics in texts that display a wonderful command of (but little sense of self-perspective about) the dense technical language and acronyms (jargon) used by the military.

Both anthropologists and military members have also engaged with one another in a process in which the negative aspects of the interaction between them are emphasized, and those involved become more closed to new information about the other, a process that Theodore Newcomb (1947) called "autistic hostility."

MILITARY ANTHROPOLOGY: AN EMERGING SPECIALTY

Despite the mutual hostilities, it turns out that anthropologists have studied and worked with the military for a long time, and militaries have also made use of anthropologists and their expertise for an equally long time (Hawkins 2003). Despite this long engagement, there is within anthropology no coherently formed subdiscipline of military anthropology as there is in the related disciplines of history, political science, psychology, and sociology. One result of this is that although the phrases "military anthropology" and "military anthropologists" are used frequently in discussions of engagement, there is no common understanding of what these entail.

In addition to my work on peace and security issues and my ethnographic research on peacekeeping, I am also a medical anthropologist, and I have found my participation in that subdiscipline instructive for thinking about military anthropology. The specialty of medical anthropology embraces a wide variety of approaches ranging from the study of ethnomedical forms of understanding of health and illness through "clinically applied medical anthropology," "applied medical anthropology," and "critical medical anthropology."[8] These coexist, though with some tension. Critical medical anthropologists have at times clashed with applied medical anthropologists, accusing them of enabling a hegemonic biomedical system that disadvantages and harms people. In this conversation critical medical anthropologists have even critiqued the categories of analysis used by other medical anthropologists, explaining, for instance, that categories like "infant mortality" are not intrinsically important but rather reflect and reinforce the hegemonic control of the Western medical profession. Despite their theoretical, epistemological, and political differences, many medical anthropologists work to effect change—whether radical re-visioning of health systems, incremental change in public policy, or change in the way health care is practiced.

There is, in fact, a nascent subdiscipline of military anthropology. It has been hard to speak about this subdiscipline in a coherent way because it, like medical anthropology, includes a wide range of research topics and perspectives on action. Yet they all share a focus on the military (in all of its heterogeneous forms) as the main subject of work. Thus they emphasize to a greater or lesser degree the social organization and cultural dimensions of military institutions and societies, as distinct from, for example, the analysis of the causes and consequences of warfare.

As Margaret Harrell (2003a; see also the useful discussion in Lucas 2009) notes, work in military anthropology runs a similar gamut, from studies of, to support of, to critique and resistance. There are a considerable number of ethnographic studies of military units, some of which include works like Ralph Linton's (1924) study of totemism in the American Expeditionary Force, Pearl Katz's (1990) study of emotional metaphors among drill sergeants, my own studies of group formation and dynamics among military peacekeepers (Rubinstein 1993), Anna Simons's (1997) study of the US Army Special Forces, and Eyal Ben-Ari's (1998) use of cultural models to examine an Israeli military unit. As well, there are studies of the social and cultural organization of military communities, such as Alexander Randall's (1986) and John Hawkins's (2001) analyses of social dislocation in the culture of military enclaves, or Linda Pulliam's (1988) and Harrell's (2003b) analyses of gender expectations in the navy and army communities. Catherine Lutz's (2001) study of the effects of militarization on Fayetteville, North Carolina, Lionel Caplan's (1995) examination of Gurkhas in Western narratives and the impact of their service at home, and Hugh Gusterson's (2007) recent review of militarism and anthropology take critical perspectives on military organizations and their representation in society and on anthropologists working with the military. In contrast, several anthropologists have worked in ways designed explicitly to contribute to professional

military education (Fujimura 2003; Selmeski 2007) or to improve operational effectiveness (for example, Kilcullen 2006; M. McFate 2005b; Salmoni
and Holmes-Eber 2009; Varhola and Varhola 2006).

It is evident that the range of things legitimately considered military
anthropology is quite broad, and also that this range is analogous in many
ways to the range of variation within medical anthropology. The analogy is
strengthened by the fact that in both disciplines anthropologists engage
matters of life and death, hegemony and resistance. Pushing this analogy a
little further, I find approaches in medical anthropology that can also
inform work in military anthropology.

HARM REDUCTION: A STRATEGY, NOT A SLOGAN

How should one act in the face of an oppressive system that harms and
kills people? The answers to this question are, of course, complex, and they
vary depending upon who is answering them and in what contexts. It follows that there would be many responsible actions, and that these actions
would differ depending upon the particular perspective from which that
action is taken. From a political perspective, one legitimate response might
be to act in a way that sharpens the injustice of the system, hoping to
advance its collapse. Alternatively, from a disciplinary perspective, one
might use the data and perspectives of anthropology to ameliorate the
harms done to people as a result of the oppressive system. A third alternative would be to seek to change the system, destabilizing it by introducing
concepts of cultural relativism and the legitimacy of diverse ways of living.
Each of these alternative courses of action require balancing the long-term
and short-term benefits of action with the harms that will result. All of these
paths lead to a trade-off between these two sets of harms and benefits. Since
creating both long-term and short-term harms for the people we study is
proscribed by cannons of anthropological responsibility, there is, in my
view, no invariably good alternative, no pure path. Deciding which course
to take and how to combine anthropological understanding with a citizen's
political action thus requires careful individual assessment rather than universal pronouncement. Those assessments should be made in light of the
trade-off between an anthropologist's independence and his or her dependence on state structures. For instance, in their discussions of peace building, NGOs, and civil society, Catherine Barnes (2005) and Simon Fisher
and Lada Zimina (2008) describe the range of ways in which engagement
may take place (see figure 7.1). Moreover, during the course of a career, a
person may move among the different forms of engagement depending
upon the projects he undertakes.

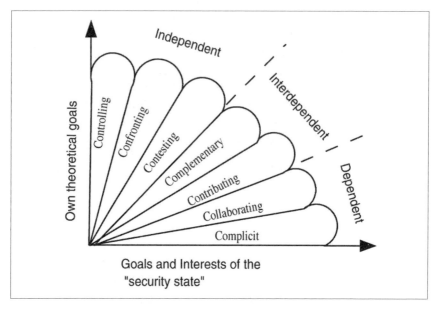

Figure 7.1.

Anthropology–Security State Relations. Adapted from Barnes 2005:10 and from Fisher and Zimina 2008:23.

Discussions about anthropology's engagement with the military can be seen as analogous to efforts at "harm reduction" in the area of health policy and practice. Medical anthropologists, among others, have played important roles in identifying and developing ways to reduce the morbidity and mortality experienced by people as a result of harmful health policies (see, for example, Singer and Baer 2007:20). This work has been carried out in a context in which many of these policies "further U.S. geopolitical and geo-economic interests" (Singer 2004:295). Originally developed in the context of drug policies (Inciardi and Harrison 2000; Lenton and Single 1998) and often having the character of insurgent social movements, the strategies involve health workers and others to change standard practice or to reframe the general understanding of a problem (Keefe, Lane, and Swars 2006; Lane et al. 2000). Harm reduction has expanded now to a more general approach. Key to this approach is that while acknowledging that it would be far preferable for the causes of the harm to be eliminated, the primary focus is on reducing the harms that result from misguided policies by using safer interventions to put actual peoples' lives above an abstract principle (Lenton and Single 1998:214–216). Changes to the system would come about as a result of changes in practice.

Robust debates regarding harm reduction strategies have occurred since they were first introduced in the 1960s (for instance, see Hathaway 2001; Inciardi and Harrison 2000; Keane 2003; Lane et al. 2000; Lenton and Single 1998). These debates pivot on the question of whether harm reduction strategies do enough good to offset the reinforcing of the structures of domination and inequality that promote the harm in the first place. This is a major dimension of the debate about harm reduction in drug literature.

This concern also appears in discussions of what to do about slavery in the contemporary world. In the context of slavery there are disagreements regarding slave redemption as a kind of harm reduction activity. On the one hand, those who would engage in slave redemption see it as an important mechanism for immediately improving the situations of individual abductees. On the other hand, those who oppose slave redemption suggest that it simply reinforces the practice of slave taking by creating a market for slavery. The latter group argues that what is needed is a fundamental change in the way slavery is addressed by the international community (see Appiah and Bunzl 2007). The ethnographic reality of slave redemption turns out to be more complicated and varied. For instance, in the Sudan where slavery is used as a war tactic, "from an empirical perspective there is no evidence that slave redemptions have led to increased raiding, or have increased volume of slaves taken since the [redemption] programs began" (Jok 2007:147).

In the context of military anthropology this analogy suggests that it is mistaken to view the strategic, operational, and tactical levels of action as sharply separated from one another.

STRATEGIC SCAFFOLDING

Especially in the current debate about Human Terrain Teams, it is often asserted that opposing the teams is wrong because they deal with soldiers on the ground who do not make strategic policy. From my work with peacekeeping I have concluded that this is a false argument. Rather, what takes place on the ground has an effect on strategic policy, just as strategic policy affects what is done in the field. I call this essential relationship "strategic scaffolding" (Rubinstein 2008:51–52).

For example, despite the broad scope of peacekeeping, individual actions play an important part in the success or failure of each mission. Because there is a reciprocal and contingent relationship among the levels of organization expressed in peacekeeping, the overarching structure of peacekeeping helps to shape and direct individual actions. At the same time, individual actions are important to maintaining the overarching structure of peacekeeping.[9]

Peacekeeping routinely addresses matters of life and death. These matters are not addressed simply by the abstract corporate entities that comprise the mission. Rather, these matters of life and death are faced every day by individual peacekeepers—whether military, humanitarian, or civil servant—in real contexts. How these individuals respond to the challenges they meet determines not only the outcome of the specific encounter, but also contributes to maintaining the social capital of the particular mission and of peacekeeping generally. In this sense peacekeeping is an emergent process because what individuals do is shaped by the social structural constraints within which they work, while at the same time their actions alter those social structural constraints in a pattern of repetitive, reciprocal structural coupling (Maturana and Varela 1988:193).

It follows as well from a variety of social theories that changing practices can create culture change (Rubinstein 2008:45–48). It has long seemed to me that engagement with the military that promotes a respect for others; lauds the value of diversity; uses an anthropological perspective to call into question the value of unilateral, militarized foreign engagements; and supports those within the military who share such views is both a harm reduction strategy and an effort at culture change. The military—and the security sector more broadly—is an important institution in American society. As an anthropologist who advocates that part of US foreign policy ought to involve a willingness to engage with and talk to our adversaries (especially since such engagement could lead to the reframing of that relationship), I do not think it anthropologically responsible to eschew speaking to the military. Like all culture change interventions, this requires engaging one's interlocutor "where they are." Even so, the results are not always as quick or in the direction desired.

WOULD YOU SPEAK TO THE CIA?

In 1999 I received an invitation to participate in a conference on the "Nature of Modern Conflict." The conference was motivated by the observation that despite increasing globalization, especially economically and in communication technology, the conference conveners were genuinely puzzled by the emergence of communal and other conflicts taking place within states. They said they wanted an anthropological perspective on this issue to help them come to terms with something they didn't understand. The first day of the conference at which I was being invited to speak was to be open to the public and thus not classified in any way, but the main audience would be people from the intelligence and defense communities. The person inviting me added, almost as an afterthought, that the conference was being convened on behalf of the CIA's Strategic Assessments Group.

This last bit of information gave me pause. I made a series of calls to my anthropological colleagues, especially those with whom I had worked in establishing the International Union of Anthropological and Ethnological Sciences Commission on Peace and Human Rights. Uniformly, the response was that if we really believed that anthropologists ought to be heard by the international security community, the only way to do this was to talk with them. As long as the conference was not covert in any way, they agreed it would be a good thing to do. I thought so too.

So I went to the conference. I was the first presenter of the day, speaking to about seventy-five people from a variety of agencies and services. I presented a paper that explored the role of identity in contemporary conflicts, and I focused especially on the ways in which women and children bore disproportionate harms in these conflicts. I discussed issues concerning rape during conflict as well as the use other coercive means of controlling women's reproductive lives and how these issues linked to communal conflicts (see Rubinstein and Lane 2002).

The immediate, almost instantaneous, response to my paper was an objection: "Western armies don't rape. In the entire history of the Civil War, there are only two recorded instances of rapes of white women!"[10]

This remark left me momentarily speechless. One might have expected at least one objection from the audience, but instead there were merely murmurs of agreement. I shortly responded that like other social phenomena, the official reporting of the Civil War was contingent and contextual; what was recorded and how it was reported are matters of power, interest, and perspective. I found it all the more stunning that the quality of US war historical reporting was viewed as straightforwardly accurate and unproblematic since my paper was given on the morning that the front page of the *New York Times* carried news that the long-denied killings of civilians at the Bridge of No Gun Ri, Korea, had in fact taken place, as confirmed by Pentagon records that had only lately, and under pressure, been discovered (Becker 1999; Choe, Hanley, and Mendoza 1999; Dobbs and Suro 1999).

Following this exchange, the audience and I had a good discussion of the issues raised in my paper, especially about the need to focus on conflict issues "below the level of the state." Observing the interaction patterns in the room, it became clear that I was the only speaker during the day who was not already known to the organizers. Following me was a series of speakers, each of whose presentations focused in some way on interstate conflict and did so in ethnocentric ways. Several of the subsequent speakers invoked the "well, I'm not a tenured professor, so…" formula. This served the double purpose of cleaving them to the "in group" and exempting them from having to critically test their assumptions.

But some people in the room did engage my presentation honestly and openly. I was reconfirmed in my belief that to break the cycle of autistic hostility between anthropologists and institutions of the national security state one had to engage with them in open conversation. This seemed especially so when, during our coffee and lunch breaks, a number of people thanked me for my talk and told me they shared these professional views, had been pushing them as minority voices, and appreciated the support that my talk offered to their cause.

MULTIPLE ENCOUNTERS, MULTIPLE VOICES

One lesson I take from my relative lack of success in engaging the audience at the "Nature of Modern Conflict" conference is that institutional and culture change is a complicated and long-term process. Clearly, many in the room would not give a second thought to the considerations that I raised in my talk. Yet a few would. It seems to me that institutional change requires persistence and multiple encounters. I mentioned this lesson at our SAR seminar, where the resulting conversation focused on whether institutional change is possible at all. I was asked, "Have you ever seen your work, or work you are familiar with, make a difference in institutional practice?"

In response to this query, I made the following two brief observations. Throughout the 1990s, and continuing today, there was a considerable amount of work directed at bringing the concerns of women affected by conflict into planning peacekeeping missions and peace-building efforts. These analyses argued that the organization of peacekeeping operations and peace-building efforts often took place absent an understanding of the experiences and concerns of women in conflict and postconflict settings (see, for example, Withworth 2004). The results of these efforts have been incremental, but very real, changes in the way that the international community addresses gender issues in conflict (Rehn and Sirleaf 2002), including efforts to "mainstream" gender. Developments on this front are moving in the "right" direction, although the destination has not been reached.

The second brief observation I made in response to the query was from my own work. When I first began studying peacekeeping, my suggestion that culture matters for peace operations was met with a kind of bemused response. Yet, as I described earlier, cultural issues, especially those involving the organizational cultures of military and NGO organizations, was salient enough in the community that I was asked to help design a handbook for the administration of peace operations. Several years later the UNDPKO invited me to submit a white paper on cultural considerations in designing the UN mission in Sudan. While I do not know how fully the materials in that white paper contributed to the mission design, I do know that the importance of cultural knowledge for mission planning had spread throughout UNDPKO. Some years after I had submitted the white paper a class of mine was being briefed at the UNDPKO Situation Center. An anthropologist colleague, Catherine Lutz, was with us. In a conversation with the center coordinator, Catherine asked whether any cultural information was used in mission planning and was told that an anthropologist had consulted on the planning of the Sudan mission. It shortly emerged that the coordinator was referring to the work I had done with her UNDPKO colleagues—again, evidence of incremental change in the "right" direction.

A second lesson from the "Nature of Modern Conflict" conference is that language matters. As we all know, and as Carol Cohn (1987) demonstrated in her now classic paper, "Sex and Death in the Rational World of Defense Intellectuals," language helps us to construct our worlds. In doing so it allows us to leave unchallenged fundamental assumptions. In many conversations about culture and military training there is a struggle over how we ought best to talk about culture in military training. I will return to this issue below, when I speak about the nature of partnership and the tensions between servicing and serving, but here I want to note only that avoiding each other's language simply reinforces mutual ethnocentrisms. I will follow up on this, but first, a brief excursion into the third topic of the SAR seminar, citizenship.

CITIZENSHIP'S RESPONSIBILITIES

Dealing as an anthropologist with subjects that are part of the contemporary experience of citizens means that there is a "diminution of cultural barriers [that] leads to increased personal visibility of the anthropologist" (Ablon 1977:70). When this happens, one must balance one's responsibilities as an anthropologist with one's responsibilities as a citizen. It turns out that the obligations of citizenship are as contested as are disciplinary ethics.

In the citizenship literature there is general agreement that a citizen "is a member of a political community who enjoys the rights and assumes the duties of membership."[11] Yet the specifics of what this general view entails and how the rights and duties should be enacted are the subject of considerable debate. In addition to rights and obligations, membership in a political community also affects identity at some level (Pinxten, Cornelis, and Rubinstein 2007). Thus I am not just an anthropologist, I am an American anthropologist. This is so no matter what I may feel about the importance of good global governance and the value of multilateral institutions, or how much I seek to distance myself from the geo-strategic policies of the US government.

As an American anthropologist I am still old-fashioned enough to believe that at some level I am responsible for the actions of my government. Comfortable though it is to separate the people from the government or administration, at some basic level this is a false distinction. So I have a responsibility to try to change that policy. As I've indicated before, there are many ways of seeking that influence. Whether through public denunciation of those policies based on anthropological analysis, reasoned engagements, or other actions, when we speak qua anthropologists, we are fulfilling a citizen's responsibilities for giving service to our community.

SERVICE, NOT SERVICING

Service is a citizen's responsibility, but it is not an end in itself or an absolute good. Rather, it requires thoughtful action. Acting as anthropologists engaging the military we must, following Ablon (1977:70), "anticipate and manage potential areas of value conflict between the anthropologist and his informants." In relation to engaging with the military, one area of potential conflict is over the reason that the interaction is taking place.

During the past few years I have had occasion to discuss with my military interlocutors the form and purpose of anthropological engagement. Too often I have heard some variant of the following claim:

> Now is an opportunity for anthropologists to make a difference, but it is a brief window of opportunity. You anthropologists should take advantage of this and the way to do that is to give us what we want in the form in which we want it. So, yeah, culture is important, but we need you to tell us how to prepare culturally sensitive soldiers in the ninety minutes we can set aside for this briefing. And, oh yeah, leave out the anthropological jargon.

While it is important to listen to such exhortations as ethnographic data—reports from the field about what the natives (or at least some of them) are thinking—anthropologists must not simply comply with them.

The idea that the military is the client and that anthropologists must "give the client what it wants" is also a native ethnographic report, but it is one that the engaged anthropologist must parse carefully and respond to appropriately. If the goals of bringing anthropology to the military table include developing harm reduction strategies and promoting culture change by introducing concepts that alter the way the military conducts business, then it is essential that anthropologists not debase what they have to offer by prostituting their contributions.

Anthropological perspectives properly understood, and as described earlier, inevitably attenuate and make less effective the mechanisms necessary for the promotion of militarism (for example, those described by Goldschmidt 1988).[12] Nevertheless, there certainly are great pressures—economic, political, and social—for using anthropological understanding in ways that anthropologists would find abhorrent. Some anthropologists are even concerned that articles and books published in scholarly literature will be used by the military for nefarious purposes. It follows, for me, that anthropologists' obligations extend to trying to influence how nonanthropological audiences use their work. In relation to institutions of the national security state this urges our engagement with them, rather than our rejection of such engagement.

Engaging institutions of the national security state in anthropological dialogue is arguably the most challenging venue where the "anthropologist must effectively deal with being the insider and outsider in his own culture" (Ablon 1977:71). Not only must military anthropologists resist the pressures to deliver caricatured and partial accounts of their work to the military, they must also navigate disciplinary efforts to enforce a disengagement from the military.

One of the concerns raised about military anthropology is that it will negatively affect anthropology's reputation among the people with whom we work. The argument is that if some of us work with (perhaps even study?) the military or with security organizations, then all anthropologists will be made suspect as a result. I think this argument is something of a red herring. All American anthropologists with whom I have spoken about their fieldwork experience have reported that at some time their informants let them know that their actions and motives were suspect, and that some in the community thought the anthropologist a spy or CIA dupe. This seems to be true no matter where or when the fieldwork took place—including in the early or mid-1970s when the AAA was passionate and vocal in its anti-Vietnam War stance. This means that independent of what other anthropologists are or are not doing, all anthropologists doing fieldwork must demonstrate to those with whom they work their sincerity and trust-worthiness.

A variant of this objection, also a red herring in my view, rests on the claim that the business of anthropology is working with people at the margins of power and those who are disenfranchised, and that allowing anthropological work with the military and other national security institutions would make it impossible for us to work with those aforementioned people, again because all anthropologists would be tarred by the affiliations of a (rotten?) few. While it is true that the preponderance of anthropological work has been done with remote peoples, it has never been the program of the discipline of anthropology as a whole to work only with those groups. Indeed, anthropologists have always to some degree studied and worked with people in powerful institutions and sectors of society. For this latter group, the disciplinary eschewing of work with the military and national security institutions would have devastating effects on their access to their research field.

As John Williams (2008) notes, pressures from within social science disciplines, our own included, to absolutely eschew working with the military create a very dangerous climate for the conduct of careful scholarship and application in this area. Anthropologists who engage with the military risk being pilloried by their colleagues, some of whom substitute their political program for empirical investigation.[13] This is another set of pressures that must be resisted if we are to fulfill our responsibilities as citizens and as anthropologists.

I close by returning to the image of the marginal person. In order to fulfill their anthropological responsibilities of reciprocity with the people they study, and to help them exercise their rights and responsibilities as citizens, it is important that military anthropologists maintain a liminal status, shuttling back and forth between the anthropological and the military worlds. Maintaining this status will also help us avoid either opting out or "going native."

Notes

1. The invitation to the SAR seminar asked that participants reflect on their own experiences as anthropologists studying, working with, or studying the consequences of interactions with the national security state. Hence this chapter is explicitly autobiographical, reporting my experiences and relating these to larger conversations within the discipline. This chapter benefited from comments made by participants at the SAR seminar. I also thank Robert Albro, Sandra D. Lane, George Lucas, and Barbara Rylko-Bauer for their helpful comments. An earlier version of this chapter was

presented at the Watson Institute for International Affairs. For comments at that time, I thank Keith Brown, Hugh Gusterson, and Catherine Lutz.

2. As Danny Hoffman (this volume) points out, military institutions are also seeking to develop their own independent capacities for using "open source" anthropological literature and data. This further complicates anthropology's relations with those institutions, as does the development of professional anthropological capabilities within these organizations themselves (see, for example, Salmoni and Holmes-Eber 2009).

3. What I identify as "master narratives" are accounts of anthropology's development as offered in synthetic history of anthropology monographs and in introductory textbooks. These narratives bear a family resemblance to the idealized accounts of what science is and how it works that dominated discussions of the history and philosophy of science in the 1950s and 1960s and led to what was called the "received view of science" (Suppe 1977). These "master narratives" of anthropology's development homogenize important distinctions and differences in practice in the same way that the received view of science gave a partial and inaccurate picture of scientific theory, method, and practice.

4. Anthropologists have worked within and for institutions of power in the United States and elsewhere. Especially prior to the boom in university employment in the 1950s and 1960s, anthropologists in the United States were often employed by, or led, government institutions such as the Smithsonian Institution, the Department of State, and the Bureau of Indian Affairs. David Price (2008b), for example, describes many of these roles, though from a critical perspective.

Bronislaw Malinowski's advance was a methodological one. It put anthropologists "on the ground" among the "natives," thus defining anthropology's standard view of fieldwork for most of the twentieth century (Rubinstein 2002). Malinowski (1954:146–147) writes:

> As regards anthropological fieldwork, we are obviously demanding a new method of collecting evidence. The anthropologist must relinquish his comfortable position in the long chair on the veranda of the missionary compound, Government station, or planter's bungalow, where, armed with pencil and notebook and at times with a whisky and soda, he has been accustomed to collect statements from informants.... He must go out into the villages, and see the natives at work in the gardens, on the beach, in the jungle.

That many of the people studied were and are at the peripheries of power derived from practical and disciplinary boundary considerations rather than from a discipline-wide political program. The abhorrence of colonialism found in the anthropological literature follows from anthropologists' exposure to the damage done by colonial exploitations, not the methodological turn. This was true as well for Malinowski (Michael Young, personal communication, June 24, 2008).

Converting feelings of support and solidarity that derive from the situated description of experiences of suffering into an axiom about disciplinary political loyalties commits a category mistake (see Ryle 1949:16–22). The shift in methods advocated by Malinowski was intended to bring anthropologists into firsthand relationships with those being studied so that they would experience as fully as possible the lifeworlds of their informants, whoever might be the community studied. Converting the abhorrence of the consequences of colonialism and other forms of abusive power developed by anthropologists in many fieldwork settings into a defining political feature of all of anthropology restricts what are the proper objects and subjects of anthropological study. It is this category mistake that Laura Nader (1972) wrote against when she urged anthropologists to "study up."

Gilbert Ryle (1949:17) observed that "the theoretically interesting category-mistakes are those that are made by people who are perfectly competent to apply concepts, at least in the situations with which they are familiar, but are still liable in their abstract thinking to allocate those concepts to logical types to which they do not belong." Tracing the reification of a private category mistake into a discipline-wide principle would repay the effort involved but is beyond the scope of this chapter.

5. The work of Gerald Hickey during the Vietnam War, discussed by Price (this volume), is an example of one anthropologist's efforts to manage these tensions.

6. Stonequist attributes the phrase "marginal man" to Robert E. Park, to whom Stonequist dedicated his book, and for which book Park contributed an introduction. In that introduction Park says, "The marginal man...is one whom fate has condemned to live in two, not merely different, but antagonistic cultures" (Stonequist 1937:xv).

7. Like all stereotypes, those about The Military found in anthropological literature and discussions homogenize, globalize, and essentialize and are offered in an unselfconscious manner (Rubinstein 2003). Broad assertions stand in for ethnographically informed understandings of the different cultural practices and diversity among military communities. For instance, the University of Foreign Military and Cultural Studies at Fort Leavenworth runs a regular "Red Team" program that is intended to raise critiques of "operations, concepts, organizations, and capabilities in the context of the operational environment" (Fontenot 2007:1). Yet a recent anthropological article asserts "the issue is not working for the military *but rather the military itself*—that they require secrecy of findings, *reject internal criticism*, lack commitment to human rights issues and ethical values" (Sluka 2010; emphasis added).

8. " Applied" and "critical" medical anthropology are somewhat arbitrary labels and need not in fact be mutually exclusive but perhaps represent end points of a

ETHICS, ENGAGEMENT, AND EXPERIENCE

continuum. Thus some work might appropriately be called "applied critical" medical anthropology or "critical applied" medical anthropology, as for example in Arachu Castro and Merrill Singer 2004 or Sandra Lane 2008. The continuous nature of engagement is discussed later.

9. Critics of anthropological involvement with some military programs often point out, as did the anonymous reviewer of this volume, that their opposition is to work that is tactical rather than strategic. The logic is that tactical programs "are controversial because they entail risk to informants." The linkages between the tactical and strategic levels that I demonstrated through empirical work on peacekeeping suggest that both levels pose direct risks to informants. Thus this easy distinction between levels should provide cold comfort for anthropologists. The anonymous reviewer of this volume found the blurring of the tactical and strategic to be "interesting" but rejected it because the distinction is "very important in the context of anthropological ethics." This intellectual move reminds me of episodes in the history of astronomy in which those comforted by the geocentric theory of planetary alignment resisted the Copernican revolution by recommitting themselves to astronomical theory that elaborated crystalline celestial spheres and epicycles to "save the phenomenon" (Kuhn 1957).

10. I subsequently learned that the objection was raised by Ralph Peters, a retired colonel and favorite analyst among military and security agencies.

11. Dominique Leydet, "Citizenship," *The Stanford Encyclopedia of Philosophy* (http://plato.stanford.edu/archives/win2006/entries/citizenship/, accessed June 1, 2008).

12. One of the anonymous reviews of this volume suggested that this claim is undercut by the collaboration between the anthropological community and the Nazi state, as described by Tomforde (this volume). To the contrary, what Tomforde's case study describes are the dangers of substituting political preferences for rigorous methodological, theoretical, and empirical analysis.

13. It is worth recalling that those anthropologists who participated on the poorly titled panel "The Empire Speaks Back" at the 2007 annual meeting of the AAA were called war criminals who should be barred from the association during the association's business meeting. This is a serious allegation and was made without empirical basis. Yet neither the chair, nor any speaker from the floor, urged less inflammatory or more careful examination of that claim. Similarly, several articles reviewing military anthropology and anthropological cooperation with the military have painted with a very broad brush, engaging in a kind of guilt by association rhetoric (see, for example, Gusterson 2007; Keenan 2009; Sluka 2010). On military anthropology as a source of ritual pollution, see Keith Brown 2009 and Rubinstein 2009.

8

Anthropology, Research, and State Violence

*Some Observations from an Israeli
Anthropologist*

Eyal Ben-Ari

As I perused the proposal for the SAR workshop on which this volume is based, I could not help but note how "American" it is.[1] By the term "American" I refer not only to its opening statement that the US military and security institutions have become increasingly interested in anthropological knowledge as a resource for understanding local contexts of conflict. Nor do I refer to the associational context of the workshop itself, located in the United States and linked to the Society for Applied Anthropology. Rather, the proposal resonated with the way terms such as "methodology" and "ethics" are often used in the American academic context as synonyms for politics: processes centered on the state and its policies and representatives, and involving impulsion toward activism. To be sure, methodology has implications beyond the methods scholars use, and ethics often entail more than the stress on individual and (especially in the American case) legal responsibility in fieldwork or afterward. But an explicit focus on politics, at least for me, raises questions about positioning in the field, contentions about the worthiness of collective action, the transformational capacities of the state, and the way belonging to different political and ideological camps is part and parcel of contemporary debates within the discipline. Following David Price (this volume), the political also includes how, given certain structural characteristics, the knowledge we produce may be wielded by the military and security sectors.

Along these lines, at base of much of the current debate about ethics are deep-rooted assumptions about the political past of anthropology. For instance, after the Vietnam War when "anthropologists were accused of participating in clandestine, government-sponsored research that endangered the communities they studied, the AAA adopted a code of ethics. These guidelines demand that anthropologists put the interests of their research subjects first and protect the anonymity of their informants" (Lamphere 2003:156). At base of this account of the relation between politics and ethics is the premise that anthropologists study, and are committed to, subordinate groups. But what if one studies soldiers, the professional perpetrators of violence? What kind of allegiance do we owe them in terms of placing their interests first? What kind of ethical and political considerations must we take into account when studying them?

It would seem to be relatively easy to protect solders' anonymity and maintain confidentiality about our findings. But in my reading it seems that underlying the genuine commitment to "do no harm" and even "do good" to the people anthropologists study is a political agenda broadly termed "postcolonial": to "just-ing," to redeeming the past of anthropology. Thus, for example, Carolyn Fluehr-Lobban (2003:13) argues for a "new professional ethics based on research premises reflecting postcolonial realities and transformed relations with the people studied." And Gerald Berreman (2003:73) makes an even clearer case in proposing to combine ethical anthropology and practical relevance as part of public interest anthropology, one that furthers an agenda dealing with social problems such as war, poverty, racism, sexism, or environmental degradation and the necessity for work with citizens in promoting change.

Rather than pandering to an anti-American streak found among some scholars outside the United States (and within it) by criticizing the contradictions of American anthropology, I would like to use my observations as an external, somewhat peripheral, observer to do the following things. Firstly, I situate the current controversy over relations between anthropologists and the military (and more broadly, security forces) as a peculiarly American rendering of global *academic* processes marking our discipline. Secondly, I contend that while heavily colored by American biases, this debate nevertheless carries implications for scholars around the world because of the structural centrality of American academia. Thirdly, I maintain that anthropologists have a political and moral duty to continue studying the military and processes of militarization and militarism, *including* studies enabled by the armed forces, because of what they may reveal about the bases for using state-mandated armed force around the world. Fourthly, I explain how fieldwork such as I have been carrying out among Israeli troops and commanders implicates a number of rather particular issues and necessitates a careful process of dialogue with the subjects of our study.

WHAT IS WORTHY OF STUDY ACCORDING TO AMERICAN ACADEMIC CENTERS

Much recent discussion in the United States centers on the help anthropologists have given, or can give, the armed forces in terms of acting within zones of conflict (Gusterson 2007; Price 2002b). These debates are an outgrowth, of course, of a situation in which anthropologists (among other social scientists) have been actively recruited into the security frameworks of the forces fighting in Afghanistan and Iraq. But as Keith Brown (2008) underscores, given anthropology's past, the current relationship between the military and anthropology has become essentially adversarial. To follow Hugh Gusterson (2007:164), "Not since World War II had military consulting been endorsed so publicly; not since Vietnam had it been condemned so fiercely." While the attitudes of a generation of anthropologists during and after World War II were shaped by the "good war" against fascism (Gusterson 2007:157), for the past few decades, within our discipline the US military has been essentially viewed in terms of the Vietnam debacle and anthropologists' participation in that war.

These kinds of antagonistic relations are not unique to anthropology. The ties between humanitarian and human rights movements and the military in various peace-support operations bear similar features (Winslow 2002). In both cases collaboration with the military is viewed with (often justified) suspicion and distrust. In the case of humanitarian organizations these worries are centered on whether "armed social work" for particular parts of the local population is actually a form of support for the US regime. In the case of anthropology this concern is related to the establishment of databases with dangerous precedents in the discipline's history of cooperation with security forces. More widely, feelings of intense wariness and often outright condemnation are related to anthropology's identification with the underdog and commitment to "liberal" values (itself a very "American" political label—see Nader 1972); the continued echoing of current debates with anthropology's painful relations with colonialism (Ben-Ari 1999); and the legacy of American imperialism in Southeast Asia and Latin America (Price 2000). Indeed, the title of Price's (2002b) editorial makes this point clearly: "Past Wars, Present Dangers, Future

Anthropologies." Yet the severity of the tone with which the current controversy is handled may be related to an American penchant for moralizing issues (related conceivably to its Puritan origins), and the current acuteness of US partisan politics within which the majority of anthropologists lean toward the left and the government is sometimes to the right.

In this respect, however, the Israeli context differs from that of the United States. The main problem many US anthropologists see with current circumstances is that anthropologists have been mobilized by the military to "know" societies within which conflict is being waged and thus to make armed action more effective. In Israel, however, this role has been the province of the "Orientalists" (Eyal 2005) and only very rarely of anthropologists. Historically, the coalition of anthropologists with the Israeli state has most often centered on the "absorption" of (Jewish) immigrants. The realm of security had entailed a practical monopoly by experts (overwhelmingly historians) carrying out research and teaching in an area called "Middle East Studies." These individuals wanted to marry the pursuit of purely academic knowledge with influence on policy. As a group it is closely allied with military officers in the Israel Defense Forces' (IDF) Intelligence Corps and is part of a wider network of actors, resources, and models centered on knowing the "Arab other" (Eyal 2005:150). However, only two Israeli anthropologists of Arab societies ever belonged to this broad coalition (Eyal 2005:134 n. 54) and one (Emanuel Marx) later became a vocal advocate of the Bedouin tribes of Israel.

Against this background it may be clear that my work, and to an extent some of my colleagues', is focused elsewhere: on the study *of* (rather than for) the military. By the standards of some US-based scholars (and some Israeli ones as well), however, this focus does not quite get me off the proverbial political or ethical hook. Some US-based commentators have generalized from the direct involvement of anthropologists in Iraq to *any* work with the military that does not fit their political agenda. In a wide-ranging review article on "anthropology and militarism" (actually focused *only* on the United States), Gusterson (2007:164) invokes a dichotomy between the "good" and the "bad" anthropologists. Thus the virtuous scholars are those who have focused on the "deformative features of American militarism" and include Carolyn Nordstrom (1997), Catherine Lutz (2001), and himself (Gusterson 1996). The anthropologists who are to be condemned are those who are "contracted to, enabled by, or in a broad sense allied with the military" (Gusterson 2007:164). In this group Gusterson includes such scholars as John Hawkins (2001) and Anna Simons (1997), or the anthropologists appearing in the volume edited by Pamela Frese and

Margaret Harrell (2003). It seems that not only anthropologists who work as subcontractors for the military bother Gusterson, but most anthropologists studying within it. Ironically, this simplistic dichotomy based on a clear vision of moral and political worthiness seems to replicate (in inverse form) the tidy division of the world into "good" and "evil" as espoused by George W. Bush's administration. If I am not mistaken, scholars who, like me, are sometimes enabled by the military are seen within this view as polluted by the very subjects of our study, state perpetrators of violence. Along these lines, for scholars such as Gusterson, such anthropologists as those participating in Human Terrain System project in contemporary Iraq are cultural anomalies who must be "purified" in order to re-create the moral boundaries of the discipline.

More broadly, within the debate among American anthropologists there seem to be two political camps distinguished by views regarding the policies of the US regime. But a closer look reveals that the camps are not equal in political terms. Anthropologists "enabled" by the military have considerable power since they are allied with state agents. Many such scholars seek the recognition of the state and wish to influence policy and its implementation. But within the discipline these anthropologists are often in a position of relative weakness. According to the status hierarchy within the discipline, "messy" applied anthropology is ranked lower than the "purer" academically oriented anthropology. While it is permissible to do fieldwork at home, I would argue that in American academic centers it is still second-best (thus best pursued in the latter parts of one's career). In fact, I agree with Erve Chambers (1987:309) that

> Applied endeavor in anthropology is typically viewed as lacking in intellectual rigor, ethically suspect, unimaginative, bereft of theoretical sophistication, and somehow essential to our future.... [A]pplication is almost inevitably viewed as a partial and dependent of expression of discipline, generally of use to some other perhaps "purer" inquiry.

The current controversy among US anthropologists, then, is marked by more highly ranked scholars who represent "pure" academic pursuits critiquing lower-placed scholars.

It is within this context that I am worried about my anthropology being harmed. I am seriously worried not only by my work being mobilized by the hegemonic powers of Israel but no less significantly by my possible subservience to a broad political camp within American anthropology. I state this since I have found that when presenting papers about the Israeli military in the United States and (increasingly) in Europe, I encounter an almost compulsory indignation that must be sounded by many anthropologists before any academic discussion of current conflicts in Afghanistan and Iraq and Israel-Palestine. This obligatory ire, moreover, is often accompanied by marks of political allegiance through the very use of scholarly jargon ("empire" and "multitude" are my favorites). I find this trend troubling not only because it stifles open discussion and exchange, but also because of the structural dependence of Israeli academia on external centers.

Let me explain. Syed Farid Alatas (2003) talks about a hierarchical global division of social scientific labor expressed through the dependence of peripheral or more peripheral academic centers on the metropolitan hubs in terms of ideas, academic media, or aid for research. Within this model Israel would be classed as a sort of semi-periphery that is dependent primarily on academic centers in the United States for funding, promotion (through evaluation letters), and subjects taught. Let me be clear that I do not wish to simplistically reduce processes of producing academic knowledge to intradisciplinary power relations (see also Tomforde and Price, this volume) or to Israel's less central place in the global system of academe. Nor do I wish to explain anthropological research as simply replicating internal US hierarchies between more and less prestigious universities or between theoretically driven and applied anthropology. But these circumstances are of central import for understanding the ways in which scholarly authority is created, definitions of what is worthy of research are constructed, and political positioning by scholars is necessitated.

Over the past twenty years I find myself framing my writing in different ways for scholars of the military (mainly sociologists, psychologists, and political scientists) and for scholars of violence (overwhelmingly anthropologists). Based on reviewers' letters regarding articles submitted to anthropological journals, writing recommendation letters, and reactions to talks given in the United States, I have had to theoretically justify my focus on the Israeli military in the following manner. My work has been much more easily accepted among anthropologists when I formulated it as related to the problematics of war and less on the military as an organization. To be fair, publishing about the Israeli military has become easier with the recent proliferation of anthropological writings about violence, suffering, and the body. Again, to be clear, my words are not sounded as a complaint. I think that I have been relatively successful in publishing outside of Israel and have often found that the challenge to theorize my findings in ways dictated by American reviewers has benefited me. Rather, I voice my concern in order to point out how in pursuing my career in Israel—which is dependent to a great degree on publishing in the United States and Britain—I have had to tailor my work to external standards, to notions of what is worthy of study and of how to study it.

A POLITICAL IMPERATIVE TO STUDY THE MILITARY

Here, however, I would like to take my argument in a different direction to suggest that it is imperative that anthropologists study the military. In her review of the development of warfare, Simons (1999) suggests that two subjects are still absent: processes of militarization and the military establishments of the industrial democracies. Their absence is surprising because violence has been the object of intense anthropological scrutiny over the past decade or so. Accordingly, if we want to understand, control, or guide the state, it would be irresponsible not to study these powers. In this respect, while anthropologists have begun studying militarization and militarism in the United States (Gusterson 2007; Lutz 2001) and outside it (Altinay 2004; Lomsky-Feder and Ben-Ari 1999), the missing subject is still very much the armed forces.

Accordingly, my argument is that one needs to study both victims *and* perpetrators if one wants to understand violence (the study of the Holocaust underwent a similar kind of shift), and not only broad processes of militarization. Indeed, if violence is an interaction, how can we cede the study of perpetrators to other disciplines and be content with portraying the terrible suffering they have wrought (a genre pursued by such scholars as Nancy Scheper-Hughes and Philippe Bourgois [2004]). Hence, and in contrast to psychologists, sociologists, political scientists, and historians, anthropologists have paid little attention to the military in complex industrialized societies. To be sure, anthropologists have long been aware of the power of state security forces (including the military), but anthropological analyses of the state's use of violent force have tended to focus almost exclusively on victims of state actions or on movements of resistance against the state (Nordstrom 1997; Sluka 2000). As Gusterson (1996:60) proposes, the proclivity of US ethnographers to study the underdog and the marginal has left the study of elites and the mainstream (including the military) outside the discipline.

The study of the military is not only important because it is another hegemonic institution. It is important because the military is *the* organization most strongly identified with the socially defined, if contested, legitimate use of violence (Boene 1990). Without such a focus the analysis of victims of suffering does not inform us about what moves military organizations to participate in inflicting violence and what makes different publics accept the perpetration of violence. What needs examining are the specific ways in which the military's expertise in handling—managing, controlling, or effecting—violence is represented, played out, and has concrete personal and social implications. It is here that I differ from Gusterson, since as I have shown elsewhere (Ben-Ari 2004, 2008), while "enabled" by the military—whether in terms of gaining access or being funded—recent ethnographic work about the United States (Linford-Steinfeld 2003; McCaffrey 2002; Simons 1997) and other places such as former Yugoslavia (Macek 2001), Turkey (Altinay 2004), Israel (Ben-Ari 1998), Canada (Winslow 1997), Britain (Kirke 2000), and peacekeeping forces (Rubinstein 2003; Sion 2004) has done much to shed light on these issues. Indeed, the projects carried out by Hana Cervinkova (2006) and John P. Hawkins (2001) that were allowed by the Czech and US militaries, respectively, offer devastating critical analyses of internal military dynamics and their relation to wider cultural processes.

RESEARCH ENABLED BY THE MILITARY

Against this background I argue that the relevant set of problems centers on how—and not whether—to work with the military (*the* institution comprised of specialists in the organized use of violence, often the very embodiment of the state, and closely linked to corporate interests). In this endeavor I follow Hanna Arendt who cautions us to work with "thoughtfulness" so that we can distinguish in our work between what is good and evil in political and moral terms. This move entails being clear about our principles and the implications of our practices in war and conflict zones (Herta Nobauer, personal communication, May 2008). This kind of process enhances transparency and accountability in the research process and provides opportunities for exploring such issues as personal motivations for accepting grants from military funders or interviewing a "captive" sample of troops. In this spirit I now outline my route into studying the Israeli military and three cases in which my research projects were enabled by the military. I do so not in order to devolve into an amateur form of self-analysis (popular a decade ago among American anthropologists), but because my experience may bear some lessons for others.

To the best of my knowledge I am probably the Israeli anthropologist who is most identified with the study of the armed forces. Yet I should note that I have primarily followed women who served in the Israeli military, as did I (and one man who did not actually serve), who opened up critical questions about the IDF. Their research is related, I think, to their relative outsiderness, which has allowed them a critical perspective on the Israeli military (Helman 1997; Izraeli 1997; Kimmerling 1993; Lomsky-Feder 1998; Sasson-Levy 2002). After being a conscript for four years in the 1970s and ending my service as an officer, I then served for twenty-two years in the reserves and was promoted to the rank of major. The seeds of my work on the military were sown during the war of 1973 when I was an infantry soldier and wounded by an Egyptian sniper in the city of Suez. It was during that war that I began (at that time only vaguely) to be aware of questions about Israel's military might (and vulnerability) and my own political commitments.

The actual beginnings of my research into things military lie in my experiences as a member of a battalion of infantry reserves at the end of the 1980s and the beginning of the 1990s. Deployed during the first Palestinian Intifada, my unit performed all of the "usual" activities IDF units were entrusted with in the occupied territories at the time: setting up roadblocks, maintaining patrols, and carrying out arrests. During that period the combination of deeply troubled citizen and anthropologist that accompanied me since returning from my doctoral studies (about Japan) in England a few years earlier guided me in asking questions about how army reservists reconcile their experiences of serving in the occupied territories with those of living their "normal" everyday Israeli lives. A few months after the first deployment I attempted to answer these questions by writing a piece (Ben-Ari 1989) in which I argued that despite circumstances that necessitated police-like activities, the military ethos soon drew soldiers and officers to define their role through an essentially military orientation, as "just" another military mission (like missions carried out in any "regular" war).

But as I wrote this piece I felt that I needed to ask wider questions about the significance of military service, the transition between civilian and army lives, and the justification of violence used by troops. Hence between 1987 and 1992 (when I left Israel for a sabbatical) I undertook a systematic study of the battalion. This effort culminated in an ethnography that can be characterized, curiously, to take off from Brown and Lutz (2007), as a form of "grunt ethnography" (an ethnography of a serving soldier) of the unit in which I served (Ben-Ari 1998). The ethnography covered the ethno-models troops used to make sense of their environment and wider questions about manhood and motivation related to the military.

Why did I turn reflective about the Israeli army? To be sure, it is generally the case that the powerful (in terms of class, ethnicity, or gender) have little reason to reflect on their position as normal, just, or inevitable.

But in times of crisis at least some members of a society's dominant categories (and I belong to them in Israel) are forced to consider anew their position. For me, the Palestinian Uprising (the First Intifada) was just that, a crisis necessitating meaning. In addition, it may be that at that stage of my life (my late thirties) I was mature enough to reflect about my relationship with the military in a way that I could not before.

In 1992, when I returned from my sabbatical and after having already established my disciplinary credentials with publications about Japan, I made a strategic career decision to develop an interest in the anthropology and sociology of the military by seeking funds for research, supervising graduate students, organizing workshops, and teaching relevant courses. Allow me to mention a few of the projects I have been involved with as background to the succeeding analysis. With colleagues I have organized a number of seminars centered on the relations between the military and militarism, with a special emphasis on the critical question of the extent to which Israel can be characterized as a militaristic society (Lomsky-Feder and Ben-Ari 1999; Maman, Rosenhek, and Ben-Ari 2001). I have also carried out more focused work, almost always with colleagues, on sexual orientation in the Israeli army (Kaplan and Ben-Ari 2000), small group dynamics (Ben-Shalom, Lehrer, and Ben-Ari 2005; Sion and Ben-Ari 2005), and managing organizational death (Vinitzky-Seroussi and Ben-Ari 2000). In these works we have described and analyzed not only the ways in which the military and wars have become natural elements of contemporary (Jewish) Israeli society and culture, but also the social processes by which military service has become a desired part of one's (male) life course. Finally, the work of my students has included focusing on the political role of bereaved parents (as a lobby petitioning for their material interests and symbolic importance), training of assassination squads (to carry out state-mandated killings), the experience of being military occupiers (and thus reproducing the taken-for-granted nature of Israel's military occupation), and the reproduction of militarized gender relations in civilian society.

Most of my students carried out their work by interviewing reserve soldiers outside the military context without explicit military authorization. A few, as I presently explain, were integrated into projects enabled by the military. As my work developed, I found my interest broadening beyond the specific context of Israel to include military leadership in industrial democracies, cultural diversity in multinational forces, and peace-support operations. I have also joined my growing expertise in the military with my knowledge of Japan to work and publish on war memory and the contemporary Japanese military and the normalization of violence in that context.

Finally, over the years I have been directly involved with the Israeli military while conducting three main research projects, one applied and two more strictly academic in orientation.

The Ground Forces in the Al-Aqsa Intifada

In the spring of 2000 I was approached by the behavioral sciences department of the IDF ground forces to carry out research with three serving officers who were, respectively, a sociologist, a social psychologist, and an anthropologist (Ben-Ari et al. 2009). The project centered on the Israeli army's combat companies, and its aim was to analyze their social structures and leadership patterns. This was a period when Israel had withdrawn from southern Lebanon and when, we assumed, the main operational assignments of the IDF would continue to be policing the territories and implementing the Oslo Accords. Three months after we began the project the Second Palestinian Uprising, the Al-Aqsa Intifada, erupted and marked the IDF's critical transition into a state of prolonged conflict with Palestinian armed groups. We consequently found ourselves in a rather "advantageous" (if peculiar) position of being able to chart this transition and accompany the development of the conflict. We decided to continue our research by observing the units within the renewed clashes. For social scientists, the Al-Aqsa Intifada provided a rare opportunity to witness how military forces shift quickly from routine activities into sudden, often violent, action.

The volume that emerged from this project (ending in 2006) encompasses a number of issues: the creation of ad hoc units; combat in urban environments; the relations between gender and military technology along the separation barrier; and the combination of violent practices and limits characterizing the Israeli armed forces that we termed, following James Ron (2000), "savage restraint." We ended the volume by examining the strong emphasis on precision warfare and new rules of engagement alongside limiting factors such as the activities of the media, human rights movements, and judicial involvement in tactical decisions.

Funding for this project was provided by the Israeli military and used for hiring research assistants (my students). The university provided space for discussion and brainstorming. Because the project involved me in a cooperative venture with serving officers, I found myself wary as never before of the constraints of military censorship. Thus, for instance, we formulated research questions in abstract terms such as "new forms of tactical organizations" or conceptual frameworks suitable to the "new wars." In effect, however, the final text included a heavy emphasis on the problems of dealing with civilians, fighting insurgents, how global human rights have impacted local level troops, and the dire impact of Israeli policy on Palestinian lives. To my mind there was no way I could have gained access to the kind of data we gathered if I were solely dependent on interviewing soldiers outside the military context.

Checkpoints

In 2003 two army officers approached me to help improve the military's work at checkpoints (arrayed around the occupied territories) (Ben-Ari et al. 2004). For the vast majority of Palestinians, checkpoints are *the* symbol of the occupation, of aggression, and of humiliation. For this reason I agreed to cooperate with the army on the basis of my hope that I could ease the plight of Palestinians moving through checkpoints and secured funding through a large German foundation. A few months after completing our report I appeared before a military committee appointed to look into the checkpoints. Perhaps as a consequence of our project (among others) the army adopted new training programs for soldiers staffing checkpoints and initiated improvements in their infrastructure.

I am aware that there may be critical readings of this project. Firstly, instituting improvements at checkpoints is akin to teaching soldiers to be polite when interacting with Palestinians. In psychological terms such measures can be seen as a sort of defense mechanism for they allow a self-image of soldiers as humane while allowing them to continue performing their roles. Secondly, sociologically, by making the checkpoints more compassionate, the argument would go that I actually contributed to reproducing the occupation. In other words, by making the occupation take on a more "humane" expression, our research group simply gave it a "good face," thus allowing the prolongation of the occupation. While aware of such potential criticisms, I made a clear choice to try to ease the everyday experiences of Palestinians at checkpoints. More widely, the dilemma that I faced centered on the question of whether to work within the system or outside of it. I decided to work within the system to make a difference to people's lives, to reduce harm (Rubinstein, this volume).

Diversity and the Reproduction of Inequality

In 2005 my friend and colleague Edna Lomsky-Feder and I were approached by officers to carry out a project on how the Israeli military manages diversity (the rhetoric, institutional arrangements, and practices for dealing with the needs and demands of groups defined as distinct). We were approached based on an article we had previously published about this subject (Lomsky-Feder and Ben-Ari 1999). In the former project we used publicly available material (mainly newspapers) to develop our analysis. In the new project we were promised access to units to observe the ways in which military policies were actually implemented. With military funds we recruited a number of research assistants and interviewed fifty relevant individuals. At the same time we jointly taught a seminar for graduate students at the Hebrew University of Jerusalem to which we belong about the management of diversity in the military.

In most of the scholarly literature on the management of diversity in the armed forces, the underlying problematic is one of how social differences may be handled so that the military's effectiveness is not impaired and that its reputation does not hamper the potential for recruitment and retention. By contrast, from the beginning of the project both of us felt that it represented a good opportunity to use the concept of "managing diversity" to learn about how the military reproduces wider inequality and treats weaker members of society. We were willing to pay the price of potential censorship for access to the units and the soldiers since we felt hearing their voices was crucial for understanding this reproduction of inequality. We are currently still waiting for the military's response in regard to what part of our text we will be allowed to publish.

STUDYING THE MILITARY: CAUTIONS AND DIALOGUES

My engagement with the IDF raises questions about professional conduct in interacting with the armed forces. I now examine a number of issues related to the methods, ethics, and politics of working with the military.

Fieldwork in the Security Sector

Most important, the military is marked by secrecy and closed-ness implying control over access. This situation first implied that the behavioral sciences department of the IDF had to authorize our research projects. Since the military had approached me in all three endeavors, this was never a problem. Secondly, in all the projects we were dependent on our military hosts for access to sites and interviewees. Most often we allied ourselves with units' organizational consultants and created a dialogue with local commanders about our research themes. To the best of my knowledge, except in instances that involved risk to our lives, we never encountered problems in gaining access to soldiers. In the interviews soldiers were sometimes wary because of the political views they seem to have attributed to us as representatives of academia. After seeing that we were not judgmental they almost always opened up and talked about a variety of often controversial issues (such as using violence against Palestinians).

But the uniqueness of the military lies in control centered on that general category of "national security." Hence the texts we wrote, based on data gathered within the military, were subject to two tiers of control: the military censor in charge of operational information and the IDF spokesperson responsible for the institution's "image." While we have never had the IDF censor reject any text submitted, one chapter dealing with checkpoints in the ethnography of the Al-Aqsa Intifada was excised by the second tier, the IDF spokesperson (presumably because it was critical of the military). Thus as far as I understand, it was disallowed not because it contained state secrets but because it contained descriptions that were seen as damaging to the public image of the IDF. In this sense not only are our subjects powerful and literate agents who read what we say (Gusterson 1996:17) but also they may use a variety of formal frameworks to limit publication of academic texts. The solution to this problem, we have found, is a dialogue with the IDF spokesperson about drafts of our texts. Moreover, since the IDF is not a homogenous organization, we have often been aided by military partners who had an interest in such publications.

Mixing with Military Elites

Antonius Robben (1995), who carried out research on Argentinean officers from a military dictatorship, cautions anthropologists to be aware of seduction by professional perpetrators of violence. In my case this allurement was less evident in terms of research, for I only rarely had interviews with senior commanders. Rather, I found the problem appeared in regard to my participation in high-ranking committees about military matters, appearing as an "expert" in front of other committees, or simply presenting talks to senior officers. As I reflect on it, my motivation for participating in such forums combined a belief that officers should be educated about issues facing them, a conviction that through committee work I could make a difference to policy, the pleasures of mixing with senior commanders (I learned a lot), and a sense of self-importance. But in only two cases did I feel that my participation had made a difference: in committees established to look into the reserve and conscript components of the IDF. Recently, I have cut back on my involvement because I feel that I am not making enough of a difference and that I am often invited merely as an academic "ornament."

Native Anthropology and Insider Research

For me, studying the IDF has also involved anthropology at home. Indeed, in the context of Israel—given conscription and reserve service—

the majority of scholars of the IDF have had direct experience in the military, or their family members, friends, or students have had such experience. With this anthropology at home one of the main problems I have encountered is creating a critical distance from my own native understandings and assumptions. In the ethnography I wrote about my battalion I found that I needed to devise techniques not so much for getting *into* a new culture as for getting *out* of all too familiar surroundings. To be sure, the advantages of participation in the unit center on being closest to the way military meanings are "naturally" actualized and my ability to use my native understandings of soldiering as a resource. Yet the major disadvantage is the lack of proper "distance" from the unit and very basic (emotionally loaded) issues such as masculine identity, citizenship, militarism, or nationhood. Among the methods I used to achieve this distancing was the study of language. I found myself making extensive use of military and vernacular dictionaries to translate military argot and informal slang. I also deliberately attempted to defamiliarize my material by linking my data to explanations of small-group formation in the US Army in Korea and Vietnam and to the Wehrmacht in World War II or to the social scientific study of emotions. All of these moves forced me to reflect about my data from a more detached vantage point.

A Public Science and Dialogue

In insider research one often has to make an intentional effort to maintain a critical edge, not to become an advocate for organizational interests or legitimizing the powers that be (Ortner 2000:987). I found that I was aided in such moves by the character of anthropology as a public discipline. The very need to publish my work in scholarly journals and to appear in various academic forums, as indeed in the SAR forum itself, have forced me to constantly reflect about my positions and responsibility as a scholar and citizen. Such moves should be placed within a wider model of dialogue: an ongoing exchange between anthropologists and the military about creating and adjusting expectations about the conditions of research, researched groups, funding, and knowledge produced. As I found in my own projects, the terms of research are negotiable, and researchers can balance funds for research and making the result available to the people studied and the general public. Yet in dialoguing with the IDF, I have found that the most serious problems center on ownership of the knowledge produced. While I did not exactly carry out proprietary anthropology (receiving no income for research), I found the problem to be one of balancing responsibility to military funders with what I see as my responsibility to the discipline and the wider public. Concretely, this exchange has involved dialogue in regard to publication and, as explained, sometimes I have had to make compromises.

ANTHROPOLOGY ENGAGED WITH THE MILITARY

Many calls for a publicly engaged anthropology have recently been sounded, and I strongly sympathize with them. The participation of anthropologists in public discussions about war and the military is crucial if we are to understand our contemporary world. Here, I would like to emphasize two main points: the particular contribution that anthropology can make to the study of such issues and the special problems of working with the military.

Sherry Ortner (2000) suggests that the distinctive contribution of our discipline lies in fieldwork as method, ethnography as textual practice, inequality as a focus of study, and culture as an organizing term. In studying armed conflict, our disciplinary perspective can uncover how state-mandated violence is actualized in concrete situations, provide soldierly points of view (without necessarily accepting them), and uncover contradictions between official pronouncements and actual behavior (McNamara, this volume). Here, I have argued that sometimes such sustained work is only possible by being enabled by the military. Indeed, recent years have seen the publication of a number of ethnographies that very successfully express the kinds of emphases as I have shown through my text by citing such scholars as Lutz, Ayse Gul Altinay, Hawkins, and Cervinkova.

But the problem of working with, or being enabled by, the military centers on an internal disciplinary dialogue about what can be called "proper" anthropology" and our commitment to social issues. Until the 1960s American anthropologists saw themselves as contributing to the betterment of assorted societies in various applied projects. This commitment had no doubt much to do with the optimistic 1950s and 1960s. But with the Vietnam War various "alliances" with the state began to be seen as inherently suspicious. Perhaps current debates may ironically signal a rethinking of these alliances and a more reflective mode of working with the state and state agents. Thus any relations between anthropologists and the military must be accompanied by a sustained reflection of how the knowledge we produce (the intentions of individuals not withstanding) may become part of waging wider conflicts (Price, Ferguson, this volume).

In this vein I follow Chambers (2005:319) in arguing for the moral necessity of work outside of academia and the potential of anthropological inquiry to contribute responsibly to understanding social issues. But the problem is, of course, that any work with external organizations involves risks. McNamara (2007a:25) talks about the need to consider the trade-off between the risks of engagement in ethically fraught environments and the benefits to the discipline of knowledge produced therein. I would cautiously add that the balance also includes the possibility of organizational change. For instance, as explained before, I have found that the IDF, like any large organization, encompasses potential coalition partners for effecting change. In the project on diversity we found officers wanting to open up questions of inequality produced by the military. One could contend that by being enabled by the military I am collaborating with it. I would counter that it would be easy to keep away from any involvement and thus keep my hands clean, my reputation as a morally upright individual intact, and my allegiance to a certain political camp upheld. Thus I am sure that for some more radically inclined colleagues and friends I have not gone far enough, but from a personal perspective, I have traveled a significant way toward a critical understanding of the Israeli military. To follow Rubinstein (this volume), in studying the Israeli military I have found myself in a liminal position: I am still personally and organizationally attached to the IDF (my two sons served in combat units during the last decade), but as a scholar wielding anthropological frames of reference I am an outsider to this institution.

Note

1. I wish to thank Herta Neubauer for discussions about the military and anthropology and Efrat Ben-Ze'ev and Nurit Stadler for comments on an earlier draft of this chapter.

9

Anthropology, War, and Peace

Hobbesian Beliefs within Science, Scholarship, and Society

Douglas P. Fry

In researching war and peace, I have noticed a bias toward exaggerating, overemphasizing, and magnifying warfare in comparison to peace. In this chapter I will argue that the cultural traditions and beliefs of the researchers themselves contribute to this bias. Several case studies that raise questions relevant to the issue of research bias will be presented in support of this thesis: (1a) Does Australian Aborigine rock art really show warfare? (1b) Why have researchers assumed that it does? (2a) Do Yanomamö killers really have more offspring than nonkillers? (2b) Why does the suggestion that they do grab so much attention? (3a) Why are nomadic hunter-gatherer societies often assumed to be warlike? (3b) How can we explain certain questionable sampling and methodological decisions in one oft cited study of hunter-gatherer war? (4a) Were South African australopithecines really killer apes? (4b) Why were they assumed to be? (5a) Will all societies make war if attacked? (5b) Why was this the default assumption of researchers conducting a large cross-cultural study of war?

A consideration of these five cases support the thesis that there is strong bias in the West, and certainly in US society in particular, that sometimes affects perceptions, research methods, and interpretations related to war and peace. It is important to raise such issues because aside from academic implications, broadcasting warlike images of humanity can contribute to the self-fulfilling prophecy that war is inevitable.

ANTHROPOLOGICAL FINDINGS ON WAR AND PEACE

Cross-cultural survey research suggests that about 5 to 8 percent of societies do not engage in warfare (Gregor 1990:106–107; Otterbein 1968; Wright 1942). Ethnographic examples of cultures lacking war come from all parts of the world and include, for instance, the Andaman Islanders of South Asia, the Arunta of Australia, the Buid of the Philippines, the Cayapa of South America, the Chewong of Malaysia, the Copper Inuit of North America, the Gosiute and Kaibab Paiute of North America, the Polar Inuit of Greenland, the Punan of Borneo, the Saulteaux of North America, the Semai of Malaysia, the Tikopian Islanders of the western Pacific, the Todas of India, the Yanadi of Eurasia, and various other cultures (Dentan 1968; Fabbro 1978; Gibson 1989; Gilberg 1984; Howell 1989; Keeley 1996; Lesser 1968; Montagu 1978; Ross 1993; Service 1971; van der Dennen 1995). I have compiled lists documenting more than seventy non-warring societies (Fry 2006, 2007).

In addition, some neighboring societies constitute peace systems, meaning that they do not make war on each other (and sometimes not with outsiders either). For example, the aboriginal inhabitants of the central Malaysia Peninsula; the Inuit of Greenland; the Montagnais, Naskapi, and Cree bands of Canada's Labrador Peninsula; the societies of India's Nilgiri and Wynaad Plateaus; the tribes of the Upper Xingu River basin in Brazil; Australian Aborigines; and even the European Union exemplify peace systems (Fry, Bonta, and Baszarkiewicz 2008; Miklikowska and Fry 2010). The existence of non-warring societies and peace systems contradicts the assumptions that humans are naturally warlike and that war is inevitable.

Furthermore, Johan van der Dennen (1995) points out that many cultures practice only *defensive* warfare. The Papago of the North American Southwest, for example, fit this pattern (Ross 1993). Van der Dennen (1995:595) has compiled a list of nearly *two hundred* cultures that are "highly unwarlike," that is, "war [is] reported as absent or mainly defensive." Clearly, pro-militaristic values or motivations involving resource acquisition are not the only factors prompting a society to engage in warfare —self-defense seems to be a common concern as well.

A cross-cultural perspective shows that some cultures are more warlike than others. Some cultures shun warrior values, such as the tribes of Brazil's Upper Xingu River basin (Fry 2006). On the other hand, some societies promote warrior values such as bravery and fortitude. For instance, equestrian societies of the North American plains began training boys at an early age to be courageous warriors (Hoebel 1967). Anthropology also shows that the likelihood and severity of warfare correlates positively with increased sociopolitical complexity (Fry 2006, 2007).

THE UNITED STATES, WAR, AND VALUES

Turning the focus to the United States, one can ask: Do Americans perceive themselves as warlike or as having warrior values? Living outside of the United States, in Finland, I periodically hear Europeans refer to Americans as militaristic or even belligerent. Italian thinker Umberto Eco is quoted in *Time* magazine as saying, "Sure Europe is old. But age brings advantages, like experience. Unfortunately with our Continent's tragic history we've lived through centuries of massacres, and maybe our nerves are steadier for it. Not to be flip, but 3,000 died in the Twin Towers, and 6 million in the Holocaust. Europe's old age is one of wisdom, not of Alzheimer's" (Israely 2005:47).

Turning to insider views, Leslie Sponsel (1998:101) writes of the United States, "Whatever the noble truths about the history of America, there are also the ignoble truths that the country was built on violence, e.g., the genocide, ethnocide, and ecocide against indigenous peoples...and numerous wars, e.g., the War of Independence, the Civil War, the Spanish-American War, World War I and World War II, the Korean War, the Vietnam War, and the Gulf War." Joel Andreas (2004:7) points out that between 1898 and 1934, US Marines invaded Honduras seven times; Nicaragua five times; Columbia, Cuba, and the Dominican Republic four times each; Mexico three times; Haiti and Panama twice; and Guatemala once.

In her paper for the second SAR seminar, Clementine Fujimura pointed out how an emphasis on competition in US culture goes hand-in-hand with militarism: "The US military wants to compete, and whether or not there is a war to be fought, the military competes at every level" (Fujimura 2011). Currently, the United States has more military forces deployed around the world, more military bases, and more military alliances, and is involved in training and arming more foreign armies than any other nation on earth (Paige 2002:8). The United States is fighting wars in both Afghanistan and Iraq. And the United States is the only country to have ever used nuclear weapons. To get a comparative perspective, the Global Peace Index (2008) provides ranks for 140 countries. The lower the rank, the more peaceful the country. Iceland, Denmark, and Norway hold ranks of one, two, and three, respectively, whereas the United States ranks 97 and Iraq 140. Based on evidence such as this, a strong case could be made that America is a warlike society. Americans are well accustomed to war, which would seem to make the waging of new wars all the easier. As I will next consider, many but not all Americans hold views of human nature that are conducive to accepting war as an inevitable, though perhaps regrettable, fact of life.

CULTURAL BELIEFS: HUMAN NATURE AND WAR

In separate studies university students from Florida and Connecticut completed attitude surveys that assessed beliefs about human nature and war (Adams and Bosch 1987; Fry and Welch 1992). The students were asked if "human beings have an instinct for war" and whether "war is an intrinsic part of human nature." Approximately half the respondents in each place connected war to instinct and human nature.

One can see such beliefs reflected in pop culture too. A *Murphy Brown* TV episode includes dialogue about the inevitability and naturalness of war. In a *Six Foot Under* episode, one character says, "Males are hardwired to be aggressive and territorial." And in academic writings one can find statements like the following by noted biologist Edward O. Wilson (2001:14): "Are human beings innately aggressive?…The answer to it is yes. Throughout history, warfare, representing only the most organized technique of aggression, has been endemic to every form of society, from hunter-gatherer bands to industrial states."

Such statements would seem to reflect shared cultural beliefs that war is natural and inevitable. Cultural belief systems contain "notions of the nature and attributes of humanity. They decide whether we are good, evil, or neutral" (Grunkemeyer 1996:126). As shared aspects of culture, "belief systems tend for the most part to reside at the level of assumptions and presuppositions" (Grunkemeyer 1996:125). In other words, people rarely check the validity of their beliefs against data. Indeed, people pick up beliefs as part of their cultural heritage. As Fujimura observed in the second SAR seminar, "through daily interactions, people shape, are being shaped by, and strengthen their cultural systems. In effect, we are continuously dynamically engaged in enculturation, learning and teaching culture, at times consciously, other times subconsciously" (Fujimura 2011). Statements such as Edward O. Wilson's about innate aggression and the endemic nature of war may reflect a common, shared belief in US culture, the veracity of which is taken for granted, as ongoing wars in Afghanistan and Iraq would seem to substantiate.

Taking a historical perspective, viewing war as part and parcel of human nature has a long tradition in Western thinking. Thomas Hobbes (1946) philosophized in *Leviathan*, originally published in 1651, on the natural state of war; renowned psychologist William James viewed humans as naturally aggressive; Sigmund Freud devised a death instinct to explain human destructiveness (see Fry 1985). However, scientists and scholars are members of a culture too (Tomforde, this volume). Like everybody else, scientists and scholars learn cultural traditions and beliefs that influence their thinking and perceptions. As David Price (this volume) says, the generation and application of all knowledge, science and social science included, is embedded within social contexts. When cultural beliefs hold that human beings are innately bellicose, inevitably violent, instinctively warlike, and so on, people socialized in such circumstances, whether scientists or nonscientists, tend to take on these cultural beliefs without much question. Perhaps it is easier to "see" this phenomenon outside one's own cultural world. For example, the Semai tend not to question whether supernatural spirits called *mara'* actually exist—they have grown up in a culture where everybody believes that mara' exist (Robarchek 1989). Similarly, Zapotecs tend not to question the belief that being subjected to a frightening event can cause an illness called *susto*, or fright sickness (Fry 2004). Cultural beliefs are generally accepted by cultural insiders—including scientists and scholars—most of the time.

THE SNAKE EATS ITS OWN TAIL: APPLYING ANTHROPOLOGICAL CONCEPTS TO ANTHROPOLOGY

To apply the anthropological concept of belief system to anthropology itself, there are many examples of how anthropological findings, and those from other fields, have been interpreted within the context of cultural beliefs about war and human nature. I will now present five cases in illustration of this theme.

The first case comes from Australia, where rock art depicting animals, humans, and mythological beings has been found across Arnhem Land. Most scenes with humans show daily nonviolent activities, but some art portrays men amidst flying boomerangs and spears. Paul Taçon and Christopher Chippindale (1994) draw the seemingly obvious interpretation that warfare is being depicted. They title their article "Australia's Ancient Warriors" and explain that "some of the paintings depict fighting, warriors, aspects or the results of warfare, and even elaborate, detailed battle scenes" (1994:214).

However, there are two important reasons to doubt whether this rock art actually portrays warfare at all. Firstly, warfare was very rare in aboriginal Australia. For instance, Ronald Berndt and Catherine Berndt (1996:362) conclude that "warfare in the broader sense is infrequent in Aboriginal Australia, and most examples which have been classified as such are often no more than feud," and E. Adamson Hoebel (1967:306) correspondingly specifies, "Among the Australians it is clearly a matter of feud."

The second reason for doubting Taçon and Chippindale's (1994) war-oriented interpretations of the scenes comes from a consideration of the rock art itself vis-à-vis ethnographic knowledge about Australian Aborigines. The majority of the rock art scenes depicting spears or boomerangs are consistent with ethnographic descriptions of events that have nothing to do with *warfare*, namely, (a) revenge killings and other homicides, (b) the punishment of wrongdoers by spearing them in the thigh, and (c) especially, ceremonial duels that are a well-documented form of Australian Aborigine conflict resolution. Let me focus on each of the above events in turn.

Firstly, regarding homicides, Australian Aborigine ethnographies report with some regularity that individuals may be killed from time to time. Therefore, when a rock art scene described by Taçon and Chippindale (1994) shows a *single* individual with a spear through his torso, this is an image more ethnographically concordant with the aftermath of a homicide than a battle. After all, why would a war scene portray one, and only one, victim?

Secondly, turning to a typical Australian Aborigine style of punishing wrongdoers, the delivery of nonfatal wounds to the thigh or other nonvital parts of the body recur in ethnographic reports. For example, among the Mardu, someone who has violated a taboo or committed some other offense will "offer himself submissively, head bowed down and thigh held motionless, ready to receive the initial clubbing and jabs from staffing spears carefully directed to avoid arteries" (Tonkinson 2004:98). Similarly, the punishment inflicted on a Tiwi man who seduced another man's wife was to dodge the spears thrown at him by the angry husband. After about ten minutes the wrongdoer was supposed to allow himself to be hit by a spear—thus receiving his punishment for the seduction. "A fairly deep cut on the arm or thigh that bled a lot but healed quickly was the most desirable wound,…and when blood gushed from such a wound the crowd yelled approval and the duel was over" (Hart and Pilling 1979:82). Thus when Taçon and Chippindale (1994) report that a rock art scene shows a *single* figure who has been speared in the thigh, this image is totally consistent with ethnographic accounts of how Aboriginal Australians inflict socially sanctioned punishments.

Thirdly, many Australian societies used ceremonial or ritualized fights to settle conflicts. Such fights could superficially resemble war, but the typical aim was to settle disputes, not to kill anybody (Fry 2006). The Tiwi, for instance, met in groups to haggle, throw spears, and vent their emotions;

they also at the same time camped together, socialized, and exchanged gossip (Hart and Pilling 1979:83–87). The Murngin of Arnhem Land engaged in a ceremonial peacemaking fight called the *makarata*. W. Lloyd Warner (1969:163) explains, "It is a kind of general duel and a partial ordeal which allows the aggrieved parties to vent their feelings by throwing spears at their enemies or by seeing the latter's blood run in expiation." The makarata was not always successful at restoring the peace, but over the two decades of Warner's research, nobody was ever killed during a makarata. In fact, the elders reminded the younger men throwing spears "to be careful not to kill or hurt anyone" (Warner 1969:164). Clearly, the ritualized makarata was not warfare. It was an instance of Australian Aborigine–style conflict resolution.

Returning to the rock art scenes that Taçon and Chippindale interpret in martial terms, another basis for skepticism that these portrayals have anything to do with warfare is that most scenes show only a few individuals, a pattern reminiscent of duels and punishments, but *not* intergroup warfare. In writing about so-called dynamic figures, Taçon and Chippindale (1994:120) explain, "In most cases where actual combat is suggested only two or three figures are engaged in some sort of encounter. *There are many examples of two opposed figures*" (emphasis added). In contrast to these abundant two-person dueling scenes, images of two groups confronting one another are relatively rare. Given the ethnographic literature on ceremonial group fights like the makarata and two-person duels, the interpretation of rock art as warfare, even in group scenes, is dubious.

In conclusion, the body of ethnographic evidence from Aboriginal Australia contradicts the assumption that these rock art scenes are portraying *warfare*. Instead, the ethnographic context suggests that homicides, socially sanctioned punishments, expiatory duels, and similar grievance settlement procedures are being represented in the rock art (see, for example, Berndt 1965; Berndt and Berndt 1996; Hart and Piling 1979; Spencer and Gillen 1927). Given, firstly, that most disputes in foraging band societies are personal in nature (Fry 2006), and, secondly, that duels, contests, and other ritualized modes of grievance resolution are regularly used by Australian Aborigines, and, thirdly, the paucity of war in the Australian Aborigine cultural context, then shouldn't the assumption that rock art shows war be viewed with skepticism?

The point is that the *concept of war* enters the picture in this Australian case not from the minds of the original artists themselves, but from interpretations of the artwork by cultural outsiders. Westerners have a tendency to take warfare for granted, since war is an established aspect of Western cultural tradition and, therefore, in this case, Western archaeologists inappropriately project martial conceptions onto rock art from a very different cultural tradition within which war is an anomaly. In their publication, Taçon and Chippindale (1994) use unambiguous war terms about seventeen times as often as they employ conflict resolution terminology (eighty-seven versus five). This emphasis on war is markedly out of step with ethnographically documented conflict resolution procedures that were common in Aboriginal Australia and with the paucity of war among the societies on this continent. It seems that Taçon and Chippindale's (1994) use of the word "warriors" in the title of their article coupled with the fact that their article make copious use of war terminology reflect the impact of a Western cultural tradition on scientific interpretation wherein the antiquity and naturalness of war are taken for granted.

DO YANOMAMÖ KILLERS REALLY HAVE MORE CHILDREN?

Napoleon Chagnon (1983:214) has advanced the Yanomamö as "our contemporary ancestors." David Buss (1999:300) claims that Yanomamö warfare highlights "key themes in the evolution of human aggression." If a Yanomamö man participates in a killing, he must take part in a purification ceremony and thereafter is referred to as *unokai*. Chagnon (1990:95; 1992:239–240) has emphasized that unokais average more than two times the wives and more than three times the number of offspring as non-unokais of the same age.

Upon publication, the report that killers out-reproduce nonkillers made the news. The amount of scholarly and public attention paid to this particular finding is noteworthy. An article in the *U.S. News and World Report*, for example, stated that Chagnon's finding "lends new credence" to the idea that "war arises from individuals struggling for reproductive success" (Allman 1988:57–58). Recently, Malcolm Potts and Thomas Hayden (2008:162) and Azar Gat (2006:58), among others, have rebroadcast the message. In fact, sources that cite and reiterate Chagnon's findings are simply too numerous to track (see Fry 2006). Steven Pinker (2003:116) explains that differences in reproductive success between killers and nonkillers is "provocative because if that payoff was typical of the pre-state societies in which humans evolved, the strategic use of violence would have been selected over evolutionary time." So again we see a Hobbesian interpretation that purports to explain how lethal aggression in humans has been propelled by evolutionary forces.

Contrary to Chagnon's assertions, his groups of unokais and non-unokais actually are *not* the same age (Ferguson 1989, 1995; Fry 2006). This

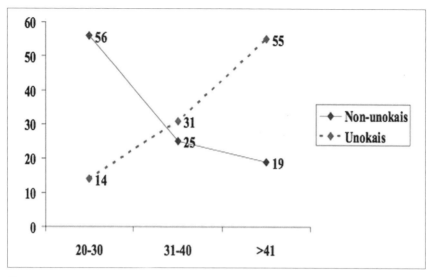

FIGURE 9.1.

*Age distributions for Non-*unokais *and* unokais *expressed in terms of percent for each distribution separately. Notice that 56 percent of the non-unokais are twenty to thirty years of age; by contrast, 55 percent of unokais are at least forty-one years of age. As a group, unokais are older than non-unokais. (Data used to make this figure are from Chagnon 1988, tables 2 and 3; this chart adapted from Fry 2007.)*

is readily apparent in figure 9.1, which is based on Chagnon's own data. Some calculating shows that group for group, the unokais are *at least* 10.4 years older than non-unokais (Fry 2006:184–199, 288–305) It is not surprising that an older group of Yanomamö men would average more children than a younger group of men, simply because older men have had more years of life to father offspring. But a false claim that ages are comparable between the two groups of men is not the only problem with Chagnon's (1988) analysis. Headmen among the Yanomamö tend to have more wives and children than non-headmen. This fact also must be taken into consideration.

Inspired by R. Brian Ferguson's (1989, 1995) skepticism over Chagnon's (1988) findings, I conducted a mathematical reanalysis that shows that neither the effects of age nor headman status were adequately taken into account in Chagnon's study. Without a doubt, the reported difference in reproductive success between unokais and non-unokais has been greatly exaggerated (Fry 2006). In actuality, it may be that no difference in reproductive success exists at all between the two groups. But even if some difference does exist, the mathematical reanalysis shows that it is only a fraction of the amount originally reported that has received so much attention (Fry 2006).

An interesting question is: Why has this finding gained such popularity? At least some of the enthusiastic reception and bountiful citation of the 1988 Chagnon study may be because the study is perceived to offer "scientific confirmation" of widely shared cultural beliefs about humanity's violent, warlike nature (see, for example, Ghiglieri 1999; Smith 2007). Perhaps another reason that these findings have been so eagerly reiterated is due to a rising popularity of evolutionary discussions of behavior.

HUNTER-GATHERER WAR: DISTORTING THE PICTURE.

The next case of "seeing" more warfare in the data than actually exists involves a cross-cultural study of hunter-gatherers. Carol Ember (1978:443) clearly states her goal: "I wish to address myself to one other view of hunter-gatherers that I have reason to believe is erroneous—namely, the view that hunter-gatherers are relatively peaceful." Ember (1978:443) reported that only 10 percent of her "sample of hunter-gatherers...were rated as having no or rare warfare." Many writers quote Ember's 1978 study. Joshua Goldstein (2001:24; see also Smith 2007), for example, cites Ember to draw implications about human nature and war:

> The evidence from modern-day gathering-hunting societies, whose supposed peaceful nature was assumed to reflect peaceful human origins, in fact shows the opposite: modern gathering-hunting societies are *not* generally peaceful. Of 31 gathering-hunting societies surveyed in one study, 20 typically had warfare more than once every two years, and only three [10 percent] had "no or rare warfare."...If typical gathering-hunting societies found today represent the typical societies found before the rise of the state—as advocates of peaceful origins have claimed— then those original societies were warlike.

There are two reasons why Goldstein and others are led astray by Ember's 1978 article. Firstly, Ember defined war to include feuding and even some cases of homicide. Under her definition, a personal grudge that culminates in a homicide can be counted as an act of "war" if two or more persons commit the deed. For example, in the real ethnographic example wherein an Alacaluf husband, accompanied by his brother, kills his wife's lover (Bird 1946:71), this murder would constitute an act of "war" according to Ember (1978). The fact that Ember is defining "war" in such an unusual way is not discussed in the article itself. One must look in a different publication (Ember and Ember 1971) to discover that acts that most people would call murder are considered as acts of "war" by Ember (1978). Discovering that such an idiosyncratic definition of "war" was used in the study casts a totally different light on the findings. Why would someone define "war" in this way? Why would someone refer readers to a different article for the definition of "war," instead of just stating the definition up front?

The second serious complication with Ember's 1978 study is that, amazing as it might seem, 48 percent of the societies in the sample are not nomadic hunter-gatherers at all. The sample includes complex and equestrian hunter-gatherers, who are very different from nomadic foragers— they tend to be warlike (Fry 2006; Kelly 1995; Knauft 1991). Therefore, the findings of Ember's 1978 study cannot logically be employed to draw conclusions about nomadic hunter-gatherer bands or the nomadic foraging past, as Goldstein (2001) and others have done. If we are interested in this question, then obviously we need to examine a sample of nomadic hunter-gatherers. It might also be interesting to compare nomadic hunter-gatherers with complex and equestrian hunter-gatherers (Fry 2006, 2007).

Hunter-gatherer societies overall, not just nomadic bands, can be operationally defined as those having *at most* 5 percent subsistence dependence on agriculture and animal husbandry. By this criterion, the Standard Cross-Cultural Sample (SCCS) contains thirty-five hunter-gatherer societies based on ratings by George Murdock (1967, 1981). Murdock also has published codes for settlement type, whether or not a society has a class system and, if so, what type, and, finally, whether horses are used in the society. An examination of Murdock's codes reveals that the thirty-five hunter-gatherer societies can be subdivided into three groups. The first group consists of nomadic or semi-nomadic societies that lack class distinctions and domestic animals, including horses. This kind of society most closely resembles nomadic hunter-gatherers of the evolutionary past.

Complex hunter-gatherers are those societies that are rated as *not* being nomadic or as having social class distinctions. Finally, equestrian hunter-gatherers constitute a subgroup of very recent origin, arising after the Spanish introduced the horse into the Americas some 350 years ago. Taking these distinctions into account yields twenty-one nomadic hunter-gatherer societies, nine complex hunter-gatherer societies, and five equestrian hunter-gatherer societies (Fry 2006:table 8.2). The key finding, apparent in table 9.1, is that all the complex hunter-gatherers and equestrian hunters in the sample wage war, whereas most of the nomadic foragers

DOUGLAS P. FRY

TABLE 9.1

Presence or Absence of Warfare and Type of Society*

Hunter-Gatherers	Non-warring	Warring
Nomadic	!Kung Aranda Hadza Copper Eskimo Mbuti Andamanese Semang Saulteaux Vedda Paiute Tiwi Yahgan Slavey	Montagnais Gilyak Ingalik Botocudo Kaska Aweikoma
Others		Bella Coola Haida Gros Ventre Yurok Comanche Yokuts Chiricahua Kutenai Tehuelche Twana Klamath Eyak Eastern Pomo Aleut
	n = 13	n = 22

* Nomadic hunter-gatherers are in the top row. Other types of hunter-gatherers are in the bottom row. "War" is defined as involving armed combat between political communities and not merely as feuding and revenge homicide. (Fisher's exact test [one-tailed] probability, $p = .0001$.)

do not (Fry 2006:table 8.3). Sponsel suggests "that warfare would be absent or negligible in most foraging societies is not only *plausible* but also *probable*, if one considers that they are largely occupied with subsistence, lack sufficient food surplus to sustain a military organization and its adventures, and do not have political leadership and organization to direct warfare" (1996:107; emphasis in original).

PROJECTING HOBBESIAN VIEWS ONTO THE HOMINID PAST

The following case is a classic one. For our purposes, it has the positive feature of showing explicitly how the researcher in question, Raymond Dart, held beliefs that human nature is belligerent and violent. Dart (1953:207) interpreted fractured australopithecine skeletal remains from South Africa as evidence that humanity's early ancestors were killers, proving humanity's "carnivorous, and cannibalistic origin." Dart observed that most of the fossil baboon skulls found with the australopithecine specimens appeared to have been bashed on the head. Some of the baboon and australopithecine crania had paired depressions or holes. Dart interpreted the holes in one australopithecine cranium as a deliberate mutilation probably inflicted for ritualistic reasons (Ury 1999:33).

Joseph Birdsell tells a story of questioning Dart about what percentage of the australopithecines had been murdered and Dart responding, "Why, all of them, of course" (van der Dennen 1995:199). Perhaps Dart was being facetious, but, nonetheless, he argued that in case after case australopithecine remains showed evidence of lethal violence (Dart 1949, 1953, 1958). Dart thought, for example, that the paired depressions on australopithecine skulls were caused by these ancient murderers bludgeoning each other with animal bones. Dart (1949:12) interpreted, for instance, that one australopithecine succumbed to "a severing transverse blow [to]...the front and back halves of the broken skull." He also thought that the famous Taung child had been killed by a blow to the skull. Thus to Dart (1953:209) the australopithecines were "confirmed killers: carnivorous creatures that seized living quarries by violence, battered them to death, tore apart their broken bodies, dismembered them limb for limb, slaking their ravenous thirst with the hot blood of victims and greedily devouring livid writhing flesh."

As if Dart's use of language was not dramatic enough, playwright Robert Ardrey (1961, 1966) further scripted the "killer ape" story in books that simultaneously reflected, reinforced, and propagated this bloodthirsty take on human ancestors and, by extrapolation, on human nature. The "killer ape" story next made it to the big screen in Stanley Kubrick's 1968 hit, *2001: A Space Odyssey*. The opening scene shows an ancestral ape wreaking havoc with a bone club. A group of these human precursors then attack their rivals, beating another group's leader to death and driving their enemies away from a waterhole.

It is now clear that the Dart-Ardrey-Kubrick vision of the australopithecines was way off the mark. In fact, australopithecine bones and skulls shattered during fossilization as piles of stones and soil compressed the remains over many millennia (Brain 1970). As for the paired holes on some of the australopithecine crania, Brain (1970) concluded that much of the damage was caused by predators. An extinct species of leopard whose fossilized remains were found along with the australopithecine species had projecting canines that matched the paired puncture holes on skulls. These prehistoric leopards were feeding on both ancient baboons and the australopithecines. The forces of geology inflicted additional damage so that after a couple million years most of the australopithecine bones were shattered for reasons far removed from Dart's fanciful reconstructions of killer apes gone wild.

Dart (1953:207–208) held beliefs, often expressed in Western culture, about the natural aggressiveness of humans:

> The blood-bespattered, slaughter-gutted archives of human history from the earliest Egyptian and Sumerian records to the most recent atrocities of the Second World War accord with early universal cannibalism, with animal and human sacrificial practices or their substitutes in formalized religions and with the world-wide scalping, head-hunting, body-mutilating and necrophilic practices of mankind in proclaiming this common bloodlust differentiator, this predaceous habit, this mark of Cain that separates man dietetically from his anthropoidal relatives and allies him rather with the deadliest Carnivora.

How we interpret the past can be influenced all too easily by culturally based beliefs about human nature. Dart's views of human nature, I suggest, predisposed him to see the australopithecines as cannibalistic murderers.

As a postscript to this story, the recently described 4.4-million-year-old *Ardipithecus ramidus* specimens offer no support for killer ape scenarios. Some primate species such as chimpanzees have large projecting canine teeth, especially among males, that function as weaponry. The back, cutting side of a male chimpanzee's projecting canines are kept very sharp as they are honed through friction with the ape's lower premolar teeth as the animal opens and closes its mouth. The first point of importance is that the canines of *Ardipithecus ramidus* are relatively small, totally unlike the canine weaponry of the chimpanzee; the second point of significance is that dimorphism in canine size is virtually absent between male and female *Ardipithecus ramidus* specimens (White et al. 2009). As a general rule, in species where male-male aggressive competition has been favored by selection, males evolve fighting anatomy and larger body size than females (Darwin 1998). Tim White et al. (2009) report that there was considerable overlap between male and female body size in *Ardipithecus ramidus*. Thus the nonprojecting canines and lack of marked sexual dimorphism in this early hominid species do not support the idea that *Ardipithecus ramidus* was allied with the deadliest carnivores or for that matter engaged in the types of aggressive behavior that typify modern chimpanzees.

DISMISSING NON-WARRING SOCIETIES

The final case offered in support of this chapter's thesis involves the landmark treatise *A Study of War*, by Quincy Wright (1942). Wright rated 590 societies regarding the type of war they engaged in and found that thirty societies (5 percent of the sample) did not engage in war at all. But instead of labeling these societies as peaceful, non-warring, warless, or with some other label to convey their warlessness, most were classified by Wright as practicing *defensive war* and a couple as engaging in *social war*. All the non-warring societies were labeled as engaging in some sort of war because there simply were no non-warring alternatives in his classificatory scheme. Wright's war classification reflects once again a belief bias in Western culture that war is natural.

How does Wright justify applying the *defensive war* label to societies that are described as not engaging in any warfare or feuding? Wright (1942:546) notes that "these people have no military organization or military weapons and do not fight unless actually attacked, in which case they make spontaneous use of available tools and hunting weapons to defend themselves but regard this necessity as a misfortune." However, Wright overlooks the anthropologically documented fact that non-warring people often flee or move away if attacked, rather than take up arms.

If we consider ethnographies on the societies that Wright labels as practicing *defensive war* (for example, the Semang, Jakun, and Kubu), the typical response to threat is avoidance and retreat, *not* war. The Inuit of Greenland lack war but also were classified by Wright as engaging in *defensive war* despite the fact that they had no need either to flee or to defend themselves from any warring neighbors. More generally, avoidance and retreat responses to belligerent neighbors have been noted for many societies, including the Aweikoma, Buid, Chewong, Dogrib, Dorobo, Guayaki, Hare, Jahai, Panare, Shoshone, Siriono, Slavey, Wáiwai, and Yellowknife, among others (Fry 2006:98).

Western cultures may inculcate the value that it is cowardly to flee from danger, but not all cultures favor aggressive responses as being most desirable. Fleeing from danger is often viewed as sensible. In other words, belief systems differ markedly regarding the value they place on fighting or fleeing and regarding the acceptability of engaging in violence. In addition, Westerners such as Wright are the heirs to an agricultural tradition that is associated with owning and defending particular pieces of land, but some other societies simply lack such traditions and motivations. Thus deciding to move away from a hostile or dangerous situation may be a sensible and consciously chosen alternative to fighting. In any case, Wright greatly overemphasized the prevalence of an aggressive response, probably based on his own Western assumptions, when he assumed that non-warring societies would practice *defensive war* if attacked. The ethnographic data do not support the universal validity of this assumption.

Anthropology offers a view of humanity that spans evolutionary time and crosses cultural space. This macroscopic perspective can lead to insights, for instance, about how cultural beliefs affect our thinking (Tomforde, this volume). In this chapter I have considered how people tend to accept cultural beliefs about human nature without much question. Beliefs that war is natural are apparent in the cases reviewed and also in society more generally.

Hobbesian cultural beliefs about war and human nature also penetrate science and scholarship. We have seen that Taçon and Chippindale (1994) filled their report on Australian Aborigine rock art with war terminology and labeled dueling men as "warriors." This seems to be a clear case of projecting beliefs from one's own culture onto another culture despite the fact that ethnographic information shows they are not a good fit. I also considered the fascination with Yanomamö unokais and the eager reiteration in academic circles and beyond of the purported link between reproductive success and killing despite many flaws with the study. Similarly, the problematic hunter-gatherer study by Ember (1978) continues to be cited to corroborate Hobbesian interpretations of the human past (for example, Alexander 1979:222–230; Gat 2006:18; Goldstein 2001:24; Ghiglieri 1999:164; Konner 2006:5; Smith 2007:58; Wrangham and Peterson 1996:75). Another example of how Hobbesian beliefs manifest themselves in science is Raymond Dart's interpretation of the australopithecines as blood besplattered killer apes. Finally, Quincy Wright's (1942) application of the label *war* to all 590 societies in his cross-cultural sample once again reflects a Hobbesian cultural belief system wherein *all* cultures are assumed to make war.

Turning to society more generally, recall that about half of university student survey respondents agreed that humans have "an instinct for war" and that "war is an intrinsic part of human nature." Beliefs such as these also are reflected in everyday conversations, in entertainment, and in the media. In television shows like *Six Feet Under* and movies like *2001: A Space Odyssey*, or in popular books such as Potts and Hayden's *Sex and War* (2008) or David Smith's *The Most Dangerous Animal* (2007), the message that war is part and parcel of human nature is reiterated. In words redolent of an origin myth, Smith (2007:81) explains: "We inherited our warlike nature from prehistoric bands that were able to kill their neighbors and acquire their resources. These groups flourished while the pacifists withered on the evolutionary vine." Such beliefs may have political consequences as other peoples are perceived as natural-born killers, ready to attack us at any opportunity. The logical response is to be ready to protect ourselves, with preemptive force if necessary, in an evolved world we believe to be filled with naturally warmongering neighbors.

Leaders adopt, reflect, and may even augment the beliefs of their cultures. A presumed link between war and human nature appears in the words of former UN Secretary-General Kofi Annan (1997), "[War is] deeply rooted in human history—perhaps, even in human nature" and of President Obama (2009a), in his Nobel Peace Prize acceptance speech: "War, in one form or another, appeared with the first man. At the dawn of history, its morality was not questioned; it was simply a fact, like drought or disease— the manner in which tribes and then civilizations sought power and settled their differences." When leaders and citizens believe in large numbers that warfare is simply part and parcel of human nature, the waging of war becomes all the more likely.

This collection of anthropological and societal examples simultaneously represents and reinforces largely taken for granted cultural beliefs about the antiquity and naturalness of war (see Tomforde, this volume). Cultural beliefs enter into scientific and other writings, affecting perceptions, descriptions, and interpretations. In the global political world, such beliefs may also affect leaders' decisions whether or not to wage war. As Tomforde (this volume) illustrates using historical material from the World War II era, German anthropologists of this time period, due to the allegedly objective status of their scientific findings turned political ideas into 'given realities' and helped to legitimize them. Eventually, racist ideas and a fascist value system became part of the 'social unconscious.' In the twenty-first century, cultural beliefs, and more specifically, political ideology, may limit our views about alternative ways to achieve security and justice without war. The cases considered in this chapter suggest that we unlock assumptions about war, peace, and human nature from the largely unconscious, taken-for-granted realm of cultural beliefs and open them up to conscious scrutiny.

References

Ablon, Joan
1977   Field Methods in Working with Middle Class Americans: New Issues of Values, Personality, and Reciprocity. Human Organization 36(1):69–72.

Abu El-Haj, Nadia
2005   Edward Said and the Political Present. American Ethnologist 32(4):538–555.

Adams, David, and Sarah Bosch
1987   The Myth that War Is Intrinsic to Human Nature Discourages Action for Peace by Young People. *In* Essays on Violence. Jesús Martín Ramírez, Robert A. Hinde, and Jo Groebel, eds. Pp. 123–237. Seville, Spain: University of Seville Press.

Agar, Michael
1980   The Professional Stranger: An Informal Introduction to Ethnography. New York: Academic Press.

Ahmed, Abdel Ghaffar
1973   Some Remarks from the Third World on Anthropology and Colonialism: The Sudan. *In* Anthropology and the Colonial Encounter. Talal Asad, ed. Pp. 259–270. London, UK: Ithaca Press.

Alatas, Syed Farid
2003   Academic Dependency and the Global Division of Labor in the Social Sciences. Current Sociology 51(6):599–613.

Albro, Rob
2009   The Culture Doctrine: Military Precedents for Culture-Based Problem Solving. Paper presented at the Professor and the Spy: Area Studies and the Politics of Global Security conference, Rutgers University (New Brunswick, NJ), February 12.

Alexander, Richard
1979   Darwinism and Human Affairs. Seattle: University of Washington Press.

REFERENCES

Allman, William F.

1988   A Laboratory of Human Conflict. U.S. News and World Report, April 11:57–58.

Altinay, Ayse Gul

2004   The Myth of the Military-Nation: Militarism, Gender, and Education in Turkey. New York: Palgrave Macmillan.

American Anthropological Association

1998   Code of Ethics of the American Anthropological Association. American Anthropological Association. http://www.aaanet.org/committees/ethics/ethcode.htm, accessed October 23, 2008.

2006   Anthropologists Weigh In on Iraq, Torture at Annual Meeting. Press release. American Anthropological Association. http://aaanet.org/_cs_upload/pdf/4100_1.pdf, accessed July 30, 2010.

2007   Final Report, AAA Commission on the Engagement of Anthropology with the US Security and Intelligence Communities. American Anthropological Association. http://www.aaanet.org/pdf/FINAL_Report_Complete.pdf, accessed July 7, 2010.

Amnesty International

2009   Obama Planning to End Harsh Interrogations? Human Rights Now (blog), January 16. http://blog.amnestyusa.org/waronterror/obama-planning-to-end-harsh-interrogations/, accessed September 30, 2009.

Andreas, Joel

2004   Addicted to War: Why the U.S. Can't Kick Militarism. Oakland, CA: AK Press.

Annan, Kofi

1997   Secretary-General Kofi Annan's closing plenary address. World Federalist: The Quarterly Newsletter of the World Federalist Association, July (special insert):6.

Antweiler, Christoph

2005   Ethnologie: Ein Führer zu populären Medien. Berlin, Germany: Dietrich Reimer.

Appiah, Kwame Anthony, and Martin Bunzl, eds.

2007   Buying Freedom: The Ethics and Economics of Slave Redemption. Princeton, NJ: Princeton University Press.

Ardrey, Robert

1961   African Genesis. New York: Dell.

1966   The Territorial Imperative. New York: Atheneum.

Arquilla, John

2003   9/11: Yesterday and Tomorrow: How We Could Lose the War on Terror. San Francisco Chronicle, September 7: D1.

Bacevich, Andrew

2008   The Petraeus Doctrine. The Atlantic, October 2008. http://www.theatlantic

.com/ magazine/archive/2008/10/the-petraeus-doctrine/6964/, accessed March 4, 2009.

Barkan, Elazar

1992   The Retreat from Scientific Racism: Changing Concepts of Race in Britain and the United States between the World Wars. Cambridge, UK: Cambridge University Press.

Barnes, Catherine

2005   Weaving the Web: Civil-Society Roles in Working with Conflict and Building Peace. *In* People Building Peace II: Successful Stories of Civil Society. Paul van Toneren, Malin Brenk, Marte Hellema, and Juliette Verhoeven, eds. Pp. 7–24. Boulder, CO: Lynne Rienner.

Barnet, Richard

1985   The Ideology of the National Security State. Massachusetts Review 26(4):483–500.

Bateson, Mary Catherine

1988   Compromise and the Rhetoric of Good and Evil. *In* The Social Dynamics of Peace and Conflict: Culture in International Security. Robert A. Rubinstein and Mary L. Foster, eds. Pp. 35–46. Boulder, CO: Westview Press.

Beaver, Diane

2002   Memorandum for Commander, Joint Task Force 170: Legal Brief on Proposed Counter-Resistance Strategies (JTF170-SJA), October 11, 2002. US Department of Defense Joint Task Force, Guantánamo Bay, Cuba.

Becker, Elizabeth

        Pentagon Says It Can Find No Proof of Massacre. New York Times, September 30:16.

Begg, Moazzam

2006   Enemy Combatant: My Imprisonment at Guantanamo, Bagram, and Kandahar. New York: New Press.

Bell, Allan

1991   The Language of News Media. Oxford, UK: Blackwell.

Ben-Ari, Eyal

1989   Masks and Soldiering: The Israeli Army and the Palestinian Uprising. Cultural Anthropologist 4(4):372–389.

1998   Mastering Soldiers: Conflict, Emotions, and the Enemy in an Israeli Military Unit. Oxford, UK: Berghahn Books.

1999   Colonialism, Anthropology and the Politics of Professionalization: An Argumentative Afterword. *In* Anthropology and Colonialism in Asia and Oceania. Jan van Bremen and Akitoshi Shimizu, eds. Pp. 384–411. London, UK: Curzon Press.

2004   The Military and Militarization in the United States. American Ethnologist 31(3):340–348.

2008   War, the Military and Militarization around the Globe. Social Anthropology
            16(1):90–99.

Ben-Ari, Eyal, Zev Lehrer, Uzi Ben-Shalom, and Ariel Vainer
2009   Rethinking the Sociology of Combat: Israel's Combat Units in the Al-Aqsa
            Intifada. Albany: State University of New York Press.

Ben-Ari, Eyal, Meirav Maymon, Nir Gazit, and Ron Shatzberg
2004   From Checkpoints to Flow-points: Sites of Friction between the Israel Defense
            Forces and Palestinians. Harry S. Truman Research Institute for the Advance-
            ment of Peace, Peace Publication #31. Jerusalem: Hebrew University.

Ben-Ari, Eyal, and Jan van Bremen
2005   Asian Anthropologies and Anthropologies in Asia: An Introductory Essay. *In*
            Asian Anthropology. Jan van Bremen, Eyal Ben-Ari, and Syed Farid Alatas,
            eds. Pp. 3–39. London, UK: Routledge.

Bennet, John T.
2008   Deputy CO: Airlifters Top AFRICOM Equipment Needs. DefenseNews, May 27.
            http://www.defensenews.com/story.php?i=3549321, accessed October 7, 2008.

Ben-Shalom, Uzi, Zev Lehrer, and Eyal Ben-Ari
2005   Cohesion during Military Operations? A Field Study on Combat Units in the
            Al-Aqsa Intifada. Armed Forces and Society 32(1):63–79.

Bercuson, David
1996   Significant Incident: Canada's Army, the Airborne, and the Murder in
            Somalia. Toronto, ON: McClelland and Stewart.

Bergen, Robert
2009   Censorship: The Canadian News Media and Afghanistan: A Historical
            Comparison with Case Studies. Calgary Papers in Military and Strategic
            Studies, Occasional Paper Number 3. Calgary, AB: Centre for Military and
            Strategic Studies.

Bergerud, Erick
1991   The Dynamics of Defeat: The Vietnam War in Hau Nghia Province. Boulder,
            CO: Westview Press.

Berndt, Ronald M.
1965   Law and Order in Aboriginal Australia. *In* Aboriginal Man in Australia:
            Essays in Honour of Emeritus Professor A. P. Elkin. Ronald M. Berndt and
            Catherine H. Berndt, eds. Pp. 167–206. London, UK: Angus and Robertson.

Berndt, Ronald M., and Catherine H. Berndt
1996   The World of the First Australians. 5th edition. Canberra, Australia:
            Aboriginal Studies Press.

Berreman, Gerald D.
1968   Is Anthropology Alive? Social Responsibility in Social Anthropology. Current
            Anthropology 9(5):391–396.
2003   Ethics versus "Realism" in Anthropology Redux. *In* Ethics and the Profession

of Anthropology. Carolyn Fluehr-Lobban, ed. Pp. 51–83. Walnut Creek, CA: AltaMira Press.

Besteman, Catherine
2008   "Beware of Those Bearing Gifts": An Anthropologist's View of AFRICOM. Anthropology Today 24(5):20–21.
2009   Counter AFRICOM. *In* The Counter-Counterinsurgency Manual. Network of Concerned Anthropologists Steering Committee, ed. Pp. 115–132. Chicago, IL: Prickly Paradigm Press.

Bhattacharjee, Yudhiji
2007   Pentagon Asks Academics for Help in Understanding Its Enemies. Science 316:534–535.

Bill and Bob's Excellent Afghan Adventure
2009   Picasso Pelton: Old Blue's Paint by Numbers. Bill and Bob's Excellent Afghan Adventure (blog), February 24. http://billandbobsadventure .blogspot.com/2009/02/picasso-pelton-old-blues-paint-by.html, accessed September 7, 2009.

Binnendijk, Hans, and Patrick Cronin, eds.
2008   Civilian Surge: Key to Complex Operations. Washington DC: National Defense University Press.

Bird, Junius
1946   The Alacaluf. *In* Handbook of South American Indians, vol. 1: The Marginal Tribes. Julian Steward, ed. Pp. 55–80. Washington DC: United States Printing Office.

Blatchford, Christie
2006   Canadian Dies in Afghan Battle: Soldiers Engaged in Lethal Two-day Game of Cat and Mouse with Taliban Fighters. Globe and Mail, July 10: A1.
2007   Fifteen Days: Stories of Bravery, Friendship, Life and Death from Inside the New Canadian Army. Scarborough, ON: Doubleday Canada.

Boas, Franz
1919   Scientists as Spies. The Nation, December 20: 797.

Boene, Bernard
1990   How Unique Should the Military Be? A Review of Representative Literature and Outline of Synthetic Formulation. European Journal of Sociology 31(1):3–59.

Bond, Charles F., and Bella M. De Paulo
2006   Accuracy of Deception Judgments. Personality and Social Psychology Review 10(3):214–234.

Borum, Randy
2006   Approaching Truth: Behavioral Science Lessons on Educing Information from Human Sources. *In* Educing Information: Interrogation: Science and Art. Intelligence Science Board, Phase 1 Report. Pp. 17–44. Washington DC: National Defense Intelligence College.

REFERENCES

Bourdieu, Pierre

1993   Sozialer Sinn: Kritik der theoretischen Vernunft. Frankfurt, Germany: Suhrkamp.

Boyer, Dominic, and Ulf Hannerz

2006   Introduction: Worlds of Journalism. Ethnography 7(1):1–17.

Bradbury, Steven G.

2009   Memorandum for the Files RE: Status of Certain OLC Opinions Issued in the Aftermath of the Terrorist Attacks of September 11, 2001, January 15. United States Department of Justice: Office of Legal Council, Office of the Principal Deputy Assistant Attorney General.

Brain, C. K.

1970   New Finds at the Swartkrans Australopithecine Site. Nature 225:1112–1119.

Braun, Jürgen

1995   Eine deutsche Karriere: Die Biographie des Ethnologen Hermann Baumann (1902–1971). Munich, Germany: Akademischer.

Bräunlein, Peter J.

1995   Ethnologie an der Heimatfront: Zwischen Heilslehre, Kriegswissenschaft und Propaganda. Margaret Mead, die amerikanische cultural anthropology und der II. Weltkrieg. *In* Krieg und Frieden: Ethnologische Perspektiven. Peter J. Bräunlein and Andrea Lauser, eds. Pp. 11–64. Bremen, Germany: Sonderband.

Brown, Keith

2008   All They Understand Is Force: Debating Culture in Operation Iraqi Freedom. American Anthropologist 110(4):443–453.

2009   Polluting Practices: Anthropology in/of Wartime. Paper presented at the Professor and the Spy: Area Studies and the Politics of Global Security conference, Rutgers University (New Brunswick, NJ), February 12.

Brown, Keith, and Catherine Lutz

2007   Grunt Lit: The Participant-Observers of Empire. American Ethnologist 34:322–328.

Bulmahn, Thomas

2006   Bevölkerungsbefragung des Sozialwissenschaftlichen Instituts der Bundeswehr. Internal Report. Strausberg, Germany: SOWI.

Bulmahn, Thomas, and Rüdiger Fiebig

2007   Erste Ergebnisse der Bevölkerungsbefragung 2007 des Sozialwissenschaftlichen Instituts der Bundeswehr. SOWI.NEWS 4:1–3.

Bunn, Geoffrey C.

2007   Spectacular Science: The Lie Detector's Ambivalent Powers. History of Psychology 10(2):156–178.

Burkeman, Oliver

2009   Obama Administration says Goodbye to "War on Terror." The Guardian,

March 25. http://www.guardian.co.uk/world/2009/mar/25/obama-war-terror-overseas-contingency-operations, accessed September 20, 2009.

Buss, David

1999   Evolutionary Psychology: The New Science of the Mind. Boston, MA: Allyn and Bacon.

Byer, Doris

1995   Zum Problem eindeutiger Klassifikation: Diskursanalytische Perspektiven der Forschungen über Völkerkunde und Nationalsozialismus. *In* Lebenslust und Fremdenfurcht: Ethnologie im Dritten Reich. Thomas Hauschild, ed. Pp. 62–84. Frankfurt, Germany: Suhrkamp Taschenbuch.

Caplan, Lionel

1995   Warrior Gentlemen: "Gurkhas" in the Western Imagination. New York: Berghahan Books.

Carstens, Uwe

2007   Franz Boas' "Offener Brief" an Paul von Hindenburg. Tönnies-Forum 16:70–75.

Castro, Arachu, and Merrill Singer, eds.

2004   Unhealthy Health Policy: A Critical Anthropological Examination. Lanham, MD: AltaMira Press.

Caton, Steven C.

2006   Coetzee, Agamben, and the Passion of Abu Ghraib. American Anthropologist 108(1):114–123.

Center for Technology and National Security Policy

2008   Words and Deeds: Strategic Communications in Complex Operations. Center for Technology and National Security Policy Seminar, October 14–15. http://www.ndu.edu/CTNSP/docUploaded//Stab Ops 14-15Oct08 Agenda.pdf, accessed September 10, 2010.

Cervinkova, Hana

2006   Playing Soldiers in Bohemia: An Ethnography of NATO Membership. Prague, Czech Republic: Set Out.

Chagnon, Napoleon A.

1983   Yanomamö: The Fierce People. 3rd edition. New York: Holt, Rinehart and Winston.

1988   Life Histories, Blood Revenge, and Warfare in a Tribal Population. Science 239:985–992.

1990   Reproductive and Somatic Conflicts of Interest in the Genesis of Violence and Warfare among Tribesmen. *In* The Anthropology of War. Jonathan Haas, ed. Pp. 77–104. Cambridge, UK: Cambridge University Press.

1992   Yanomamö: The Last Days of Eden. San Diego, CA: Harcourt Brace and Company.

References

Chambers, Erve

1987 Applied Anthropology in the Post-Vietnam Era: Anticipations and Ironies. Annual Review of Anthropology 16:309–337.

2005 Epilogue: Archeology, Heritage, and Public Endeavor. *In* Places in Mind: Public Archeology as Applied Anthropology. Paul A. Shackel and Erve J. Chambers, eds. Pp. 193–208. New York: Routledge.

Chatterjee, Partha

2004 The Politics of the Governed: Reflections on Popular Politics in Most of the World. New York: Columbia University Press.

Choe, Sang Hun, Charles J. Hanley, and Martha Mendoza

1999 G.I.'s Tell of a U.S. Massacre in Korean War. New York Times, September 30: 1.

Christensen, Maya M., and Mats Utas

2008 Mercenaries of Democracy: The "Politricks" of Remobilized Combatants in the 2007 General Elections, Sierra Leone. African Affairs 107(429):515–539.

Cohn, Carol

1987 Sex and Death in the Rational World of Defense Intellectuals. Signs 12(4):687–718.

Canadian Expeditionary Force Commander

N.d. Op Athena-Media Embed Program (MEP) Instructions. Unpublished document. www.forces.gc.ca/site/newsroom/mep_e.pdf, accessed April 8, 2008.

Condominas, Georges

1977 We Have Eaten the Forest. New York: Kodansha America.

Connable, Ben

2009 All Our Eggs in a Broken Basket: How the Human Terrain System is Undermining Sustainable Military Cultural Competence. Military Review (March–April):57–64.

Conroy, John

2000 Unspeakable Acts, Ordinary People: The Dynamics of Torture: An Examination of the Practice of Torture in Three Democracies. Berkeley: University of California Press.

Conte, Edouard

1988 Völkerkunde und Faschismus? *In* Kontinuität und Bruch: 1938–1945–1955: Beiträge zur österreichischen Kultur- und Wissenschaftsgeschichte. Friedrich Stadler, ed. Pp. 229–264. Vienna, Austria: LIT Verlag.

Cotter, John

2006 "Grunts in the Mist": Canadian Soldiers in Afghanistan Share Stories with Anthropologist. Edmonton Sun (Alberta), July 4:30.

Cottle, Simon

2006 Mediatized Conflict: Developments in Media and Conflict Studies. Maidenhead, UK: Open University Press.

Cowan, Jane
2006   Culture and Rights after *Culture and Rights*. American Anthropologist 108(1):9–24.

Cramer, Janet, and Michael McDevitt
2004   Ethnographic Journalism. *In* Qualitative Research in Journalism: Taking It to the Streets. Sharon Iorio, ed. Pp. 127–144. Mahwah, NJ: Lawrence Erlbaum.

Dart, Raymond A.
1949   The Predatory Implemental Technique of Australopithecines. American Journal of Physical Anthropology 7:1–38.
1953   The Predatory Transition from Ape to Man. International Anthropological and Linguistic Review 1:201–218.
1958   The Minimal Bone-Breccia Content of Makapansgat and the Australopithecine Predatory Habit. American Anthropologist 60:923–931.

Darwin, Charles
1998[1871]   The Descent of Man. Amherst, NY: Prometheus Books.

Defense Science Board
2009   Report of the Defense Science Board Task Force on Understanding Human Dynamics. Washington DC: Office of the Undersecretary of Defense for Acquisition, Technology, and Logistics.

Dentan, Robert K.
1968   The Semai: A Nonviolent People of Malaya. New York: Holt, Rinehart and Winston.

DeYoung, Karen
2009   Civilians to Join Afghan Buildup. "Surge" Is Part of Larger U.S. Strategy Studied by White House. The Washington Post, March 19. http://www.washingtonpost.com/wp-dyn/content/article/2009/03/18/AR2009031802313.html, accessed May 4, 2009.

Diewald-Kerkmann, Gisela
1995   Politische Denunziation im NS-Regime oder Die kleine Macht der "Volksgenossen." Bonn, Germany: Dietz.

Dobbs, Michael, and Roberto Suro
1999   U.S. Army Files Support Accounts of Korean Massacre. Ottawa Citizen, October 1:11.

Donnell, John C., and Gerald C. Hickey
1962   The Vietnamese "Strategic Hamlets": A Preliminary Report. US Air Force, Project RAND Research Memorandum, RM-3208-ARPA. Santa Monica, CA: The RAND Corporation. http://www.rand.org/pubs/research_memoranda/2006/RM3208.pdf, accessed July 7, 2010.

Dostal, Walter
1994   Silence in the Darkness: An Essay on German Ethnology during the National Socialist Period. Social Anthropology 2(3):251–262.

REFERENCES

Deutsche Prese-Agentur (DPA)
2008   US Forces Find Footing in Afghanistan's "Human Terrain." Earthtimes, October 13 http://www.earthtimes.org/articles/news/236694,us-forces-find-footing-in-afghanistans-human-terrain—feature.html, accessed September 5, 2010.

Dreyfus, Hubert, and Paul Rabinow
1987   Michel Foucault: Jenseits von Strukturalismus und Hermeneutik. Frankfurt, Germany: Athenäum.

Dunlap, Charles
2007   Shortchanging the Joint Fight? An Airman's Assessment of FM 3-24 and the Case for Developing Truly Joint COIN Doctrine. Montgomery, AL: Air University Monograph.
2008   We Still Need the Big Guns. New York Times, July 7:19.

Dunlap Jr., Charles J.
2001   Law and Military Interventions: Preserving Humanitarian Values in 21st Century Conflicts. Paper presented at Humanitarian Values in Military Intervention conference at the Carr Center for Human Rights Policy, Kennedy School of Government, Harvard University, Washington DC. November 29–30. http://www.hks.harvard.edu/cchrp/programareas/conferences/november2001.php#workingpapers, accessed December 29, 2010.
2007   Lawfare Amid Warfare. Washington Times, August 3. http://www.washingtontimes.com/news/2007/aug/03/lawfare-amid-warfare/, accessed December 29, 2010.
2009   Lawfare: A Decisive Element of 21st Century Conflicts? Joint Forces Quarterly 54(3):34–39.

Eisenstadt, Michael
2007   Iraq: Tribal Engagement Lessons Learned. Military Review (September–October):16–31.

Elkins, Caroline
2005   The Wrong Lesson. Atlantic Monthly, July/August. http://www.theatlantic.com/magazine/archive/2005/07/the-wrong-lesson/4052/, accessed December 18, 2010.

Ellis, Stephen
1999   The Mask of Anarchy: The Religious Dimensions of an African Civil War. New York: New York University Press.

Ember, Carol
1978   Myths about Hunter-Gatherers. Ethnology 17:439–448.

Ember, Melvin, and Carol Ember
1971   The Conditions Favoring Matrilocal Versus Patrilocal Residence. American Anthropologist 73:571–594.

Embree, John
1945   Applied Anthropology and Its Relationship to Anthropology. American
          Anthropologist 47(4):635–637.

Ephron, Dan, and Silvia Spring
2008   A Gun in One Hand, a Pen in the Other. Newsweek, April 12. http://www
          .newsweek.com/2008/04/12/a-gun-in-one-hand-a-pen-in-the-other.html,
          accessed October 17, 2010.

Eyal, Gil
2005   The Disenchantment of the Orient: A History of Orientalist Expertise in
          Israel. Jerusalem: Van Leer Institute and Hakibbutz Hameuchad Publishing
          House.

Fabbro, David
1978   Peaceful Societies: An Introduction. Journal of Peace Research 15:67–83.

Falk, Richard A., and Samuel S. Kim, eds.
1980   The War System: An Interdisciplinary Approach. Boulder, CO: Westview
          Press.

Farah, Douglas
2004   Blood from Stones: The Secret Financial Network of Terror. New York:
          Broadway Books.

Featherstone, Steve
2008   Human Quicksand for the U.S. Army: A Crash Course in Cultural Studies.
          Harper's Magazine, September:60–68.

Fein, Robert A.
2006   US Experience and Research in Educing Information: A Brief History. *In*
          Educing Information: Interrogation: Science and Art, Intelligence Science
          Board. Pp. xi–xii. Washington DC: National Defense Intelligence College.

Ferguson, R. Brian
1989   Do Yanomamö Killers Have More Kids? American Ethnologist 16:564–565.
1995   Yanomami Warfare: A Political History. Santa Fe, NM: SAR Press.
forthcoming Full Spectrum: The Military Invasion of Anthropology. *In* Virtual War and
          Magical Death: Technologies and Imaginaries for Terror and Killing. Neil L.
          Whitehead and Sverker Finnstrom, eds. Durham, NC: Duke University Press.

Ferguson, R. Brian, and Neil Whitehead, eds.
1992   War in the Tribal Zone: Expanding States and Indigenous Warfare. Santa Fe,
          NM: SAR Press.

Ferme, Mariane, and Danny Hoffman
2004   Hunter Militias and the International Human Rights Discourse in Sierra
          Leone and Beyond. Africa Today 50(4):73–95.

Feuchtwang, Stephan
1973   The Colonial Formation of British Social Anthropology. *In* Anthropology and
          the Colonial Encounter. Talal Asad, ed. Pp. 259–270. London, UK: Ithaca Press.

REFERENCES

Finney, Nathan
2008   Human Terrain Team Handbook. Fort Leavenworth, KS: Human Terrain System.

Fischer, Hans
1988   Anfänge, Abgrenzungen, Anwendungen. *In* Ethnologie: Einführung und Überblick. Hans Fischer, ed. Pp.3–38. Berlin, Germany: Dietrich Reimer.
1990   Völkerkunde im Nationalsozialismus: Aspekte der Anpassung, Affinität und Behauptung einer wissenschaftlichen Disziplin. Berlin, Germany: Dietrich Reimer.
1991   Völkerkunde in Hamburg 1933 bis 1945. *In* Hochschulalltag im "Dritten Reich": Die Hamburger Universität 1933–1945, Hamburger Beiträge zur Wissenschaftsgeschichte, 3 vols. Holger Fischer, Eckart Krause, and Ludwig Huber, eds. Pp. 589–606. Berlin, Germany: Dietrich Reimer.

Fisher, Simon, and Lada Zimina
2008   Just Wasting Our Time? An Open Letter to Peacebuilders. *In* Berghoff Handbook for Conflict Transformation. Martina Fischer and Norbert Ropers, eds. Berlin, Germany: Berghof Research Center for Constructive Conflict Management.

Fluehr-Lobban, Carolyn
2003   Dialogue for an Ethically Conscious Practice. *In* Ethics and the Profession of Anthropology. Carolyn Fluehr-Lobban, ed. Pp. 225–245. Walnut Creek, CA: AltaMira Press.
2006   Ethical Challenges, New and Old: In National Security and the Global War on Terror. Anthropology News 47(3):5.

Fontenot, Greg
2007   Red Team Leader's Course. RTLC 07-002 Advance Book, July. Fort Leavenworth, KS: University of Foreign Military and Cultural Studies.

Forte, Maximilian
2008   Priming the Propaganda Pumps: Four More Sales Pitches for the Spreading Human Terrain System (2.0). Zero Anthropology (blog), October 17. http://zeroanthropology.net/2008/10/17/priming-the-propaganda-pumps-more-sales-pitches-for-the-spreading-human-terrain-system/, accessed September 5, 2010.
2009a   Bumming a Ride with the Occupation Parade: A Look at Human Terrain Teams in Afghanistan. Zero Anthropology (blog), January 23. http://zeroanthropology.net/2009/01/23/bumming-a-ride-with-the-occupation-parade-a-look-at-human-terrain-teams-in-afghanistan/, accessed September 5, 2010.
2009b   Questions and Allegations about Robert Young Pelton's Reporting on a Human Terrain Team in Afghanistan. Zero Anthropology (blog), February 24. http://zeroanthropology.net/2009/02/24/questions-and-allegations-about-robert-young-peltons-reporting-on-a-human-terrain-team-in-afghanistan/, accessed September 5, 2010.

Foster, George M.
2000   An Anthropologist's Life in the Twentieth Century: Theory and Practice at
        UC Berkeley, the Smithsonian, in Mexico, and with the World Health
        Organization, An Oral History Conducted in 1998 and 1999 by Suzanne B.
        Riess. Berkeley, CA: Regional Oral History Office, The Bancroft Library,
        University of California.

Foster, George M., Peter Hinton, and A. J. F. Köbben
1971   To the Editors. New York Review of Books, April 8. http://www.newyork
        books.com/articles/archives/1971/apr/08/anthropology-on-the-warpath-an-
        exchange/?page=1, accessed September 5, 2010.

Foster, Mary LeCron, and Robert A. Rubinstein, eds.
1986   Peace and War: Cross-Cultural Perspectives. New Brunswick, NJ: Transaction
        Publishers.

Foucault, Michel
1970   The Order of Things. New York: Random House.

1978   Dispositive der Macht: Über Sexualität, Wissen und Wahrheit. Berlin,
        Germany: Merve.

1980   Power/Knowledge: Selected Interviews and Other Writings, 1972–1977. New
        York: Pantheon.

FoxNews.com
2009   Obama Scraps "Global War on Terror" for "Overseas Contingency
        Operation." FoxNews.com, March 25. http://www.foxnews.com/politics/
        elections/2009/03/25/report-obama-administration-backing-away-global-war-
        terror/, accessed September 20, 2009.

Frese, Pamela R., and Margaret C. Harrell, eds.
2003   Anthropology and the United States Military: Coming of Age in the Twenty-
        first Century. New York: Palgrave Macmillan.

Fried, Morton, Marvin Harris, and Robert Murphy, eds.
1967   War: The Anthropology of Armed Conflict and Aggression. Garden City, NY:
        Natural History Press.

Fromm, Erich
1962   Beyond the Chains of Illusion: My Encounter with Marx and Freud. New
        York: Simon and Schuster.

Fry, Douglas P.
1985   Utilizing Human Capacities for Survival in the Nuclear Age. Bulletin of
        Peace Proposals 16:159–166.

2004   Multiple Paths to Peace: The "La Paz" Zapotec of Mexico. In Keeping the
        Peace: Conflict Resolution and Peaceful Societies around the World. Graham
        Kemp and Douglas P. Fry, eds. Pp. 73–87. New York: Routledge.

2006   The Human Potential for Peace: An Anthropological Challenge to
        Assumptions about War and Violence. New York: Oxford University Press.

REFERENCES

2007   Beyond War: The Human Potential for Peace. New York: Oxford University
            Press.

Fry, Douglas P., Bruce D. Bonta, and Karolina Baszarkiewicz
2008   Learning from Extant Cultures of Peace. *In* Handbook on Building Cultures
            of Peace. Joseph DeRivera, ed. Pp. 11–26. New York: Springer.

Fry, Douglas P., and James Welch
1992   Beliefs about Human Nature and Conflict: Implications for Peace
            Education. Paper presented at the Annual Meeting of the American
            Anthropological Association, San Francisco, CA, December 2–6.

Fujimura, Clementine
2003   Integrating Diversity and Understanding the Other at the U.S. Naval
            Academy. *In* Anthropology and the United States Military: Coming of Age in
            the Twenty-first Century. Pamela R. Frese and Margaret C. Harrell, eds. Pp.
            147–151. New York: Palgrave Macmillan.
2011   Navigating the Cultures of the Military. *In* Anthropologists in the
            SecurityScape. Robert Albro, George Marcus, Laura A McNamara, and
            Monica Schoch-Spana, eds. Walnut Creek, CA: Left Coast Press.

Galeano, Eduardo
1995   Zehn geläufige Irrtürmer oder Lügen über Literatur und Kultur in
            Lateinamerika. Quetzal 12(13):2–5.

Gat, Azar
2006   War in Human Civilization. Oxford, UK: Oxford University Press.

Gates, Robert
2008   Speech given at Annual Meeting of Association of American Universities,
            Washington DC, April 14. http://www.defenselink.mil/speeches/
            speech.aspx?speechid=1228, accessed March 4, 2009.

Gberie, Lansan
2005   A Dirty War in West Africa: The RUF and the Destruction of Sierra Leone.
            Bloomington: Indiana University Press.

Geis, Anna
2007   Der Funktions- und Legitimationswandel der Bundeswehr und das "fre-
            undliche Desinteresse" der Bundesbürger. *In* Friedensgutachten 2007.
            Bruno Schoch, ed. Pp. 39–50. Berlin, Germany: LIT Verlag.

Gerecht, Reuel Marc
2008   Out of Sight. New York Times, December 13. http://www.nytimes.com/
            2008/12/14/opinion/14gerecht.html, accessed December 29, 2010.

Gerwehr, Scott
2007   Enhancing Interviewing and Deception Detection Skills in Counter-
            Terrorism Efforts. Paper presented at the Annual Meeting of the
            International Studies Association, Chicago, March 2.

Ghiglieri, Michael P.

1999   The Dark Side of Man: Tracing the Origins of Male Violence. Reading, MA: Perseus.

Gibson, Thomas

1989   Symbolic Representations of Tranquility and Aggression among the Buid. *In* Societies at Peace: Anthropological Perspectives. Signe Howell and Roy Willis, eds. Pp. 60–78. London, UK: Routledge.

Gilberg, Rolf

1984   Polar Eskimo. *In* Handbook of North American Indians, vol. 5: Arctic. David Damas and William C. Sturtevant, eds. Pp. 577–594. Washington DC: Smithsonian Institution.

Gill, Lesley

2004   The School of the Americas: Military Training and Political Violence in the Americas. Durham, NC: Duke University Press.

2005   The School of the Americas: Military Training and Political Violence in the Americas. Journal of Latin American Anthropology 10(2):472–473.

Gingrich, André

2005   The German-Speaking Countries: Ruptures, Schools, and Nontraditions: Reassessing the History of Sociocultural Anthropology in Germany. *In* One Discipline, Four Ways: British, German, French, and American Anthropology. Fredrik Barth, Andre Gingrich, Robert Parkin, and Sydel Silverman, eds. Pp. 61–153. Chicago, IL: University of Chicago Press.

Giroux, Henry A.

2007   The University in Chains: Confronting the Military-Industrial-Academic Complex. Boulder, CO: Paradigm.

Given, James B.

2001   Inquisition and Medieval Society: Power, Discipline, and Resistance in Languedoc. Ithaca, NY: Cornell University Press.

Glenn, David

2007   Former Human Terrain System Participant Describes a Program in Disarray. Campus Watch, December 5. http://www.campus-watch.org/article/id/4586, accessed March 28, 2008.

Global Peace Index

2008   Global Peace Index. Vision of Humanity. http://www.visionofhumanity.org/gpi/results/rankings.php, accessed July 7, 2010.

Goldschmidt, Walter

1988   Inducement to Military Participation in Tribal Societies. *In* The Social Dynamics of Peace and Conflict: Culture in International Security. Robert A. Rubinstein and Mary L. Foster, eds. Pp. 47–65. Boulder, CO: Westview Press.

Goldstein, Joshua
2001   War and Gender: How Gender Shapes the War System and Vice Versa. Cambridge, UK: Cambridge University Press.

González, Roberto
2007a   Phoenix Reborn? The Rise of the Human Terrain System. Anthropology Today 23(6):21–22.
2007b   Towards Mercenary Anthropology? The New US Army Counterinsurgency Manual FM 3-24 and the Military-Anthropology Complex. Anthropology Today 23(3):14–19.
2008a   From Anthropologists to Technicians of Power. Paper presented at the Annual Meeting of the Society for Applied Anthropology, Memphis, TN, March 28.
2008b   "Human Terrain": Past, Present and Future Applications. Anthropology Today 24(1):21–26.
2009a   American Counterinsurgency: Human Science and the Human Terrain. Chicago, IL: Prickly Paradigm Press.
2009b   Anthropologists or "Technicians of Power"? Examining the Human Terrain System. Practicing Anthropology 31(1):34–37.

Gregor, Thomas
1990   Uneasy Peace: Intertribal Relations in Brazil's Upper Xingu. In The Anthropology of War. Jonathan Haas, ed. Pp. 105–124. Cambridge, UK: Cambridge University Press.

Griffin, Marcus
2007   From an Anthropological Perspective. Marcusgriffin.com (blog), September 18. http://marcusgriffin.com/blog/2007/09/aerial_survey_2.html, accessed September 27, 2007.

Grunkemeyer, Marilyn T.
1996   Belief Systems. In Encyclopedia of Cultural Anthropology, vol. 1. David Levinson and Melvin Ember, eds. Pp. 125–130. New York: Henry Holt and Company.

Grüttner, Michael
1997   Wissenschaft. In Enzyklopädie des Nationalsozialismus. Wolfgang Benz, Hermann Graml, and Hermann Weiß, eds. Pp. 135–153. Stuttgart, Germany: Kett-Cotta.

Gulfnews.com
2009   The Real and Ethical Minefield of Afghanistan. Gulfnews, March 13. http://archive.gulfnews.com/articles/09/03/14/10294598.html, accessed April 7, 2009.

Gusterson, Hugh
1996   Nuclear Rites: A Weapons Laboratory at the End of the Cold War. Berkeley: University of California Press.
2007   Anthropology and Militarism. Annual Review of Anthropology 36:155–176.

2008   The U.S. Military's Quest to Weaponize Culture. Bulletin of the Atomic
          Scientists, June 20. http://thebulletin.org/web-edition/columnists/hugh-
          gusterson/the-us-militarys-quest-to-weaponize-culture, accessed July 7, 2010.

Guttman, Matthew, and Catherine Lutz
2010   Breaking Ranks: Iraq War Veterans Speak Out Against the War. Berkeley:
          University of California Press.

Haberland, Eike
1974   Hermann Baumann, 1902–1972, Schriftleiter der Zeitschrift für Völkerkunde
          von 1928 bis 1941. Zeitschrift für Ethnologie 99:1.

Haller, Dieter
2005   dtv-Atlas Ethnologie. Munich, Germany: Deutscher Taschenbuchverlag.

Hammes, Thomas
1994   The Evolution of War: The Fourth Generation. Marine Corps Gazette
          78:35–44.

Hannerz, Ulf
1996   Transnational Connections: Culture, People, Places. London, UK: Routledge.
1998   Reporting from Jerusalem. Cultural Anthropology 13(4):548–574.

Harrell, Margaret C.
2003a   Conclusion. In Anthropology and the United States Military: Coming of Age
          in the Twenty-first Century. Pamela R. Frese and Margaret C. Harrell, eds.
          Pp. 147–151. New York: Palgrave Macmillan.
2003b   Gender- and Class-based Role Expectations for Army Spouses. In
          Anthropology and the United States Military: Coming of Age in the Twenty-
          first Century. Pamela R. Frese and Margaret C. Harrell, eds. Pp. 69–94. New
          York: Palgrave Macmillan.

Hart, C. W. M., and Arnold Pilling
1979   The Tiwi of North Australia, Fieldwork Edition. New York: Holt, Rinehart
          and Winston.

Hathaway, Andrew D.
2001   Shortcomings of Harm Reduction: Toward a Morally Invested Drug Reform
          Strategy. International Journal of Drug Policy 12(2):125–137.

Hauschild, Thomas
1994   Unter der Last der Vergangenheit. Anthropos 89:567–571.
1995a   Dem lebendigen Geist Warum die Geschichte der Völkerkunde im, Dritten
          Reich, auch für Nichtethnologen von Interesse sein kann. In Lebenslust und
          Fremdenfurcht: Ethnologie im Dritten Reich. Thomas Hauschild, ed. Pp.
          13–61. Frankfurt, Germany: Suhrkamp Taschenbuch.
1995b   Vorwort. In Lebenslust und Fremdenfurcht: Ethnologie im Dritten Reich.
          Thomas Hauschild, ed. Pp. 7–11. Frankfurt, Germany: Suhrkamp
          Taschenbuch.

2001 Army of Hope, Army of Alienation: Culture and Contradiction in the American Army Communities of Cold War Germany. Westport, CT: Praeger.

2003 Preface. *In* Anthropology and the United States Military: Coming of Age in the Twenty-first Century. Pamela R. Frese and Margaret C. Harrell, eds. P. ix. New York: Palgrave Macmilllan.

Helbig, Zenia

2008 Subject: US Army Human Terrain System Malfeasance. Letter to Jake Wiens, Project on Government Oversight, March 28. http://pogoarchives.org/m/wi/hts-statement-20080328.pdf, accessed April 7, 2009.

Helman, Sara

1997 Militarism and the Construction of Community. Journal of Political and Military Sociology 25:305–332.

Herlihy, Peter, Jerome Dobson, Miguel Aguilar Robledo, Derek Smith, John Kelly, and Aida Ramos Viera

2008 A Digital Geography of Indigenous Mexico: Prototype for the American Geographical Society's Bowman Expeditions. Geographical Review 98:395–415.

Hersh, Seymour

2004a Torture at Abu Ghraib. New Yorker, May 10. http://www.newyorker.com/archive/2004/05/10/040510fa_fact, accessed June 15, 2009.

2004b Chain of Command. New Yorker, May 17. http://www.newyorker.com/archive/2004/05/17/040517fa_fact2, accessed June 15, 2009.

2004c The Gray Zone. New Yorker, May 24. http://www.newyorker.com/archive/2004/05/24/040524fa_fact, accessed June 15, 2009.

2004d Chain of Command: The Road from 9/11 to Abu Ghraib. New York: Harper Collins.

2005 The Coming Wars: What the Pentagon Can Now Do in Secret. New Yorker, January 24: 40–47.

Hickey, Gerald C.

1959 The Social Systems of Northern Vietnam. PhD dissertation, Department of Anthropology, University of Chicago.

1964 The Major Ethnic Groups of the South Vietnamese Highlands. RAND Corporation, ARPA Memorandum RM-4041-ARPA. Santa Monica, CA: The RAND Corporation. http://www.rand.org/pubs/research_memoranda/2008/RM4041.pdf, accessed July 7, 2010.

1965 The American Military Advisor and His Foreign Counterpart: The Case of Vietnam. With the assistance of W. P. Davison. RAND Memorandum, RM-4482-ARPA. Santa Monica, CA: The RAND Corporation. http://www.rand.org/pubs/research_memoranda/2007/RM4482.pdf, accessed July 7, 2010.

1967 The Highland People of South Vietnam: Social and Economic Development. Prepared for Advanced Research Projects Agency, ARPA Order No. 189-1.

RM-5381/1-ARPA. Santa Monica, CA: The RAND Corporation. http://www
.rand.org/pubs/research_memoranda/2005/RM5281.1.pdf, accessed July 7,
2010.

1969   U.S. Strategy in South Vietnam: Extrication and Equilibrium. RAND no. D-
          19736-ARPA. Project No. 9793. Santa Monica, CA: The RAND Corporation.
          http://www.rand.org/pubs/documents/2006/D19736.pdf, accessed July 7,
          2010.

1971   Some Recommendations Affecting the Prospective Role of Vietnamese
          Highlands in Economic Development. Santa Monica, CA: The RAND
          Corporation. http://www.rand.org/pubs/papers/2008/P4708.pdf, accessed
          July 7, 2010.

2002   Window on a War: An Anthropologist in the Vietnam Conflict. Lubbock:
          Texas Tech University Press.

Hilsman, Roger

1998   Interview by the National Security Archive, December 6. http://www.gwu
          .edu/~nsarchiv/coldwar/interviews/episode-11/hilsman1.html, accessed July
          30, 2010.

Hobbes, Thomas

1946[1651] Leviathan: Or the Matter, Form and Power of a Commonwealth,
          Ecclesiastical and Civil. Oxford, UK: Basil Blackwell.

Hobson, Sharon

2007   The Information Gap: Why the Canadian Public Doesn't Know More about
          Its Military. Calgary, AB: Canadian Defence and Foreign Affairs Institute.

Hodge, Nathan

2009   Help Wanted: "Human Terrain" Teams for Africa. Wired, "Danger Room"
          (blog), January 12. http://blog.wired.com/defense/2009/01/help-wanted-
          hum.html, accessed July 7, 2010.

Hoebel, E. Adamson

1967   The Law of Primitive Man: A Study in Comparative Legal Dynamics.
          Cambridge, MA: Harvard University Press.

Hoffman, Danny

2003   Frontline Anthropology: Research in a Time of War. Anthropology Today
          19(3):9–12.

2004a   The Civilian Target in Sierra Leone and Liberia: Political Power, Military
          Strategy, and Humanitarian Intervention. African Affairs 103(411):211–226.

2004b   The Submerged Promise: Strategies for Ethnographic Writing in a Time of
          War. Anthropological Quarterly 77(2):323–330.

2007a   The City as Barracks: Freetown, Monrovia, and the Organization of Violence
          in Postcolonial African Cities. Cultural Anthropology 22(3):400–428.

2007b   The Meaning of a Militia: Understanding the Civil Defense Forces of Sierra
          Leone. African Affairs 106(425):639–662.

Holden, Constance
2001   Polygraph Screening: Panel Seeks Truth in Lie Detector Debate. Science,
        February 9:967.

Horowitz, Irving Louis, ed.
1967   The Rise and Fall of Project Camelot: Studies in the Relationship between
        Social Sciences and Practical Politics. Cambridge, MA: MIT Press.

Howe, Herbert
2001   Ambiguous Order: Military Forces in African States. Boulder, CO: Lynne
        Rienner.

Howell, Signe
1989   To Be Angry Is Not to Be Human, but to Be Fearful Is. *In* Societies at Peace:
        Anthropological Perspectives. Signe Howell and Roy Willis, eds. Pp. 45–59.
        London, UK: Routledge.

Human Terrain System
2008a   HTS Mission. http://humanterrainsystem.army.mil/missionstatement.html,
        accessed September 8, 2009.

2008b   HTS Impact on the Military. http://humanterrainsystem.army.mil/impacts
        .html, accessed September 5, 2010.

Hymes, Dell, ed.
1972   Reinventing Anthropology. New York: Pantheon.

Inbau, Fred E., John E. Reid, Joseph P. Buckley, and Brian C. Jayne
2001   Criminal Justice Interviewing and Detection of Deception. Gaithersburg, MD:
        Aspen.

Inciardi, James A., and Lana D. Harrison, eds.
2000   Harm Reduction: National and International Perspectives. Thousand Oaks,
        CA: Sage.

Intelligence Science Board
2006   Educing Information: Interrogation: Science and Art. Washington DC:
        National Defense Intelligence College.

Irwin, Anne
1993   Infantry Platoon Commanders and the Emergence of Leadership. MA thesis,
        Department of Anthropology, University of Calgary, Alberta, Canada.

2002   The Social Organization of Soldiering: A Canadian Infantry Company in the
        Field. PhD dissertation, Department of Social Anthropology, University of
        Manchester, UK.

Isenberg, David
2009   Dogs of War: The Good, the Bad and the Contractor. UPI.com, March 27.
        http://www.upi.com/Emerging_Threat/2009/03/27/Dogs-of-War-The-good-
        the-bad-and the-contractor/UPI-57071238162194/, accessed September 8, 2009.

Isikoff, Michael, and Mark Hosenball
2009   War on Words: Why Obama May Be Abandoning Bush's Favorite Phrase.

Newsweek, February 4. http://www.newsweek.com/id/183251, accessed July 7, 2010.

Israely, Jeff

2005   A Resounding Echo. Time, June 5. http://www.time.com/time/magazine/article/0,9171,1069054,00.html, accessed July 7, 2010.

Izraeli, Dafna

1997   Gendering Military Service in the Israeli Defense Forces. Israel Social Science Research 12(1):129–166.

Jaffer, Jameel, and Amrit Singh

2007   Administration of Torture: A Documentary Record from Washington to Abu Ghraib and Beyond. New York: Columbia University Press.

Jasanoff, Sheila

1987   Contested Boundaries in Policy-Relevant Science. Social Studies of Science 17:195–230.

Jaschik, Scott

2006   If CIA Calls, Should Anthropology Answer? Inside Higher Ed, September 1. http://insidehighered.com/news/2006/09/01/anthro, accessed July 7, 2010.

2008   A Pentagon Olive Branch to Academe. Inside Higher Ed, April 16. http://www.insidehighered.com/news/2008/04/16/minerva, accessed May 12, 2008.

Jelinek, Pauline

2009   US Lacks Civilians for Afghan "Civilian Surge." USA Today, April 23. http://www.usatoday.com/news/washington/2009-04-23-afghanistan-surge_N.htm, accessed July 7, 2010.

Johnson, Eric Michael

2007   Anthropology Goes to War, Part 3. The Primate Diaries (blog), October 10. http://primatediaries.blogspot.com/2007/10/anthropology-goes-to-war-part-3.html, accessed September 6, 2010.

Jok, Jok Madut

2007   Slavery and Slave Redemption in Sudan. *In* Buying Freedom: The Ethics and Economics of Slave Redemption. Kwame Anthony Appiah and Martin Bunzl, eds. Pp. 143–157. Princeton, NJ: Princeton University Press.

Jones, Delmos

1967   Cultural Variation among Six Lahu Villages, Northern Thailand. PhD dissertation, Department of Anthropology, Cornell University.

1971a   Reply to Jorgensen & Wolf. New York Review of Books, July 22. http://www.nybooks.com/articles/archives/1971/jul/22/anthropology-on-the-warpath-an-exchange/, accessed July 7, 2010.

1971b   Social Responsibility and the Belief in Basic Research: An Example from Thailand. Current Anthropology 12:347–350.

1976   Applied Anthropology and the Application of Human Knowledge. Human Organization 35:221–229.

Jones, Terry

2002   Why Grammar Is the First Casualty of War. London Daily Telegraph, January 12. http://www.commondreams.org/views02/0112-02.htm, accessed December 29, 2010.

2005   Terry Jones's War on the War on Terror. New York: Nation Books.

Jorgensen, Joseph G., and Eric Wolf

1970   Anthropology on the Warpath in Thailand. New York Review of Books, November 19:27–35. http://www.nybooks.com/articles/archives/1970/nov/19/a-special-supplement-anthropology-on-the-warpath-i/, accessed July 7, 2010.

1971   Joseph Jorgensen and Eric Wolf Reply. New York Review of Books, April 8. http://www.newyorkbooks.com/articles/archives/1971/apr/08/anthropology-on-the-warpath-an-exchange/?page=1, accessed September 6, 2010.

Junger, Sebastian

2010   War. New York: Harper Collins.

Kaplan, Danny, and Eyal Ben-Ari

2000   Engaging or Building Walls? Managing Gay Identity in Combat Units of the Israeli Army. Journal of Contemporary Ethnography 29(4):396–432.

Kaplan, Robert

2003   Supremacy by Stealth: Ten Rules for Managing the World. Atlantic Monthly, July/August:66–83.

Kaschuba, Wolfgang

2006   Fremde Nähe—nahe Fremde? evifa.de, May, 13. http://edoc.hu-berlin.de/evifa/documents/books/Beitrag_Kaschuba_13-05-06.pdf, accessed November 24, 2010.

Kassin, Saul M., Richard A. Leo, Christian A. Meissner, Kimberly D. Richman, Lori H. Colwell, Amy-May Leach, and Dana La Fon

2007   Police Interviewing and Interrogation: A Self-Report Survey of Police Practices and Beliefs. Law and Human Behavior 31(4):381–400.

Katel, Peter

2008   Rise in Counterinsurgency: Will New Tactics Weaken the Military? CQ Researcher 18(5):697–720.

Katz, Perl

1990   Emotional Metaphors, Socialization, and the Roles of Drill Sergeants. Ethos 18(4):457–480.

Keane, Helen

2003   Critiques of Harm Reduction, Morality and the Promise of Human Rights. International Journal of Drug Policy 14(3):227–232.

Keefe, Robert H., Sandra D. Lane, and Heidi Swars

2006   From the Bottom Up: Tracing the Impact of Four Health-Based Social

Movements on Health and Social Policies. Journal of Health and Social Policy 21(3):55–69.

Keeley, Lawrence H.
1996   War before Civilization: The Myth of the Peaceful Savage. Oxford, UK: Oxford University Press.

Keen, David
2005   Conflict and Collusion in Sierra Leone. New York: Palgrave Macmillan.

Keenan, Jeremy
2008   US Militarization in Africa: What Anthropologists Should Know about AFRICOM. Anthropology Today 24(5):16–20.
2009   Under Construction: Making Homeland Security at the Local Level: Where Ethics and Politics Intertwine. Times Higher Education, January 29. http://www.timeshighereducation.co.uk/story.asp?sectioncode=26&storycode=405203&c=1, accessed July 7, 2010.

Kelly, Robert L.
1995   The Foraging Spectrum: Diversity in Hunter-Gatherer Lifeways. Washington DC: Smithsonian Institution.

Keren, Michael
2005   Narrative and Image in the Commemoration of War: The Blog of L. T. Smash. Journal of Military and Strategic Studies 7:1–25.

Kilcullen, David
2006   Twenty-Eight Articles: Fundamentals of Company-Level Counterinsurgency. Military Review 86(3):103–108.

Kimmerling, Baruch
1993   Patterns of Militarism in Israel. European Journal of Sociology 34:196–223.

Kipp, Jacob, Lester Grau, Karl Prinsloo, and Don Smith
2006   The Human Terrain System: A CORDS for the Twenty-first Century. Military Review (September–October):8–15.

Kirke, Charles
1999   A Model for the Analysis of Fighting Spirit in the British Army. In The British Army: Manpower and Society into the Twenty-first Century. Hew Strachan, ed. Pp. 227–241. London, UK: Frank Cass.

Knauft, Bruce
1991   Violence and Sociality in Human Evolution. Current Anthropology 32:391–428.

Knorr-Cetina, Karin
1999   Epistemic Cultures: How the Sciences Make Knowledge. Cambridge, MA: Harvard University Press.

Kohl-Larsen, Ludwig
1943   Auf den Spuren des Vormenschen. Forschungen, Fahrten, und Erlebnisse in Deutsch-Ostafrika. Band I. Stuttgart, Germany: Strecker & Schröder.

Konner, Melvin

2006   Human Nature, Ethnic Violence, and War. *In* The Psychology of Resolving Global Conflicts: From War to Peace, vol. 1: Nature versus Nurture. Mari Fitzduff and Chris Stout, eds. Pp. 1–39. Westport, CT: Praeger Security International.

Kornelius, Stefan

2009   Die afghanische Zäsur. Süddeutsche Zeitung, September 7:4.

Kuhn, Thomas S.

1957   The Copernican Revolution: Planetary Astronomy in the Development of Western Thought. Cambridge, MA: Harvard University Press.

Kühne, Winrich

2007   Deutschland und die Friedenseinsätze–vom Nobody zum weltpolitischen Akteur. ZIF, Aufsatz 12/07, Zentrum für Internationale Friedenseinsätze: Berlin. http://www.zif-berlin.org/fileadmin/uploads/analyse/dokumente/veroeffentlichungen/Deutschland_und_die_Friedenseinsaetze_12_07.pdf, accessed November 24, 2010.

Kümmel, Gerhard, and Heiko Biehl

2000   Anforderungen an die deutsche Außen-, Sicherheits- und Verteidigungspolitik an der Schwelle zum 21. Jahrhundert. *In* Die Bundeswehr an der Schwelle zum 21. Paul Klein and Dieter Walz, eds. Pp. 11–49. Baden-Baden, Germany: Nomos-Verlag.

Lagouranis, Tony, and Allen Mikaelian

2007   Fear Up Harsh: An Army Interrogator's Dark Journey through Iraq. New York: NAL Caliber.

Lamphere, Louise

2003   The Perils and Prospects for an Engaged Anthropology: A View from the United States. Social Anthropology 11(2):153–168.

Landers, Jim

2009a   Anthropologist from Plano Maps Afghanistan's Human Terrain for Army. Dallas Morning News, March 8. http://www.dallasnews.com/sharedcontent/dws/news/world/stories/DN-afghanculture_08int.ART.State.Edition2.48b1d26.html, accessed September 6, 2010.

2009b   Her Mission Orders in Afghanistan: Map the Human Terrain. Dallas Morning News, March 13. Originally accessed on www.bostonherald.com, later available on http://www.leatherneck.com/forums/showthread.php?t=80629, accessed September 6, 2010.

Lane, Sandra D.

2008   Why Are Our Babies Dying? Pregnancy, Birth, and Death in America. Boulder, CO: Paradigm.

Lane, Sandra D., Peter Lurie, Benjamin Bowser, Jim Kahn, and Donna Chen

2000   The Coming of Age of Needle Exchange: A History through 1993. *In* Harm

Reduction: National and International Perspectives. James A. Inciardi and
Lana D. Harrison, eds. Pp. 47–68. Thousand Oaks, CA: Sage.

Latham, Andrew
2002   Warfare Transformed: A Braudelian Perspective on the "Revolution in
        Military Affairs." European Journal of International Relations 8(2):231–266.

Lave, Jean
1988   Cognition in Practice. Cambridge, MA: Harvard University Press.

Lave, Jean, and Etienne Wenger
1991   Situated Learning: Legitimate Peripheral Participation. Cambridge, UK:
        Cambridge University Press.

Lenton, Simon, and Eric Single
1998   The Definition of Harm Reduction. Drug and Alcohol Review
        17(2):213–220.

Leo, Richard A.
1992   From Coercion to Deception: The Changing Nature of Police Interrogation
        in America. Crime, Law and Social Change 18:35–59.
2008   Police Interrogation and American Justice. Cambridge, MA: Harvard
        University Press.

Leo, Richard A., and Jerome H. Skolnick
1992   The Ethics of Deceptive Interrogation. Criminal Justice Ethics 11.
        http://papers.ssrn.com/sol3/papers.cfm?abstract_id=1141390, accessed June
        28, 2009.

Leonhard, Nina, and Jacqueline Werkner
2005   Einleitung: Militär als Gegenstand der Forschung. In Militärsoziologie–Eine
        Einführung. Jacqueline Wernker and Nina Leonhard, eds. Pp. 13–22.
        Wiesbaden, Germany: VS Verlag für Sozialwissenschaften.

Lesser, Alexander
1968   War and the State. In War: The Anthropology of Armed Conflict and
        Aggression. Morton Fried, Marvin Harris, and Robert Murphy, eds. Pp.
        92–96. Garden City, NY: Natural History Press.

Levin, Carl
2008   Senate Armed Services Committee Hearing: The Origins of Aggressive
        Interrogation Techniques. http://levin.senate.gov/newsroom/release
        .cfm?id=299242, accessed September 6, 2010.

Leyendecker, Hans
2008   Ein bisschen Krieg: Deutschland ist weltweit drittgrößter Rüstungsexporteur.
        Süddeutsche Zeitung, May16:1.

Linford-Steinfeld, Joshua
2003   Weight Control and Physical Readiness among Navy Personnel. In
        Anthropology and the United States Military: Coming of Age in the Twenty-
        first Century. Pamela R. Frese and Margaret C. Harrell, eds. Pp. 115–112.
        New York: Palgrave Macmillan.

REFERENCES

Linton, Ralph
1924   Totemism and the AEF. American Anthropologist 26(2):296–300.

Lomsky-Feder, Edna
1998   As If There Was No War: The Life Stories of Israeli Men. Jerusalem: Magnes.

Lomsky-Feder, Edna, and Eyal Ben-Ari
1999   "The People in Uniform" to "Different Uniforms for the People": Profession-
        alism, Diversity and the Israel Defence Forces. *In* The Management of
        Diversity in the Armed Forces. Jan van der Meulen and Joseph Soeters, eds.
        Pp. 157–188. Tilburg, Netherlands: Tilburg University Press.

Loue, Sana
2000   Textbook of Research Ethics: Theory and Practice. New York: Springer.

Lucas, George
2009   Anthropologists in Arms: The Ethics of Military Anthropology. Lanham,
        MD: AltaMira Press.

Lutz, Catherine
2001   Homefront: The Military City and the American Twentieth Century. Boston,
        MA: Beacon Press.
2002   Making War at Home in the United States: Militarization and the Current
        Crisis. American Anthropologist 104:723–735.
2009   The Bases of Empire: The Global Struggle against U.S. Military Posts. New
        York: New York University Press.

Macek, Ivana
2001   Predicament of War: Sarajevo Experiences and Ethics of War. *In*
        Anthropology of Violence and Conflict. Bettina Schimdt and Ingo Schröder,
        eds. Pp. 197–224. London, UK: Routledge.

Mackey, Chris, and Greg Miller
2004   The Interrogators: Inside the Secret War Against al Qaeda. New York: Little,
        Brown and Company.

Macnamara, Don, and Thomas Adams
2008   Strategic Profile: Canada 2008. Toronto, ON: Canadian International
        Council.

Malinowski, Bronislaw
1954   Magic, Science and Religion and Other Essays. Garden City, NY: Doubleday.

Maman, Daniel, Zeev Rosenhek, and Eyal Ben-Ari
2001   War, Politics, and Society in Israel: Theoretical and Comparative
        Perspectives. New Brunswick, NJ: Transaction.

Mann, Morgan
2007   The Power Equation: Using Tribal Politics in Counterinsurgency. Military
        Review (May–June):104–108.

Marcus, George
1999   Foreword. *In* Cultures of Insecurity: States, Communities, and the

Production of Danger. Jutta Weldes, Mark Laffey, Hugh Gusterson, and Raymond Duvall, eds. Pp. vii–xv. Minneapolis: University of Minnesota Press.

Maturana, Humberto R., and Francisco J. Varela

1988 The Tree of Knowledge: The Biological Roots of Human Understanding. Boston, MA: New Science Library.

McCaffrey, Katherine T.

2002 Military Power and Popular Protest: The U.S. Navy in Vieques, Puerto Rico. New Brunswick, NJ: Rutgers University Press.

McCoy, Alfred

2006 A Question of Torture: CIA Interrogation, from the Cold War to the War on Terror. New York: Henry Holt.

McFate, Montgomery

2005a Anthropology and Counterinsurgency: The Strange Story of Their Curious Relationship. Military Review (March–April):24–38.

2005b The Military Utility of Understanding the Adversary Culture. Joint Forces Quarterly 38:43–45.

2007 Building Bridges or Burning Heretics? Anthropology Today 23(3):21.

McFate, Montgomery, and Steve Fondacaro

2008 Cultural Knowledge and Common Sense. Anthropology Today 24(1):27.

McFate, Sean

2007 The Art and Aggravation of Vetting in Post-Conflict Environments. Military Review (July–August):79–87.

2008 US Africa Command: Next Step or Next Stumble? African Affairs 107(426):111–120.

McLeary, Paul

2008 Future Face of Conflict: Human Terrain Teams. World Politics Review, October 14. http://www.worldpoliticsreview.com/article.aspx?id=2774, accessed September 8, 2009.

McMichael, William

2008 AfriCom Goes Operational. Army Times, October 2. http://www.armytimes.com/news/2008/09/military_africacommand_100108w/, accessed October 7, 2008.

McNamara, Laura

2007a SAR Hosts Seminar on the Anthropology of Military and National Security. Anthropology News (May):24–25.

2007b Culture, Critique, and Credibility: Speaking Truth to Power during the Long War. Anthropology Today 23(2):20–21.

Melman, Seymour

1986 The War-Making Institutions. In Peace and War: Cross-Cultural Perspectives. Mary L. Foster and Robert A. Rubinstein, eds. Pp. 193–208. New Brunswick, NJ: Transaction Books.

REFERENCES

Metcalf, Peter
2001   Global "Disjuncture" and the "Sites" of Anthropology. Cultural Anthropology 16(2):165–182.

Michel, Ute
1995   Neue ethnologische Forschungsansätze im Nationalsozialismus? Aus der Biographie von Wilhelm Emil Mühlmann (1904–1988). *In* Lebenslust und Fremdenfurcht: Ethnologie im Dritten Reich. Thomas Hauschild, ed. Pp. 141–167. Frankfurt, Germany: Suhrkamp Taschenbuch.

Middle East Online
2008   U.S. Military, Oblivious of Iraqi Culture, Enlists Anthropologists for Occupation. Alternet, January 19. http://www.alternet.org/story/74326/, accessed June 15, 2008.

Miklikowska, Marta, and Douglas P. Fry
2010   Values for Peace: Lessons from the Semai of Malaysia and the Mardu of Australia. Beliefs and Values 2(2):124–137.

Miles, Steven
2006   Oath Betrayed: Torture, Medical Complicity, and the War on Terror. New York: Random House.
2007a   Medical Ethics and the Interrogation of Guantanamo 063. American Journal of Bioethics 7(4):5–11.
2007b   Science and Torture. Archives of General Psychiatry 64(3):275–276.

Milhauser, Steven
2008   The Next Thing. Harper's Magazine, May:71–78.

Miller, Greg
2009   Obama Preserves Renditions as Counterterrorism Tool. Los Angeles Times, February 1. http://articles.latimes.com/2009/feb/01/nation/na-rendition1, accessed December 29, 2010.

Miller, Greg, and Julian Barnes
2009   Obama Overturns Bush Tactics in War on Terrorism. Los Angeles Times, January 23. http://articles.latimes.com/2009/jan/23/nation/na-obama-guantanamo23, accessed June 28, 2009.

Mohamed, Feroze B., Scott H. Faro, Nathan J. Gordon, Steven M. Plate, Harris Ahmad, and J. Michael Williams
2006   Brain Mapping of Deception and Truth Telling about an Ecologically Valid Situation: Functional MR Imaging and Polygraph Investigation—Initial Experience. Radiology 238(2):679–88.

Montagu, Ashley
1978   Introduction. *In* Learning Non-Aggression: The Experience of Non-Literate Societies. Ashley Montagu, ed. Pp. 3–11. Oxford, UK: Oxford University Press.

Mosen, Markus

1991   Der koloniale Traum: Angewandte Ethnologie im Nationalsozialismus. Bonn, Germany: Holos.

MTC Technologies

2008   Human Terrain System (HTS) Update. HTS Newsletter, April 7:1–2.

Mühlmann, Wilhelm E.

1970[1933]   Die Hitler-Bewegung: Bemerkungen zur Krise der bürgerlichen Kultur. Zeitschrift für Völkerkunde und Soziologie 9. Stuttgart, Germany: Kohlhammer.

1936   Rassen- und Völkerkunde: Lebensprobleme der Rassen, Gesellschaften und Völker. Braunschweig, Germany: Vieweg.

1940   Krieg und Frieden: Ein Leitfaden politischer Ethnologie: Mit Berücksichtigung völkerkundlichen und geschichtlichen Stoffes. Heidelberg, Germany: Carl Winter's Universitätsbuchhandlung.

Mulrine, Anna

2007   The Culture Warriors. US News and World Report, December 10:34–37.

Münkler, Herfried

2002   Die neuen Kriege. Reinbek, Germany: Rowohlt.

2009   Durch den Sehschlitz: Man mache sich nichts vor–Der Westen kann den Krieg in Afghanistan nicht gewinnen. Süddeutsche Zeitung, April 6:11.

Murdock, George P.

1967   Ethnographic Atlas: A Summary. Ethnology 6:109–236.

1981   Atlas of World Cultures. Pittsburgh, PA: University of Pittsburgh Press.

Mychalejko, Cyril, and Ramor Ryan

2009   U.S. Military Funded Mapping Project in Oaxaca. Z Magazine, April 1. http://www.zmag.org/zmag/viewArticle/21044, accessed September 9, 2009.

Nader, Laura

1972   Up the Anthropologist—Perspectives Gained from Studying Up. *In* Reinventing Anthropology. Dell H. Hymes, ed. Pp. 284–311. New York: Pantheon Books.

Nagengast, Carole

1994   Violence, Terror, and the Crisis of the State. Annual Review of Anthropology 23:109–136.

Nagl, John

2007   Institutionalizing Adaptation: It's Time for a Permanent Army Advisor Corps. Washington DC: Center for New American Security.

Nature

2008   Failure in the Field (editorial). Nature 456(11):676.

Network of Concerned Anthropologists Steering Committee, ed.

2009   The Counter-Counterinsurgency Manual. Chicago, IL: Prickly Paradigm Press.

REFERENCES

Newcomb, Theodore M.
1947   Autistic Hostility and Social Reality. Human Relations 1(1):69–86.

Nordstrom, Carolyn
1997   A Different Kind of War Story. Philadelphia: University of Pennsylvania Press.

Nordstrom, Carolyn, and Antonius Robben, eds.
1995   Fieldwork Under Fire: Contemporary Studies of Violence and Survival. Berkeley: University of California Press.

Norwitz, Jeffrey H.
2005   Defining Success at Guantanamo: By What Measure? Military Review (July–August):79–83.

Obama, Barack
2009a   Obama's Nobel remarks. New York Times, December 10. http://www .nytimes.com/2009/12/11/world/europe/11prexy.text.html?_r=2, accessed November 18, 2010.

2009b   Executive Order 13,491, Ensuring Lawful Interrogations, Federal Register 74(16):4893–4896.

2009c   Executive Order no. 13,492, Review and Disposition of Individuals Detained at the Guantánamo Bay Naval Base and Closure of Detention Facilities. Federal Register 74(16):4897–4900.

2009d   Executive Order 13,493, Review of Detention Policy Options. 27 Federal Register 74(16):4901–4902.

Ortner, Sherry
1999   Some Futures of Anthropology. American Ethnologist 26(4):984–991.

Otis, Pauletta
2006   Educing Information: The Right Initiative at the Right Time by the Right People. *In* Educing Information: Interrogation: Science and Art. Intelligence Science Board. Pp. xv–xx. Washington DC: National Defense Intelligence College.

Otterbein, Keith F.
1968   Internal War: A Cross-Cultural Study. American Anthropologist 70:277–289.

Paige, Glenn D.
2002   Nonkilling Global Political Science. Bloomington, IN: Xlibris USA.

Patterson, Kevin
2007   Talk to Me Like My Father: Frontline Medicine in Afghanistan. Mother Jones (July): 39–45, 82.

Patterson, Kevin, and Jane Warren, eds.
2007   Outside the Wire: The War in Afghanistan in the Words of Its Participants. Toronto, ON: Random House Canada.

Pels, Peter
1997   The Anthropology of Colonialism: Culture, History, and the Emergence of

Western Governmentality. Annual Review of Anthropology 26:163–183.

Pelton, Robert Young

2009   Afghanistan: The New War for Hearts and Minds. Men's Journal, January 21. http://www.mensjournal.com/new-war-for-hearts-and-minds, accessed February 10, 2009.

Pengelly, Ryan, and Anne Irwin

2010   Twenty-First Century Narratives from Afghanistan: Storytelling, Morality, and War. *In* The Routledge Handbook of War and Society. Steven Carlton-Ford and Morten G. Enders, eds. Pp. 44–55. Oxford, UK: Routledge.

Peterson, Mark Allen

2003   Anthropology and Mass Communication: Media and Myth in the New Millennium. New York: Berghahn Books.

Piatetsky, Peter

2009   The Army's Controversial Anthropology Program. Boston Phoenix, March 15. http://thePhoenix.com/Boston/News/78049-Culture-wars/, accessed June 26, 2009.

Pinker, Steven

2003   The Blank Slate: The Modern Denial of Human Nature. New York: Penguin.

Pinxten, Rik, Marijke Cornelis, and Robert A. Rubinstein

2007   European Identity: Diversity in Union. International Journal of Public Administration 30:687–698.

Potts, Malcolm, and Thomas Hayden

2008   Sex and War: How Biology Explains Warfare and Terrorism and Offers a Path to a Safer World. Dallas, TX: Benbella.

Powlen, Lester J.

2007   Criminal Investigation Task Force. Military Police PB 19-07-1: 1–4 http://www.wood.army.mil/mpbulletin/pdfs/Spring%2007%20pdfs/Powlen .pdf, accessed June 28, 2009.

Price, David

2000   Anthropologists as Spies. Nation, November 2. http://www.thenation.com/ article/anthropologists-spies, accessed July 7, 2010.

2002a   Lessons from Second World War Anthropology: Peripheral, Persuasive, and Ignored Contributions. Anthropology Today 18(3):14–20.

2002b   Past Wars, Present Dangers, Future Anthropologies. Anthropology Today 18(1):3–5.

2007   Pilfered Scholarship Devastates General Petraeus's *Counterinsurgency Manual.* Counterpunch, October 30. http://www.counterpunch.org/price10302007 .html, accessed July 7, 2010.

2008a   The Military "Leveraging" of Cultural Knowledge: The Newly Available 2004 Stryker Report Evaluating Iraqi Failures. Counterpunch, March 18. http://www.counterpunch.com/price03182008.html, accessed July 7, 2010.

2008b   Anthropological Intelligence: The Deployment and Neglect of American
           Anthropology during the Second World War. Durham, NC: Duke University
           Press.

2008c   First Read of a Leaked Handbook. Counterpunch, December 12/14. http:
           //www.counterpunch.org/price12122008.html, accessed September 9, 2010.

2009   Counterinsurgency's Free Ride. Counterpunch, April 7. http://www
           .counterpunch.com/price04072009.html, accessed April 14, 2009.

2010   Soft Power, Hard Power, and the Anthropological "Leveraging" of Cultural
           "Assets": Distilling the Politics and Ethics of Anthropological
           Counterinsurgency. In Anthropology and Global Counterinsurgency. John
           D. Kelly, Beatrice Jauregui, Sean T. Mitchell, and Jeremey Walton, eds. Pp.
           245–260. Chicago, IL: University of Chicago Press.

Priest, Dana
2009   Bush "War" on Terror Comes to a Sudden End. Washington Post, January
           23. http://www.washingtonpost.com/wp-dyn/content/article/2009/01/22/
           AR2009012203929.html, accessed June 28, 2009.

Pryor, Mike
2007   Experts Help Soldiers Understand Culture. Army.Mil (website), December
           11. http://www.army.mil/-news/2007/12/11/6531-human-terrain-team-helps-
           soldiers-in-iraq-understand-cultural-landscape/, accessed August 1, 2010.

Pulliam, Linda
1988   Achieving Social Competence in the Navy Community. In The Social
           Dynamics of Peace and Conflict: Culture in International Security. Robert A.
           Rubinstein and Mary L. Foster, eds. Pp. 91–106. Boulder, CO: Westview
           Press.

Redden, Elizabeth
2009   American Counterinsurgency. Inside Higher Ed, January 29. http://www
           .insidehighered.com/news/2009/01/29/humanterrain, accessed February
           10, 2009.

Rehn, Elisabeth, and Ellen Johnson Sirleaf
2002   Women, War, and Peace. New York: United Nations Development Fund for
           Women.

Renner, Erich
2000   Ludwig Kohl-Larsen–Zur Frage von Schuld und Sühne. In Ethnologie und
           Nationalsozialismus. Bernhard Streck, ed. Pp. 115–125. Gehren, Germany:
           Escher.

Renzi, Fred
2006a   Networks: Terra Incognita and the Case for Ethnographic Intelligence.
           Military Review (September–October):16–22.

2006b   The Military Cooperation Group. MA thesis. Department of Defense
           Analysis, Naval Postgraduate School, Monterey, CA.

Richards, Paul
1996   Fighting for the Rainforest: War, Youth and Resources in Sierra Leone. Portsmouth, NH: Heinemann.

Ricks, Thomas
2009   A Military Tactician's Political Strategy. Washington Post, February 9:A1.

Robarchek, Clayton A.
1989   Hobbesian and Rousseauan Images of Man: Autonomy and Individuality in a Peaceful Society. *In* Societies at Peace: Anthropological Perspectives. Signe Howell and Roy Willis, eds. Pp. 31–44. London, UK: Routledge.

Robben, Antonius
1995   The Politics of Truth and Emotion among Victims of Perpetrators of Violence. *In* Fieldwork Under Fire. Carolyn Nordstrom and Antonius Robben, eds. Pp. 81–103. Berkeley: University of California Press.

Rohde, David
2007   Army Enlists Anthropology in War Zones. New York Times, October 5. http://www.nytimes.com/2007/10/05/world/asia/05afghan.html?pagewanted=1&hp, accessed November 20, 2010.

Ron, James
2000   Savage Restraint: Israel, Palestine and the Dialectics of Repression. Social Problems 47(4):445–472.

Ross, Marc Howard
1993   The Culture of Conflict: Interpretations and Interests in Comparative Perspective. New Haven, CT: Yale University Press.

Rötzer, Florian
2008   Anthropologisierung des Militärs. Telepolis. www.heise.de, April 21. http://www.heise.de/tp/r4/artikel/27/27769/1.html, accessed April 21, 2008.

Rubin, Alissa, and Damien Cave
2007   In a Force for Iraqi Calm, Seeds of Conflict. New York Times, December 23:A1, 14–15.

Rubin, Michael
2007   Asymmetrical Threat Concept and Its Reflections on International Security. Middle East Forum, May 31. http://www.meforum.org/article/1696, accessed July 7, 2010.

Rubinstein, Robert A.
1983   Averting International Conflict and the Policy Process: Toward a Role for Anthropologists. Forum for Correspondence and Contact 14(1):96–100.
1986   The Collapse of Strategy: Understanding Ideological Bias in Policy Decisions. *In* Peace and War: Cross Cultural Perspectives. Mary L. Foster and Robert A. Rubinstein, eds. Pp. 343–351. New Brunswick, NJ: Transaction Books.
1988   Cultural Analysis and International Security. Alternatives 13(4):529–542.

REFERENCES

1992   Culture and Negotiation. *In* The Struggle for Peace: Israelis and
        Palestinians. Elizabeth W. Fernea and Mary E. Hocking, eds. Pp. 116–129.
        Austin: University of Texas Press.
1993   Cultural Aspects of Peacekeeping: Notes on the Substance of Symbols.
        Millennium: Journal of International Studies 22(3):547–562.
1998   Methodological Challenges in the Ethnographic Study of Multilateral
        Peacekeeping. Political and Legal Anthropology Review 21(1):138–149.
2002   Doing Fieldwork: The Correspondence of Robert Redfield and Sol Tax. New
        Brunswick, NJ: Transaction.
2003   Peacekeepers and Politics: Experience and Political Representation among
        U.S. Military Officers. *In* Anthropology and the United States Military:
        Coming of Age in the Twenty-first Century. Pamela R. Frese and Margaret C.
        Harrell, eds. Pp. 15–28. New York: Palgrave Macmillan.
2006   Anthropology, Peace, Conflict, and International Security. Paper presented
        at the Annual Meeting of the American Anthropological Association, San
        Jose, CA, November 18.
2008   Peacekeeping Under Fire: Culture and Intervention. Boulder, CO:
        Paradigm.
2009   Retrospective Attribution, Ritual Pollution, and Master Narratives in
        Anthropology's Engagements with the Military. Paper presented at the
        Annual Meeting of the Society for Applied Anthropology, Santa Fe, NM,
        March 19.

Rubinstein, Robert A., and Sandra D. Lane
2002   Population, Identity and Political Violence. Social Justice: Anthropology,
        Peace and Human Rights 3(3/4):139–152.

Rubinstein, Robert A., and Sol Tax
1985   Power, Powerlessness, and the Failure of "Political Realism". *In* Native
        Power: The Quest for Autonomy and Nationhood of Indigenous People.
        Jens Brøsted, Jens Dahl, Andrew Gray, Hans Christian Gullov, Georg
        Henriksen, Jørgen B. Jorgensen, and Inge Kleivan, eds. Pp. 301–308.
        Bergen, Norway: Universitetsforlaget AS.

Rühle, Michael
2008   Am Rubikon der Kampfeinsätze. Frankfurter Allgemeine Zeitung, February
        4:8.

Ryle, Gilbert
1949   The Concept of Mind. New York: Barnes and Noble.

Saar, Eric, and Viveca Novak
2005   Inside the Wire: A Military Intelligence Soldier's Eyewitness Account of Life
        at Guantanamo. New York: Penguin.

Sabourin, Michel
2007   The Assessment of Credibility: An Analysis of Truth and Deception in a
        Multiethnic Environment. Canadian Psychology 48(1):24–31.

Sahlins, Marshall

1966 The Destruction of Conscience in Vietnam. *In* Culture and Practice: Selected Essays. Pp. 229–260. Cambridge, MA: MIT Press.

Said, Edward

1978 Orientalism. New York: Vintage.

Salmoni, Barak, and Paula Holmes-Eber

2009 Operational Culture for the Warfighter: Principles and Applications. Quantico, VA: Marine Corps University Press.

Sanders, Brian

2006 An Afghan Odyssey. Canadian Broadcasting Corporation, September 7. http://www.cbc.ca/news/viewpoint/vp_sanders/20060901.html, accessed July 5, 2009.

Sasson-Levy, Orna

2002 Constructing Identities at the Margins: Masculinities and Citizenship in the Israeli Army. Sociological Quarterly 43(3):353–383.

Scarry, Elaine

1985 The Body in Pain: The Making and Unmaking of the World. New York: Oxford University Press.

Schactman, Noah

2007 Army Social Scientists Calm Afghanistan, Make Enemies at Home. Wired, November 29. http://www.wired.com/politics/security/news/2007/11/human_terrain, accessed April 29, 2008.

2008 Montgomery McFate: Use Anthropology in Military Planning. Wired, September 22. http://www.wired.com/politics/law/magazine/16-10/sl_mcfate, accessed September 9, 2010.

2009 Mass Exodus from "Human Terrain" Program: At Least One-Third Quits (Updated). Wired, April 6. http://blog.wired.com/defense/2009/04/htts-quit.html, accessed April 7, 2009.

Schafft, Gretchen

2004 From Racism to Genocide: Anthropology in the Third Reich. Urbana: University of Illinois Press.

Schaner, Eric

2008 The Human Terrain System: Achieving a Competitive Advantage through Enhanced "Population-centric" Knowledge Flows. MA thesis, Department of Information Sciences, Naval Postgraduate School, Monterey, CA.

Scheper-Hughes, Nancy, and Philippe Bourgois, eds.

2004 Violence in War and Peace: An Anthology. Oxford, UK: Blackwell.

Schoch, Bruno

2007 Stellungnahme der Herausgeber: Aktuelle Entwicklungen und Empfehlungen. *In* Friedensgutachten 2007. Bruno Schoch, Andreas Heinemann-Grüder, Jochen Hippler, Markus Weingardt, and Reinhard Mutz, eds. Pp. 3–26. Berlin, Germany: LIT Verlag.

Schweitzer, Martin
2008   Statement of Colonel Martin P. Schweitzer before the House Armed Services Committee, Terrorism and Unconventional Threats Sub-Committee and the Research and Education Sub-Committee of the Science and Technology Committee, April 24. Human Terrain System (website). http://humanterrain system.army.mil/col_schweitzer_statement.pdf, accessed September 9, 2010.

Scott, James C.
1998   Seeing Like a State. New Haven, CT: Yale University Press.

Sedillo, Simon
2009   The Demarest Factor: The Ethics of US Department of Defense Funding for Academic Research in Mexico. El Enemigo Común (website), March 25. http://www.elenemigocomun.net/2255, accessed September 9, 2009.

Seidler, Christoph
2003   Wissenschaftsgeschichte nach der NS-Zeit: Das Beispiel der Ethnologie. Die beiden deutschen Ethnologen Wilhelm Mühlmann (1904–1988) und Hermann Baumann (1902–1972). MA thesis, Institut für Ethnologie (Department of Anthropology), Albert-Ludwigs-Universität zu Freiburg, Germany.
2005   Opfer ihrer Erregung: Die deutsche Ethnologie und der Kolonialismus. www.boell.de. http://www.boell.de/navigation/aussen-sicerheit-1991.html, accessed October 17, 2005.

Selmeski, Brian
2007   Military Cross-Cultural Competence: Core Concepts and Individual Development. Armed Forces and Society Occasional Paper Series #1. Kingston, ON: Royal Military College of Canada Centre for Security.

Sepp, Kalev
2007   From "Shock and Awe" to "Hearts and Minds": The Fall and Rise of US Counterinsurgency Capability in Iraq. Third World Quarterly 28:217–230.

Service, Elman
1971   Profiles in Ethnology. Rev. edition. New York: Harper and Row.

Shanker, Thom
2008   Command for Africa Established by Pentagon. New York Times, October 4. http://www.nytimes.com/2008/10/05/world/africa/05command.html, accessed July 7, 2010.

Shaw, Martin
2005   The New Western Way of War: Risk-Transfer War and Its Crisis in Iraq. Cambridge, UK: Polity.

Silverman, Adam
2009   The Why and How of Human Terrain Teams. Inside Higher Ed, Feb 19. http://www.insidehighered.com/layout/set/print/views/2009/02/19/humanterrain, accessed July 1, 2009.

Silverman, Barry

2007   Human Terrain Data—What Should We Do With It? Department of
        Electrical and Systems Engineering, University of Pennsylvania,
        Departmental Papers. http://repository.upenn.edu/ese_papers/298,
        accessed June 5, 2008.

Simons, Anna

1997   The Company They Keep: Life Inside the US Army Special Forces. New York:
        Free Press.

1999   War: Back to the Future. Annual Review of Anthropology 28:73–108.

Simons, Anna, and Catherine Lutz

2002   Interview by Renee Montagne. Morning Edition. National Public Radio,
        August 14.

Singer, Merrill

2004   Why Is It Easier to Get Drugs than Drug Treatment in the United States? *In*
        Unhealthy Health Policy: A Critical Anthropological Examination. Arachu
        Castro and Merrill Singer, eds. Pp. 287–301. Lanham, MD: AltaMira Press.

Singer, Merrill, and Hans Baer

2007   Introducing Medical Anthropology: A Discipline in Action. Lanham, MD:
        AltaMira Press.

Sion, Liora

2004   Changing from Grey to Blue Beret: Dutch Peacekeepers in Bosnia and
        Kosovo. PhD dissertation, Department of Social and Cultural Anthropology,
        Free University of Amsterdam, The Netherlands.

Sion, Liora, and Eyal Ben-Ari

2005   "Hungry, Weary and Horny": Joking and Jesting Among Israel's Combat
        Reserves. Israel Affairs 11(4):656–672.

Sluka, Jeffrey

2000   Introduction: State Terror and Anthropology. *In* Death Squad: The
        Anthropology of State Terror. Jeffrey Sluka, ed. Pp. 1–45. Philadelphia:
        University of Pennsylvania Press.

2010   Curiouser and Curiouser: Montgomery McFate's Strange Interpretation of
        the Relationship between Anthropology and Counterinsurgency. Political
        and Legal Anthropology Review 33(S1):99–115.

Smith, David Livingstone

2007   The Most Dangerous Animal: Human Nature and the Origin of War. New
        York: St. Martin's.

Snyder, Jack

2002   Anarchy and Culture: Insights from the Anthropology of War. International
        Organization 56(1):7–45.

Society for Applied Anthropology

1949   Report of the Committee on Ethics. Human Organization (Spring):20–21.

REFERENCES

Spencer, Baldwin, and Francis J. Gillen
1927   The Arunta: A Study of a Stone Age People. London, UK: Macmillan.

Sponsel, Leslie E.
1996   The Natural History of Peace: A Positive View of Human Nature and Its Potential. *In* A Natural History of Peace. Thomas Gregor, ed. Pp. 95–125. Nashville, TN: Vanderbilt University Press.
1998   Yanomami: An Arena of Conflict and Aggression in the Amazon. Aggressive Behavior 24:97–122.

Spöttel, Michael
1996   Hamiten: Völkerkunde und Antisemitismus. Frankfurt, Germany: Lang.

Stade, Ronald
1998   Pacific Passages: World Culture and Local Politics in Guam. Stockholm Studies in Social Anthropology. Stockholm, Sweden: University of Stockholm.

Stanton, John
2008a   Is the Human Terrain System Imploding? (Let's Hope So). Zero Anthropology (blog), November 20. http://zeroanthropology.net/2008/11/20/is-the-human-terrain-system-imploding-lets-hope-so/, accessed September 9, 2010.
2008b   Human Terrain System: Murder Charges, Espionage, Paranoia, General Sacked. Zero Anthropology (blog), November 26. http://zeroanthropology.net/2008/11/27/human-terrain-system-murder-espionage-paranoia/, accessed September 9, 2010.
2009   US Army 101st Airborne Investigative Report on Human Terrain System: Toxic at Headquarters and in Bagram. Zero Anthropology (blog), April 2. http://zeroanthropology.net/2009/04/02/us-army-101st-airborne-investigative-report-on-human-terrain-system/, accessed April 7, 2009.

Starrett, Gregory
2004   Culture Never Dies: Anthropology at Abu Ghraib. American Anthropological Association (website). http://www.aaanet.org/press/an/infocus/viewsonhumans/starrett.htm, accessed July 7, 2010.

Stockman, Farah, and Bryan Bender
2009   Afghan Plan Adds 4,000 US Troops: Obama to Include Hundreds of Civilian Advisors. Boston Globe, March 27. http://www.boston.com/news/nation/washington/articles/2009/03/27/afghan_plan_adds_4000_us_troops/, accessed September 9, 2010.

Stonequist, Everett V.
1937   The Marginal Man: A Study in Personality and Culture Conflict. New York: Charles Scribner's Sons.

Streck, Bernhard
2000   Einleitung. *In* Ethnologie und Nationalsozialismus. Bernhard Streck, ed. Pp. 7–21. Gehren, Germany: Escher.

Suppe, Frederick
1977   The Search for Philosophic Understanding of Scientific Theories. *In* The Structure of Scientific Theories. 2nd edition. Frederick Suppe, ed. Pp. 3–56. Urbana: University of Illinois Press.

Susser, Ida
2000   Delmos Jones (1936–1999). American Anthropologist 102(3):581–583.

Swire, Nathan
2008   McFate Explains Human Terrain Teams. Dartmouth, September 26. http://thedartmouth.com/2008/09/26/news/htt/print/, accessed February 10, 2009.

Taçon, Paul, and Christopher Chippindale
1994   Australia's Ancient Warriors: Changing Depictions of Fighting in the Rock Art of Arnhem Land, N.T. Cambridge Archaeological Journal 4:211–248.

Taguba, Major General Antonio M.
2004a   Annexes to Article 15-6 Investigation of the 800th Military Police Brigade, Department of the Army, U.S. Department of Defense.
2004b   Article 15-6 Investigation of the 800th Military Police Brigade, Department of the Army, U.S. Department of Defense.

Tax, Sol
1968   War and the Draft. *In* War: The Anthropology of Armed Conflict and Aggression. Morton Fried, Marvin Harris, and Robert Murphy, eds. Pp. 195–212. New York: Natural History Press.

Thompson, D. D.
2002   Memorandum for the Director for Strategic Plans and Policy Directorate, J-5, SUBJECT: Navy Planner's Memo WRT Counter-Resistance Techniques (SJS 02–06697). Washington DC: United States Department of Defense.

Tiantian, Qi, and Judee K. Burgoon
2007   An Investigation of Heuristics of Human Judgment in Detecting Deception and Potential Implications in Countering Social Engineering. *In* Proceedings of the 2007 IEEE Intelligence and Security Informatics, May 23–24, New Brunswick, NJ. Pp. 152–159. Piscataway, NJ: IEEE.

Tomforde, Maren
2005   Motivation and Self-Image among German Peacekeepers. International Peacekeeping 12(4):576–585.
2006a   Einmal muss man schon dabei gewesen sein…—Auslandseinsätze als Initiation in die "neue" Bundeswehr. *In* Armee in der Demokratie: Zum Spannungsverhältnis von zivilen und militärischen Prinzipien. Ulrich vom Hagen, ed. Pp. 101–119. Wiesbaden, Germany: VS Verlag für Sozialwissenschaften.
2006b   Wo ist denn Deine Uniform? Als Ethnologin bei der Bundeswehr. Ethnoscripts 8(2):20–1.

2008 Zu viel verlangt? Interkulturelle Kompetenz während der Auslandseinsätze der Bundeswehr. *In* Streitkräfte im Einsatz: Zur Soziologie militärischer Interventionen. Gerhard Kümmel, ed. Pp. 69–86. Baden-Baden, Germany: Nomos.

2009a "My Pink Uniform Shows I Am One of Them": Socio-Cultural Dimensions of German Peacekeeping Missions. *In* Armed Forces, Soldiers and Civil-Military Relations: Essays in Honor of Jürgen Kuhlmann. Gerhard Kümmel, Giuseppe Caforio, and Christopher Dandeker, eds. Pp. 37–57. Wiesbaden, Germany: VS Verlag für Sozialwissenschaften.

2009b Bereit für drei Tassen Tee? Die Rolle von Kultur für Auslandseinsätze der Bundeswehr. *In* Auslandseinsätze der Bundeswehr: Sozialwissenschaftliche Analysen, Diagnosen und Perspektiven. Sabine Jaberg, ed. Pp. 71–91. Berlin, Germany: Duncker and Humblot.

2009c Neue Militärkultur(en): Wie verändert sich die Bundeswehr durch die Auslandseinsätze? *In* Forschungsthema Militär. Maja Apelt, ed. Pp. 161–169. Wiesbaden, Germany: VS Verlag für Sozialwissenschaften.

2009d Ethnologie und Militär: Ein Widerspruch? *In* Berufsorientierung für Kulturwissenschaftler: Erfahrungsberichte und Zukunftsperspektiven. Bettina Beer, Sabine Klocke-Daffa, and Christina Lütkes, eds. Pp. 161–169. Berlin, Germany: Dietrich Reimer.

Tuosto, Kylie
2008 The "Grunt Truth" of Embedded Journalism: The New Media/Military Relationship. Stanford Journal of International Relations 10(1):20–31.

Tutakhel, Mariam, and Manija Gardizi
2008 Ein Plädoyer für den Einsatz in Afghanistan. Heinrich-Böll-Stiftung: Außen- & Sicherheit, February 19. http://www.boell.de/internationalepolitik/aussensicherheit/aussen-sicherheit-1991.html, accessed September 9, 2010.

Tyson, Ann Scott
2007 US Widens Push to Use Armed Iraqi Residents: Irregulars to Patrol Own Neighborhoods. Washington Post, July 28:A1, 16.

United States Army and Marine Corps
2007 The U.S. Army/Marine Corps Counterinsurgency Field Manual. Chicago, IL: University of Chicago Press.

United States Army Intelligence Center
1997 Questioning Techniques. Fort Huachuca, AZ: United States Army.

United States Central Intelligence Agency
1963 Kubark Counterintelligence Interrogation, July 1963. National Security Archive, George Washington University. http://www.gwu.edu/~nsarchiv/NSAEBB/NSAEBB122/#hre, accessed June 28, 2009.

1983 Human Resource Exploitation Training Manual—1983. National Security Archive, George Washington University. http://www.gwu.edu/~nsarchiv/NSAEBB/NSAEBB122/#hre, accessed June 28, 2009.

United States Department of Defense

1992   FM 34-52 Intelligence Interrogation. Washington DC: Department of the Army, United Stated Department of Defense.

2005a   Army Regulation 15-6: Final Report: Investigation into FBI Allegations of Detainee Abuse at Guantanamo Bay, Cuba Detention Facility (Schmidt-Furlow Report). Washington DC: Department of the Army, United States Department of Defense.

2005b   Review of DoD Directed Investigations of Detainee Abuse. Washington DC: United States Department of Defense. www.fas.org/irp/agency/dod/abuse.pdf, accessed June 21, 2009.

2006a   Counterinsurgency, Field Manual 3-24. Washington DC: Department of the Army. http://usacac.army.mil/cac2/coin/repository/FM_3-24.pdf, accessed September 5, 2010.

2006b   M 2-22.3 (FB 34-52) Human Intelligence Collector Operations. Washington DC: Department of the Army, United States Department of Defense.

2006c   Quadrennial Defense Review Report, February 6, 2006. www.defenselink.mil/pubs/pdfs/QDR20060203.pdf, accessed October 13, 2008.

United States Department of Justice

2003   Interview and Interrogation of Extremists Working Group, Critical Incident Response Group (CIRG), National Center for the Analysis of Violent Crime (NCAVC) Behavioral Analysis Unit I (BAU I). University of Minnesota Human Rights Library. http://www1.umn.edu/humanrts/OathBetrayed/FBI%203156-3165.pdf/, accessed September 9, 2010.

United States Joint Forces Command

2008   The Joe 2008: Joint Operating Environment: Challenges and Implications for the Future Joint Force. http://www.jfcom.mil/newslink/storyarchive/2008/JOE2008.pdf, accessed September 9, 2010.

Ury, William

1999   Getting to Peace: Transforming Conflict at Home, at Work, and in the World. New York: Viking.

Valentine, Douglas

1990   The Phoenix Program. New York: Avon Books.

van der Dennen, Johan M. G.

1995   The Origin of War, 2 vols. Groningen, the Netherlands: Origin Press.

Varhola, Christopher, and Laura Varhola

2006   Avoiding the Cookie-Cutter Approach to Culture: Lessons Learned from Operations in East Africa. Military Review (November–December):73–78.

Vinitzky-Seroussi, Vered, and Eyal Ben-Ari

2000   A Knock on the Door: Managing Death in the Israeli Defense Forces. Sociological Quarterly 41(3):391–412.

Vorstand und Beirat der Deutschen Gesellschaft für Völkerkunde e.V., ed.

2008   Mitteilungen der DGV, vol. 39. Frankfurt, Germany: Frobenius-Institut.

REFERENCES

Wakin, Eric
1992   Anthropology Goes to War. Madison: University of Wisconsin Press.

Warner, W. Lloyd
1969[1937] A Black Civilization: A Social Study of an Australian Tribe. Gloucester, MA: Peter Smith.

Wax, Murray
1987   Some Issues and Sources on Ethics in Anthropology. *In* Handbook on Ethical Issues in Anthropology. Joan Cassell and Sue-Ellen Jacobs, eds. Pp. 4–10. Washington DC: American Anthropological Association.

Weinberger, Sharon
2008a   Gates: Human Terrain Teams Going Through "Growing Pains." Wired, "Danger Room" (blog), April 16. http://blog.wired.com/defense/2008/04/gates-human-ter.html, accessed December 16, 2008.
2008b   The Pentagon's Culture Wars. Nature 455(2):583–585.

Weisbrod, Bernd, ed.
2002   Akademische Vergangenheitspolitik: Beiträge zur Wissenschaftskultur der Nachkriegszeit. Göttingen, Germany: Wallstein-Verlag.

Weizman, Eyal
2006   Walking Through Walls: Soldiers as Architects in the Israeli-Palestinian Conflict. Radical Philosophy 136(March–April):8–23.

Wenger, Etienne
1998   Communities of Practice: Learning, Meaning, Identity. Cambridge, UK: Cambridge University Press.

West, Bing
2009   Counterinsurgency Lessons from Iraq. Military Review (March–April):2–12.

White, Tim, Berhane Asfaw, Yonas Beyene, Yohannes Haile-Selassie, C. Owen Lovejoy, Gen Suwa, and Gilday WoldeGabriel
2009   *Ardipithecus ramidus* and the Paleobiology of Early Hominids. Science 326:75–86.

Whitehead, Neil L.
2005   War and Violence as Cultural Expression. Anthropology News (May):23–36.

Whitehead, Neil L., and Sverker Finnstrom, eds.
forthcoming Virtual War and Magical Death: Technologies and Imaginaries for Terror and Killing. Durham, NC: Duke University Press.

Whitehead, Neil L., and Laura A. McNamara
2008   Scholars, Security, and Citizenship: Seminar Proposal for SAR. Unpublished seminar proposal submitted to SAR, April 7, 2008.

Wilcox, James
2007   Precision Engagement—Strategic Context for the Long War: Weapons Technology Blueprint for the Future. PowerPoint presentation at the

Precision Strike Winter Roundtable, February 9. http://www.dtic.mil/ndia/2007psa_winter/wilcox.pdf, accessed June 29, 2009.

Williams, John Allen

2008   Our Intellectual Freedom. Armed Forces and Society 34(4):533–535.

Wilson, Edward O.

2001   On Human Nature. *In* Understanding Violence. David P. Barash, ed., Pp. 13–20. Boston, MA: Allyn and Bacon.

Wilson, Gregory

2006   Anatomy of a Successful COIN Operation: OEF-Philippines and the Indirect Approach. Military Review (November–December):2–12.

Wilson, Scott, and Al Kamen

2009   "Global War on Terror" Is Given New Name. Washington Post, March 25. http://www.washingtonpost.com/wp-dyn/content/article/2009/03/24/AR2009032402818.html, accessed June 28, 2009.

Winslow, Donna

1997   The Canadian Airborne Regiment in Somalia: A Socio-Cultural Inquiry. Ottawa, ON: Canadian Government Publishing.

2002   Strange Bedfellows: NGOs and the Military in Humanitarian Crisis. International Journal of Peace Studies 7(2):35–55.

Withworth, Sandra

2004   Men, Militarism, and UN Peacekeeping: A Gendered Analysis. Boulder, CO: Lynne Rienner.

Wrangham, Richard, and Dale Peterson

1996   Demonic Males: Apes and the Origin of Human Violence. Boston, MA: Houghton Mifflin.

Wright, Quincy

1942   A Study of War. Chicago, IL: University of Chicago Press.

Zhou, Lina, and Simon Lutterbie

2005   Deception across Cultures: Bottom-Up and Top-Down Approaches. Lecture Notes in Computer Science 3495:465–470.

Zimbardo, Philip

2007   The Lucifer Effect: Understanding How Good People Turn Evil. New York: Random House.

Zumer, John

2009   Human Terrain Teams Build Friendships, Future. American Forces Press Service, News Articles, US Department of Defense, March 2. http://www.defense.gov/news/newsarticle.aspx?id=53281, accessed March 2, 2009.

Index

8ok........stop

people studied, xvi, xix, xxx, 146–147, 149–150; responsibilities of, 153, 161–162; role of, xv–xvi, xxxi, 16–21, 39–40, 60, 73, 160–161; and science, xviii–xix, xxi; and security engagement, 124–126; social consciousness of, 148; and the state, xiv–xxi, xxiii

anthropologists: Canadian: embedded in Afghanistan, xxxi, 127–144; and ethical issues, xxx–xxxi, 131, 136, 141–143; and research, 140–142

anthropologists: German, 201; articles/books by, 82–83, 90–91, 93, 95; and the Bundeswehr, 77–79, 85, 88–96; debates/criticism among, xxix–xxx, 91–94, 99n17; and ethical issues, 77–79, 82–83, 88–89, 91–97, 99n17; liberal/left orientation of, 78, 92; and National Socialism, xxix, 78–85, 92, 94; and political issues, 77–79, 88–89, 96; in postwar era, xxix, 83–85; and race, xxix, 80–85, 94, 98n6; sociocultural, 79, 81–82, 89–91; under Third Reich, 80–86, 98n10, 165n12

anthropologists: Israeli: articles/books by, 172–173, 181–182; and censorship, 179–180; and dependence on US academia, 172; and the military, xxxi–xxxii, 170–181; and views on American anthropology, 167–169

"Anthropology on the Warpath in Thailand" (Wolf and Jorgensen), xviii

anti-Semitism, 82, 85, 98n11

Antweiler, Christoph, 88

applied anthropology, xiv–xv, 72, 171–172

"Applied Anthropology and Its Relationship to Anthropology" (Embree), xiv

Arab Mind, The (Patai), xxviii, 29–30, 39

Arabs, 29, 39, 43, 170

Archimedes Global Inc., 123

Ardipithecus ramidus specimens, 198–199

Ardrey, Robert, 197

Arendt, Hanna, 174

Arnehm Land (Australia), 189, 191

Arquilla, John, 9–10

Arunta people (Australia), 186

Asia, xv, 186. *See also* Southeast Asia

Association for Asian Studies (AAS), xviii

Association of American Universities, xxii

Australian Aborigine rock art, 185–186, 189–192, 200

"Australia's Ancient Warriors" (Taçon and Chippindale), 189–192

australopithecine specimens, 185, 197–198, 200

Austria, 80

Awakening movement (Iraq), 11, 18–20

Aweikoma people, 196, 199

Baboons, 197–198

Baghdad, Iraq, 3, 19–20, 108, 119

Balkans, 89

Barnes, Catherine, 153

Baumann, Hermann, 81–85, 96

Beaver, Diane, 50n6

belief systems, 188–189, 199–200

Bell, Allan, 139–140

Belshaw, Cyril, xxi

Ben-Ari, Eyal, xxi, xxv, xxviii, xxx–xxxii, 6, 152

Benedict, Ruth, 91–92

Berlin Wall, 77, 85, 134

Berndt, Ronald and Catherine, 189–190

Berreman, Gerald, xix, 168

biological anthropology, 81, 98n7

Birdsell, Joseph, 197

Blackwater, 11

Blatchford, Christie, xxxi, 128–129, 137, 141–142

Blix, Hans, 99n14

Boas, Franz, xx, xxx, 98n9

Boneca, Tony, 127–129, 137, 142

Borneo, 186

Bosnia, 87

Boston Herald, 116–117

Bourdieu, Pierre, 96

Bourgois, Philippe, 173

Bowman Expedition, 123

Boyer, Dominic, 140

Bradbury, Steven, 49n2

Brain, C. K., 198

Braun, Jürgen, 81

Brazil, 186

Brooks, James, xxii–xxiii

Brown, Keith, xix–xx, 169, 175

Buid people (Philippines), 186, 199

Bundeswehr Geographic Information Office, 89, 91

Bundeswehr (German Armed Forces), xxv, xxix, 77–79, 85–96

Bundeswehr Institute of Social Sciences (SOWI), 87, 89–90, 92

Bureau of Indian Affairs, 163n4

Bush, George W., 5, 24n16, 25–27, 49n1–2, 171

Buss, David, 192

Byer, Doris, 96

Camp Delta, 42, 44–46. *See also* Guantánamo Bay, Cuba

Canada's Code of Service Discipline, 135

Canada's Eight Platoon, 127–129, 133, 137–138

Canada's Public Affairs Officers (PAFFO), 134–136, 138

Canada's Task Force Orion, 133, 137

Canadian anthropologists. *See* anthropologists: Canadian

Phillips, Herbert, xvii
physical anthropology, 81
Pinker, Steven, 192
political contexts, xxx, 51–53, 60–62, 65–66, 68, 70–71, 79, 101, 153
political issues, xvi, xviii–xix, xxi, xxiii, 53, 73, 153, 170–171
politics, 18–19, 57, 88, 96, 104, 167–168, 201
polygraph, 33, 47
postconflict conditions/programs, 16, 19–21
Potts, Malcolm, 192, 201
power: anthropology's critiques of, 62; groups outside of, xxxivn2; institutions of, xxiii, xxiv–xxvi, 148, 163n4; and knowledge production, xiv, xxvi; national, 147; and politics, 51; relations, 52; scholarship in the service of, xxix; "soft," xxviii, 5
Precision Strike Winter Roundtable, 124
Price, David, xxiii, xxv, xxviii–xxix, xxxi, 29, 115, 163n4, 164n5, 167, 169–170, 189
Princess Patricia's Canadian Light Infantry (PPCLI), 130–131, 133
Project Camelot (Latin America), xvi, xix–xx, xxii, 148
Project Phoenix, xxii
Provincial Reconstruction Team (PRT), 113–114, 119
Psychological Operations Center (PSYOP Center), 89, 91, 99n15
public dialogue, 181–182
Pulliam, Linda, 152
Punan people (Borneo), 186

Quadrennial Defense Review Report (US Dept. of Defense), 9–10
Quiet American, The (Greene), 54

Racial: biology, 80–81; hierarchy, 98n6; hygiene, 81–82, 84–85; policy/ideology, xvi, xxix, 82, 94, 98n9
racism, 53, 81, 83, 168, 201
RAND Corporation, 53–54, 58–67, 72–73, 76n4
Randall, Alexander, 152
Reachback Research Cells, 102, 121
Red Cross, 47, 50n6
Reid interrogation technique, 34, 38
Renzi, Fred, 7, 11, 23n9, 123–124
reproductive success, 192–193, 200
research bias, xxiv, 150, 185, 200
resources: acquisition of, 186, 201; and cash crops, 57, 67; local ownership of, 95; trade in, 12, 15; wars for, 12; wealth of, 3. *See also* diamonds
Revolution in Military Affairs (RMA), 8
Rikhye, Indar Jit, 149
Robben, Antonius, 180

Roberts, Audrey, 106, 115–117
rock art. *See* Australian Aborigine rock art
Ron, James, 177
Rosenberg, Alfred, 98n11
Rubin, Michael, 10
Rubinstein, Robert A., xx–xxi, xxiii, xxv, xxviii, xxxi, 183
Rühle, Michael, 88
Rumsfeld, Donald, 8, 26
Russia, 99n14
Ryle, Gilbert, 164n4

Saar, Eric, 37
Sahlins, Marshall, 27, 47
Saudi Arabia, 40, 47
Saulteaux people (North America), 186, 196
Scales, Robert, 5
Scarry, Elaine, 29
Schactman, Noah, 115
Schafft, Gretchen, 81, 84
Scheper-Hughes, Nancy, 173
School for Advanced Research (SAR), xxii–xxvii
Schweitzer, Martin, 113, 115, 119
Scott, James, 56
secret: operations, 18, 68, 179; reports, 66; research, xxx, 94, 146, 164n7, 168
security, 7, 15, 24n16, 25, 95, 106, 122, 124–126; companies/contractors, 11, 13, 16, 18, 20; forces, 6, 16, 18, 20, 168–169, 173; in Germany, 79, 85–91, 95–97; and Human Terrain Teams, 111, 118; international, 79, 87–88, 147–148, 157; in Israel, 170; national, xxi, xxii, xxxivn1, 33, 146–147, 158, 180; organizations, 145–148, 161–162, 167; outsourcing of, 9, 18–19; and political ideology, 201; sector, xxviii, xxx–xxxi, 3, 8, 11, 16, 20, 89, 91, 146, 156, 168, 179–180; threats, 101, 123, 125; without war, 201. *See also* global: security; national security state
Selmeski, Brian, 18
Semai people (Malaysia), 186, 189
September 11, 2001. *See* 9/11
Sex and War (Potts and Hayden), 201
Sharp, Lauriston, xvii
Shaw, Martin, 9
Sierra Leone, xxvii–xxviii, 5, 12–16, 19–20, 23n10, 23n12
Sierra Leone's Civil Defense Forces (CDF), xxviii, 13–16, 19, 23n13
Sierra Leone's Revolutionary United Front (RUF), 12–13, 15, 23n12
Silverman, Adam, 110, 112
Simons, Anna, 11, 22, 152, 170, 173
slavery, 155

89, 103; defensive, 186, 199–200; definition of, 194–195; graphic/written documentation of, 143; and human ancestors, 197–199, 201; and human nature, xxxii, 188–189, 200–201; inevitability of, xxxii, 185–186, 188–189, 200–201; and international conventions, 17; and militarization, 18; networked, 8–10, 12, 14–15; and non-warring societies/cultures, 186, 189, 191–192, 196, 199–201; outsourcing of, xxviii, 5, 9, 16, 21; and soldiers' social relationships, 139–141; study of, xv, xvii, xxiii, xxiv, xxxi–xxxii, 90, 96, 173, 177, 185–189; and subcontractors, 4, 11, 16, 22; and Western cultural traditions, 191–192, 199–200; witnesses of, 142–144. *See also* counterinsurgency; hunter-gatherer societies; indigenous forces; specific countries

Washington Post, 3, 25–26

Wax, Murray, xv–xvi

weaponry, 8, 13, 43, 63, 95, 106, 112, 124, 198–199. *See also* disarmament

weather forecasting, xiv

Weinberger, Sharon, 113

West Africa, 5, 12–13

White, Tim, 198–199

Whitehead, Neil, xxiii, xxv, xxvii

Wilcox, John, 124

Williams, John, 162

Wilson, Edward O., 188

Wilson, Gregory, 7, 9–10, 23n6

Window on a War (Hickey), 66

Wolf, Eric, xvii–xviii, xx–xxi, 51, 71, 76n6

women, 17, 24n14, 62, 113–115, 157–158, 174–175

World Bank, 20

World Congress of Anthropolgy and Ethnology, 148

World War I, xvi, 98n4, 187

World War II, xvi, 54, 59, 62, 72, 75, 75n3, 86, 92, 169, 181, 187, 198, 201

Wright, Quincy, 199–200

Wynaad Plateaus society (India), 186

Yanadi people (Eurasia), 186

Yanomamö people (South America), xxiii, 185, 192–194, 200

Yugoslavia (former), 85–86, 174

Zadrans, 113

Zapotec people (Mexico), 189

Zeitschrift für Ethnologie (Journal of Anthropology), 91

Zimbardo, Philip, 35

Zimina, Lada, 153

School for Advanced Research Advanced Seminar Series

PUBLISHED BY SAR PRESS

CHACO & HOHOKAM: PREHISTORIC REGIONAL SYSTEMS IN THE AMERICAN SOUTHWEST
  Patricia L. Crown & W. James Judge, eds.

RECAPTURING ANTHROPOLOGY: WORKING IN THE PRESENT
  Richard G. Fox, ed.

WAR IN THE TRIBAL ZONE: EXPANDING STATES AND INDIGENOUS WARFARE
  R. Brian Ferguson & Neil L. Whitehead, eds.

IDEOLOGY AND PRE-COLUMBIAN CIVILIZATIONS
  Arthur A. Demarest & Geoffrey W. Conrad, eds.

DREAMING: ANTHROPOLOGICAL AND PSYCHOLOGICAL INTERPRETATIONS
  Barbara Tedlock, ed.

HISTORICAL ECOLOGY: CULTURAL KNOWLEDGE AND CHANGING LANDSCAPES
  Carole L. Crumley, ed.

THEMES IN SOUTHWEST PREHISTORY
  George J. Gumerman, ed.

MEMORY, HISTORY, AND OPPOSITION UNDER STATE SOCIALISM
  Rubie S. Watson, ed.

OTHER INTENTIONS: CULTURAL CONTEXTS AND THE ATTRIBUTION OF INNER STATES
  Lawrence Rosen, ed.

LAST HUNTERS–FIRST FARMERS: NEW PERSPECTIVES ON THE PREHISTORIC TRANSITION TO AGRICULTURE
  T. Douglas Price & Anne Birgitte Gebauer, eds.

MAKING ALTERNATIVE HISTORIES: THE PRACTICE OF ARCHAEOLOGY AND HISTORY IN NON-WESTERN SETTINGS
  Peter R. Schmidt & Thomas C. Patterson, eds.

CYBORGS & CITADELS: ANTHROPOLOGICAL INTERVENTIONS IN EMERGING SCIENCES AND TECHNOLOGIES
  Gary Lee Downey & Joseph Dumit, eds.

SENSES OF PLACE
  Steven Feld & Keith H. Basso, eds.

THE ORIGINS OF LANGUAGE: WHAT NONHUMAN PRIMATES CAN TELL US
  Barbara J. King, ed.

CRITICAL ANTHROPOLOGY NOW: UNEXPECTED CONTEXTS, SHIFTING CONSTITUENCIES, CHANGING AGENDAS
  George E. Marcus, ed.

ARCHAIC STATES
  Gary M. Feinman & Joyce Marcus, eds.

REGIMES OF LANGUAGE: IDEOLOGIES, POLITIES, AND IDENTITIES
  Paul V. Kroskrity, ed.

BIOLOGY, BRAINS, AND BEHAVIOR: THE EVOLUTION OF HUMAN DEVELOPMENT
  Sue Taylor Parker, Jonas Langer, & Michael L. McKinney, eds.

WOMEN & MEN IN THE PREHISPANIC SOUTHWEST: LABOR, POWER, & PRESTIGE
  Patricia L. Crown, ed.

HISTORY IN PERSON: ENDURING STRUGGLES, CONTENTIOUS PRACTICE, INTIMATE IDENTITIES
  Dorothy Holland & Jean Lave, eds.

THE EMPIRE OF THINGS: REGIMES OF VALUE AND MATERIAL CULTURE
  Fred R. Myers, ed.

CATASTROPHE & CULTURE: THE ANTHROPOLOGY OF DISASTER
  Susanna M. Hoffman & Anthony Oliver-Smith, eds.

URUK MESOPOTAMIA & ITS NEIGHBORS: CROSS-CULTURAL INTERACTIONS IN THE ERA OF STATE FORMATION
  Mitchell S. Rothman, ed.

REMAKING LIFE & DEATH: TOWARD AN ANTHROPOLOGY OF THE BIOSCIENCES
  Sarah Franklin & Margaret Lock, eds.

TIKAL: DYNASTIES, FOREIGNERS, & AFFAIRS OF STATE: ADVANCING MAYA ARCHAEOLOGY
  Jeremy A. Sabloff, ed.

PUBLISHED BY SAR PRESS

GRAY AREAS: ETHNOGRAPHIC ENCOUNTERS
WITH NURSING HOME CULTURE
Philip B. Stafford, ed.

PLURALIZING ETHNOGRAPHY: COMPARISON
AND REPRESENTATION IN MAYA CULTURES,
HISTORIES, AND IDENTITIES
John M. Watanabe & Edward F. Fischer, eds.

AMERICAN ARRIVALS: ANTHROPOLOGY
ENGAGES THE NEW IMMIGRATION
Nancy Foner, ed.

VIOLENCE
Neil L. Whitehead, ed.

LAW & EMPIRE IN THE PACIFIC:
FIJI AND HAWAI'I
Sally Engle Merry & Donald Brenneis, eds.

ANTHROPOLOGY IN THE MARGINS
OF THE STATE
Veena Das & Deborah Poole, eds.

THE ARCHAEOLOGY OF COLONIAL
ENCOUNTERS: COMPARATIVE PERSPECTIVES
Gil J. Stein, ed.

GLOBALIZATION, WATER, & HEALTH:
RESOURCE MANAGEMENT IN TIMES OF
SCARCITY
Linda Whiteford & Scott Whiteford, eds.

A CATALYST FOR IDEAS: ANTHROPOLOGICAL
ARCHAEOLOGY AND THE LEGACY OF
DOUGLAS W. SCHWARTZ
Vernon L. Scarborough, ed.

THE ARCHAEOLOGY OF CHACO CANYON: AN
ELEVENTH-CENTURY PUEBLO REGIONAL
CENTER
Stephen H. Lekson, ed.

COMMUNITY BUILDING IN THE TWENTY-
FIRST CENTURY
Stanley E. Hyland, ed.

AFRO-ATLANTIC DIALOGUES:
ANTHROPOLOGY IN THE DIASPORA
Kevin A. Yelvington, ed.

COPÁN: THE HISTORY OF AN ANCIENT MAYA
KINGDOM
E. Wyllys Andrews & William L. Fash, eds.

THE EVOLUTION OF HUMAN LIFE HISTORY
Kristen Hawkes & Richard R. Paine, eds.

THE SEDUCTIONS OF COMMUNITY:
EMANCIPATIONS, OPPRESSIONS, QUANDARIES
Gerald W. Creed, ed.

THE GENDER OF GLOBALIZATION: WOMEN
NAVIGATING CULTURAL AND ECONOMIC
MARGINALITIES
Nandini Gunewardena & Ann Kingsolver, eds.

NEW LANDSCAPES OF INEQUALITY:
NEOLIBERALISM AND THE EROSION OF
DEMOCRACY IN AMERICA
Jane L. Collins, Micaela di Leonardo,
& Brett Williams, eds.

IMPERIAL FORMATIONS
Ann Laura Stoler, Carole McGranahan,
& Peter C. Perdue, eds.

OPENING ARCHAEOLOGY: REPATRIATION'S
IMPACT ON CONTEMPORARY RESEARCH AND
PRACTICE
Thomas W. Killion, ed.

SMALL WORLDS: METHOD, MEANING, &
NARRATIVE IN MICROHISTORY
James F. Brooks, Christopher R. N. DeCorse,
& John Walton, eds.

MEMORY WORK: ARCHAEOLOGIES OF
MATERIAL PRACTICES
Barbara J. Mills & William H. Walker, eds.

FIGURING THE FUTURE: GLOBALIZATION
AND THE TEMPORALITIES OF CHILDREN AND
YOUTH
Jennifer Cole & Deborah Durham, eds.

TIMELY ASSETS: THE POLITICS OF
RESOURCES AND THEIR TEMPORALITIES
Elizabeth Emma Ferry &
Mandana E. Limbert, eds.

DEMOCRACY: ANTHROPOLOGICAL
APPROACHES
Julia Paley, ed.

CONFRONTING CANCER: METAPHORS,
INEQUALITY, AND ADVOCACY
Juliet McMullin & Diane Weiner, eds.

Participants in the School for Advanced Research short seminar "Scholars, Security, and Citizenship" co-chaired by Laura A. McNamara and Neil L. Whitehead, July 24–25, 2008. *Standing, from left*: R. Brian Ferguson, Robert A. Rubinstein, David Price, Anne Irwin, Nasser Abufarha, Maren Tomforde, Clementine Fujimura; *seated, from left*: Laura A. McNamara, Neil L. Whitehead. Photograph by Jonathan A Lewis.